PATTERNS
OF DEVELOPMENT,
1950–1970

PATTERNS
OF DEVELOPMENT,
1950–1970

Hollis Chenery and Moises Syrquin

with the assistance of

Hazel Elkington

Published for the
WORLD BANK
by
OXFORD UNIVERSITY PRESS
1975

Oxford University Press, Ely House, London W. 1

GLASGOW NEW YORK TORONTO MELBOURNE WELLINGTON
CAPE TOWN IBADAN NAIROBI DAR ES SALAAM LUSAKA ADDIS ABABA
DELHI BOMBAY CALCUTTA MADRAS KARACHI LAHORE DACCA
KUALA LUMPUR SINGAPORE HONG KONG TOKYO

CASEBOUND ISBN 0 19 920075 0
PAPERBACK ISBN 0 19 920076 9

© *International Bank for Reconstruction and Development, 1975*

Library of Congress Catalogue Card Number 74–29172

B+T

*Printed in Great Britain by
William Clowes & Sons, Limited
London, Beccles and Colchester*

FOREWORD

Better understanding of the economic and social changes in the development process is essential to continued progress in the less developed countries. This is what the World Bank is attempting to achieve through its own research, as well as by participation with other institutions engaged in the same effort.

Patterns of Development is a prime example of the work now being done under an expanded program which includes a series of comparative analyses of various aspects of structural change and development policy. Together with other studies planned and in progress, this volume should help both the Bank and its member governments come to grips more effectively with the problem of "absolute poverty" which continues to degrade the lives of some 800 million human beings in the developing world, in spite of the relatively rapid growth of their national economies.

ROBERT S. MCNAMARA
President
The World Bank

CONTENTS

Foreword   v
Tables   xi
Figures   xiii
Preface   xv

1. Bases for Comparative Analysis   3
Conceptual Framework   4
Basic Development Processes   6
Econometric Procedure and Data   10
Presentation of Results   18

2. Accumulation and Allocation Processes   23
Accumulation Processes   23
  Theoretical Background   23
  Statistical Analysis   25
  The Role of Accumulation in the Transition   31
Resource Allocation Processes   32
  Theoretical Background   32
  Statistical Analysis   34
  The Role of Resource Allocation in the Transition   42
The Interactions among External and Internal Processes   42
  Regression Analysis   43
  Shifts in Production and Trade   45
  Shifts in Accumulation and Demand   45

3. Demographic and Distributional Processes   47
Employment by Sector   48
Urbanization   53
Demographic Transition   56
Income Distribution   60

4. Alternative Patterns of Development   64
Classification of Trade Patterns   65
  Classification vs. Regression Analysis   66
  The Scale Index   67
  The Trade Orientation Index   68
  Application to Regression Analysis   69
Scale Effects: The Large-Country Patterns   74
  Scale and Resource Allocation   78
  Scale and Accumulation   88
  Other Effects of Scale   88

Resource Effects: The Small-Country Patterns   89
Variability of the Transformation   89
Effects of Primary Orientation   90
Effects of Industry Orientation   100
A Typology of Development Patterns   101
Criteria for Classification   101
Applications   105
Patterns for Developed Countries   107
Effects of Income Level on Accumulation Processes   108
Effects of Income Level on Allocation Processes   112

5. Time-series vs. Cross-section Patterns   117
Time-series Estimation   118
Average Time-series Relations   118
The Samples   119
Nature of the Results   120
Accumulation   122
Saving and Investment   122
Foreign Capital Inflow   123
Government Revenue   127
Allocation Patterns   128
Production   128
The Share of Exports   130
Adjustments to Changes in External Capital   132
Conclusions   133

6. Conclusions   135
The Nature of the Transition   135
Development Theory and Policy   136
International Development Policy   137
Future Research   138

Technical Appendix   141
Specification   141
The Functional Form   141
Nonlinearities and Multicollinearity   143
Real Income, Relative Prices, and
Exchange Rate Conversions   145
Effect of the Bias on Cross-section Estimates   146
Alternative Approaches   149
The Treatment of Time   153
The Trade Orientation Index   155
Reduced Forms and Structural Relations   158

Estimation   159
  Errors in the Variables   159
  Weighted Regression (Heteroscedasticity)   161
  Stratifying the Sample   162
    Tests of Homogeneity   163
    Statistical Accuracy   166
  Pooling of Cross-section and Time-series Data   167
    Average Cross Section   167
    Average Time Series   167
    Omitted Variables   168
The Composition of the Sample   169
  The Samples   170
  Annual Cross Sections   170
  The Share of Services   174
    Annual Cross Sections   175
    Services in Large Countries   176
    The Time Series   176

Statistical Appendix   179
  The Data   179
  Exchange Rates   179
  Definitions of Variables   180
    Accumulation Processes   180
    Resource Allocation Processes   183
    Demographic and Distributional Processes   186
Bibliography   215
Subject Index   223
Author Index   233

TABLES

1. Structural Characteristics Analyzed   9
2. 101 Countries Included in the Study, 1950–70:
   Samples for Basic Regressions   12
3. Normal Variation in Economic Structure with
   Level of Development   20
4. Basic Regressions: Accumulation Processes   30
5. Basic Regressions: Resource Allocation Processes   38
6. Effects of a Unit Increase in Exports and External Capital   44
7. Basic Regressions: Demographic and Distributional Processes   49
8. Key to Graphs   51
9. Augmented Regressions: Birth Rates   59
10. Classification of Trade Patterns (1965): Large Countries   70
11. Classification of Trade Patterns (1965):
    Small, Primary-oriented Countries   71
12. Classification of Trade Patterns (1965):
    Small, Balanced Countries   72
13. Classification of Trade Patterns (1965):
    Small, Industry-oriented Countries   73
14. Comparison of Large and Small Country Patterns   75
15. Comparison of Small Country Patterns:
    Primary and Industry-Oriented   75
16. A Classification of Allocation Patterns   103
17. Accumulation Processes: Richer Countries
    with per Capita Income Greater than $500 in 1960   110
18. Accumulation Processes: Poorer Countries
    with per Capita Income Less than $500 in 1960   111
19. Size Effects for Saving and Exports: Three-way
    Income Split   112
20. Resource Allocation and Trade Processes:
    Richer Countries with per Capita Income
    Greater than $500 in 1960   113
21. Resource Allocation and Trade Processes:
    Poorer Countries with per Capita Income
    Less than $500 in 1960   114
22. Comparison of Long-run and Short-run Patterns   121
23. Comparison of Accumulation Estimates   124
24. Comparison of Allocation Estimates   124

Tables in the Technical Appendix

T1. Tests of Homogeneity (F Tests) of Alternative
       Patterns Classified by Size, Trade Orientation,
       and Level of Development   164
T2. A Summary of Regression Results   165
T3. Average Predicted Value of Production Shares
       from Yearly Cross Sections   171
T4. Industrial Patterns by Income Groups   173
T5. Countries with High Services Share of Production
       around 1965: Main Characteristics   175

Tables in the Statistical Appendix

S1. Annual Average Exchange Rate   181
S2. Accumulation Processes: Data for 1965
       or Closest Available Year   188
S3. Resource Allocation and Trade Processes:
       Data for 1965 or Closest Available Year   192
S4. Demographic and Distributional Processes:
       Data for 1965 or Closest Available Year   196
S5. Accumulation Processes: Large Countries   200
S6. Accumulation Processes: Small Countries   201
S7. Accumulation Processes: Small, Primary-oriented
       Countries   202
S8. Accumulation Processes: Small, Industry-oriented
       Countries   203
S9. Resource Allocation and Trade Processes:
       Large Countries   204
S10. Resource Allocation and Trade Processes:
       Small Countries   205
S11. Resource Allocation and Trade Processes:
       Small, Primary-oriented Countries   206
S12. Resource Allocation and Trade Processes:
       Small Industry-oriented Countries   207
S13. Saving-Compatible Sample: Time-series Coefficients   208
S14. Regressions with Exogenous Trade Variables   210
S15. Saving and Export Patterns: Income Split   212
S16. Short-run Patterns: Full and Reduced Samples   213
S17. Structure of Production: Cross Sections   214

FIGURES

1. Investment   27
2. Government Revenue   28
3. Education   29
4. Structure of Domestic Demand   35
5. Structure of Production (Value Added)   36
6. Structure of Trade   37
7. Export Variation with Size of Population   41
8. Labor Allocation   50
9. Labor Productivity Indices—Scatter for Primary Sector
   of 39 Countries (1965)   52
10. Urbanization—Scatter for 90 Countries (1965)   55
11. Demographic Transition—Scatter for Birth Rate
   in 76 Countries (1965)   57
12. Income Distribution—Scatter for 55 Countries (1965)   63
13. Comparison of Trade Patterns: Large Countries—
   Scatter for 26 Countries (1965)   76
14. Comparison of Trade Patterns: Small Countries—
   Scatter for 60 Countries (1965)   77
15. Total Exports—Scatter for 26 Large Countries (1965)   79
16. Primary Exports—Scatter for 26 Large Countries (1965)   80
17. Manufactured Exports—Scatter for 26 Large Countries (1965)   81
18. Saving—Scatter for 26 Large Countries (1965)   82
19. Investment—Scatter for 26 Large Countries (1965)   83
20. Private Consumption—Scatter for 25 Large Countries (1965)   84
21. Government Revenue—Scatter for 23 Large Countries (1965)   85
22. Primary Share of Production—Scatter for
   25 Large Countries (1965)   86
23. Industry Share of Production—Scatter for
   25 Large Countries (1965)   87
24. Total Exports: Small Countries—Scatter for
   67 Countries (1965)   91
25. Primary Exports: Small Countries—Scatter for
   62 Countries (1965)   92
26. Manufactured Exports: Small Countries—Scatter for
   62 Countries (1965)   93
27. Saving: Small Countries—Scatter for 67 Countries (1965)   94
28. Investment: Small Countries—Scatter for 67 Countries (1965)   95
29. Private Consumption: Small Countries—Scatter for
   71 Countries (1965)   96
30. Government Revenue: Small Countries—Scatter for
   66 Countries (1965)   97

31. Primary Share of Production: Small Countries—Scatter for
    64 Countries (1965)   98
32. Industry Share of Production: Small Countries—Scatter for
    64 Countries (1965)   99
33. Saving: Three Income Groups   109
34. Total Exports: Two Income Groups   115
35. Saving and Capital Inflow   126

Figures in the Technical Appendix

T1. Industry Share of GDP: Effect of Reducing
    Transition Range by One-Half   147
T2. Normal Export Structure and the Trade-Orientation Index   157

PREFACE

The past forty years have seen numerous attempts to discover uniformities in economic behavior by a comparison of economies at different levels of income. Among the most fruitful have been Colin Clark's analysis of the changes in use of labor with rising income *(The Conditions of Economic Progress, 1940)* and Simon Kuznets's series comparing elements of the national accounts ("Quantitative Aspects of the Economic Growth of Nations," I-X, 1956-1967). Kuznets demonstrates the similarities between historical growth patterns and the intercountry patterns of the 1950s.

Many detailed comparisons have focused on individual characteristics of developing countries, notably consumption, savings, investment, taxation, industrialization, and population growth. These studies apply a variety of statistical methods to different country samples and time periods, so their results are not generally comparable. However, they do demonstrate the value of comparative analysis for a variety of purposes.

Our main objective is to provide a comprehensive description of the structural changes that accompany the growth of developing countries and to analyze their interrelations. The great increase in statistical information since 1950 makes it possible to employ a combination of cross-section and time-series analysis that was not feasible as recently as ten years ago. By comparing intercountry and intertemporal patterns, we can respond to several important questions left unanswered in previous studies—notably those concerning the stability of the observed patterns and the nature of the time trends. To these ends, a uniform statistical procedure has been developed for measuring variations in different aspects of the economic structure in relation to income level and other factors.

To achieve broad coverage of the various features of development, we selected twenty-seven variables that are included in the IBRD economic and social data bank for a large number of countries. These variables describe ten basic processes of accumulation, resource allocation, and income distribution. Analysis of these processes suggests the "stylized facts" of development that can be used in testing theoretical hypotheses as well as in policy analysis.

The first phase of the present study was completed under the Project for Quantitative Research in Economic Development at Harvard University. The Harvard-based research is reported in Chenery and Taylor ("Development Patterns: Among Countries and Over Time," 1968) and Chenery, Elkington, and Sims ("A Uniform Analysis of Development Patterns," 1970). Transfering the study to the World Bank has allowed us to integrate data collection, computation, and analysis in a way that is rarely possible in academic research.

We are indebted to a number of persons for assistance at various stages of our research. Lance Taylor and Christopher Sims collaborated in the first phase of the work and advised us on the methodology used in the present analysis. Hazel Elkington has been responsible for the collection and processing of data over the past six years and has prepared the Statistical Appendix to this volume, with generous support from the Economic Analysis and Projections Department of the World Bank. Jon Eaton provided valuable help in research and computation. We have had the benefit of criticism and comment from Irma Adelman, Manmohan Agarwal, Bela Belassa, Nicholas Carter, Simon Kuznets, Jacob Paroush, William Raduchel, Lance Taylor, Wouter Tims, Larry Westphal, Ross Williams, and Jeffrey Williamson. Teresita Kamantigue typed various drafts of the manuscript with speed and accuracy. Jane Carroll and Brian Svikhart lent editorial guidance aimed at improving the book's style and readability. The index was prepared by Arthur Gamson.

HOLLIS CHENERY
MOISES SYRQUIN

PATTERNS
OF DEVELOPMENT,
1950–1970

Chapter 1

BASES FOR COMPARATIVE ANALYSIS

INTERCOUNTRY COMPARISONS play an essential part in understanding the processes of economic and social development. To generalize from the historical experience of a single country, we must compare it in some way to that of other countries. Through such comparisons, uniform features of development can be identified and alternative hypotheses as to their causes tested.

Comparative analysis is equally important to the formulation and evaluation of development policy. Since theoretical bases for determining a range of feasible policies are limited, comparative studies provide the main source of information about possible levels of savings and taxation, the requirements for capital and labor, and achievable rates of growth. Whether acquired from personal observation or more systematic comparisons, international experience is a major ingredient in development policy in all countries.

The value of quantitative comparisons for economic analysis and policy has been recognized in a variety of separate fields, such as saving and investment, trade, taxation, industrialization, urbanization, and employment. Up to now these analyses have been made independently, using different methodologies, hypotheses, and basic data. It has therefore been difficult to combine their results into a consistent picture of development as a whole or to trace interrelations among separate processes.

The present study attempts to provide a uniform analysis of the principal changes in economic structure that normally accompany economic growth. The focus is on the major features of resource mobilization and allocation, particularly those aspects needed to sustain further growth and therefore of primary interest for policy. By treating these aspects in a uniform econometric framework, it is possible to provide a consistent description of a number of interrelated types of structural change and also to identify systematic differences in development patterns among countries that are following different development strategies.

The starting point for this study is the pioneering work of Simon Kuznets, who first demonstrated the value of quantitative intercountry analysis of economic structures.[1] Since ten years ago there were few significant time series for developing countries, Kuznets was properly skeptical of applying his cross-country results to the analysis of change over

---

[1]In a series of ten articles published in the journal *Economic Development and Cultural Change* (1956-67), Kuznets analyzed the intercountry variation in the principal components of the gross national product (GNP) and compared these results to historical changes in the developed countries over the past century or more.

time. With the benefit of the great increase in data that has taken place over the past decade, we are able to compare cross-country and time-series estimates and to establish some useful relationships between them.[2]

The establishment of a more uniform and comprehensive description of structural change opens up the possibility of identifying countries that have been following similar development strategies. The choice of a development strategy is affected not only by the structural characteristics of the economy but also by the government's social objectives and willingness to use various policy instruments. Our analysis leads to the identification of three main patterns of resource allocation, which are identified in Chapter 4 as: *large country, balanced allocation; small country, primary specialization; small country, industry specialization.* By comparing countries that are following similar development patterns, it is possible to derive more valid performance standards and also compare the policies chosen by countries under similar conditions. A basis for this type of study is provided by a typology of development patterns in Chapter 4.

CONCEPTUAL FRAMEWORK

In general terms, a development pattern may be defined as a systematic variation in any significant aspect of the economic or social structure associated with a rising level of income or other index of development. Although some variation with the income level is observable in almost all structural features, we are primarily interested in those structural changes that are needed to achieve sustained increases in per capita income. Since one can rarely prove that a given aspect of development is logically "necessary," we start with those for which a plausible case can be made on empirical grounds.

Kuznets's approach to the identification and measurement of development patterns is largely inductive. Starting with the elements of the national accounts that are recorded in a number of countries, he measures the changes in the composition of consumption, production, trade, and other aggregates as income rises. His observations are either for individual advanced countries over time or for groups of countries classified by income level. In this way he achieves comparable measures of development patterns both among countries and over time.[3]

----

[2]The value of a large-scale statistical analysis of development patterns depends heavily on the quality and comparability of the data on which it is based. This study is therefore undertaken in conjunction with the continuing development of the International Bank for Reconstruction and Development (IBRD) Economic and Social Data Bank.

[3]This methodology is summarized and applied to the analysis of production patterns in Kuznets (1971), chs. 4 and 5.

This form of analysis is further developed by examining some of the underlying growth processes that generate the observed development patterns. General models of structural change applicable to all countries can be derived from the following types of assumptions:[4]

1. Similar variation in the composition of consumer demand with rising per capita income, dominated by a decline in the share of foodstuffs and a rise in the share of manufactured goods
2. Accumulation of capital—both physical and human—at a rate exceeding the growth of the labor force
3. Access of all countries to similar technology
4. Access to international trade and capital inflows.

These basic aspects of consumer demand, technology, and trade change over time as a result of technological progress, population growth, the rising level of world income, and consequent changes in trading conditions and the supply of external capital. Rather than ignore the existence of such changes, we will estimate time trends in all structural relations during the postwar period.

Any attempt to identify the causes of structural change is complicated by the fact that supply and demand factors often interact. For example, one of the most fundamental development patterns—the shift from agriculture to industry—is promoted by the change in the composition of internal demand, by the rising level of skills, and by international shifts in comparative advantage. When the level of per capita income is the only explanatory variable used in a regression equation, it will incorporate elements of all of these factors in a single income effect. This combined relationship can be broken down, however, by allowing for independent variation in some of the elements, such as trade patterns, which depend on resource endowments and government policies as well as on the level of income.

A major objective of this study will be to separate the effects of universal factors affecting all countries from particular characteristics such as natural endowments or government policies. To the extent that this objective is achieved each aspect of a country's development pattern, such as the observed rise in saving or in the level of industry, can be described in terms of three components: (a) the normal effect of universal factors which are related to the level of income; (b) the effect of other general factors such as market size or natural resources over which the government has little or no control; (c) the effects of the country's individual history,

---

[4]Models of structural change based on these assumptions were proposed and elaborated in an intersectoral framework by Chenery (1960), Chenery (1965), and Taylor (1969). The latter two articles simulate development patterns that illustrate the interactions among systematic changes in demand, trade, and production. A similar approach based on dual economy assumptions is used by Kelley, Williamson, and Cheetham (1972).

its political and social objectives and the particular policies the government has followed to achieve them. Our primary concern here is the identification of the uniform factors (a) and (b) which affect all countries. Since these typically account for well over half the observed variation among countries in most structural characteristics, the effects of factors specific to a given country can be more readily evaluated after allowing for the uniform elements in each development pattern.

BASIC DEVELOPMENT PROCESSES

In order to separate universal factors from characteristics that are specific to individual countries, this study tries to establish testable links between empirically derived development patterns and the deductive results of development theory. In some cases the links between theory and observation are fairly simple and lead directly to causal statements as to the nature of the underlying process. For example, Arthur Lewis's dual economy theory (1954) predicts that the share of saving in GNP will rise due to the more rapid growth of the modern, capitalistic sector with its higher saving potential—a prediction that has been borne out by subsequent experience. This type of relationship between a structural characteristic such as saving and the level of income is defined here as a development process.

Engel's law provides a second example of a universal development process.[5] It specifies that the income elasticity of demand for food is less than unity, implying that the share of food in total consumption will fall as the level of income rises. When combined with other development processes, such as the accumulation of capital and skills with rising income, Engel's law also helps to explain the observed patterns of industrialization.

These examples illustrate the usefulness of assuming the existence of a set of underlying processes that may interact in different ways in different countries. The term "development process" will be used to denote these universal technological and behavioral relations. Included in this concept are some of the standard building blocks of economic models—such as consumption and investment functions—as well as demographic processes, governmental behavior, and other relations involving the level of income. In some cases the nature of a development process can be determined by aggregating behavioral relations that have been established by studies of individual or family behavior. In other cases (urbanization, for example) the existence of uniformities must be posited from observations

---

[5] A restatement and evaluation of the universality of Engel's law is given by Houthakker (1957).

of aggregate variables, and the process that is assumed is in the nature of a working hypothesis. In such cases the choice of units of analysis is largely a matter of convenience.

Although development theory does not furnish a complete guide to the identification of development processes as units for empirical study, it does provide a solid point of departure. In well-studied fields, such as consumption and saving, existing theory and econometric results suggest the choice of units, the relevant explanatory variables, and the nature of the underlying structural relations. In these cases it is possible to infer some of the properties of the underlying relations from the available intercountry evidence. There is also an adequate theoretical basis for the analysis of import substitution and industrialization, even though a comprehensive analysis of comparative advantage is not yet available.

For the present study we have selected ten basic processes that appear to be essential features of development in all countries. One test of essentiality is provided by economic theory. It is virtually impossible to construct a disaggregated model of long-term growth in which there is not some shift of resources from primary production to industry, a rise in the ratio of capital to labor, and a systematic change in the composition of imports and exports.[6] To study these processes on the basis of intercountry data the compositions of domestic demand, trade, and production are taken as the units of analysis.[7]

There is a second type of income-related change for which the available evidence suggests considerable uniformity but for which there is as yet no well-defined body of theory. Examples of such processes include the growth of the public sector's share in income and expenditure, the movement of population from rural to urban locations, and the demographic transition that results in a lowering of both death and birth rates. Since these processes have strong claims to be considered both universal and essential on the basis of the experience of more advanced countries, they are included in the present study.

The ten basic processes to be analyzed are listed in Table 1. They are defined by twenty-seven variables for which data are available for a large number of countries. The processes and the variables used to measure

---

[6]Examples of general models of development that predict the behavior of some of these variables with rising income include those of Lewis (1954), Nurkse (1959), Fei and Ranis (1964), and Kelley, Williamson, and Cheetham (1972). Disaggregated planning models lead to more concrete specifications of structural relations that can also provide a basis for theoretical analysis, as shown in Chenery, Shishido, and Watanabe (1962).

[7]Although it is customary to analyze separately individual components such as levels of investment or of industrial output, it is both theoretically and statistically preferable to analyze all the components of a given aggregate simultaneously.

them represent a compromise among four desiderata: theoretical significance, universality, data availability, and policy relevance. For example, in
defining accumulation processes it was necessary to omit direct measures
of physical and human capital and to utilize instead investment rates and
educational indices. In the case of income distribution a provisional analysis is included, based on data that is less comprehensive and reliable than
that available for the other variables, because of the importance of this
process for both theory and policy.

Taken together these ten processes describe different dimensions of the
overall structural transformation of a poor country into a rich one. Single
dimensions of the transformation — such as industrialization or urbanization — are often used to symbolize the whole set of development processes. It is more useful to consider them as separate processes of change,
however, since they may proceed at different rates even though all are
highly correlated.

Before attempting to measure these processes it is useful to consider
some of their common characteristics. Long time series of almost any of
these variables for the presently developed countries usually show a
period of fairly rapid change followed by deceleration and in some cases
even a reversal of the direction of change. Among less developed countries that have grown substantially over the past fifty years, it is often
possible to identify a period in which the rate of change has accelerated
following an earlier period of little structural change. Taken together,
these observations suggest that an S-shaped curve, characterized by an
upper and lower asymptote, will generally represent the major features of
the structural transformation. Illustrations of such curves for several
development processes are given in Chapter 4.

For almost all of the development processes considered here the existence of an upper and lower asymptote is virtually a logical necessity. No
economy can continue to exist without minimal levels of investment,
government revenue, or food consumption. It is equally necessary that
there should be an upper limit to the share of each of these components
in total income. For other processes, such as industrialization or urbanization, the lower limit may be close to zero but there is an equally strong
case for an upper asymptote. Since structural discontinuities may be ruled
out, a logistic curve, which describes a gradual transition from one limit to
the other, illustrates the type of function needed for the analysis of these
transitional processes.[8]

The concept of development as a multidimensional transition from one
relatively constant structure to another also provides a basis for analyzing

---

[8]The choice between a logistic curve and other algebraic forms as a basis for intercountry
regression analysis is considered in the Technical Appendix.

TABLE 1. Structural Characteristics Analyzed

Dependent Variable*	Symbol	Basic Regression	
		No. of Countries	No. of Obs.
Accumulation Processes			
1. *Investment (Figure 1)*			
a. Gross domestic saving as % of GDP	S	93	1,432
b. Gross domestic investment as % of GDP	I	93	1,432
c. Capital inflow (net import of goods and services) as % of GDP	F	93	1,432
2. *Government revenue (Figure 2)*			
a. Government revenue as % of GDP	GR	89	1,111
b. Tax revenue as % of GDP	TR	89	1,111
3. *Education (Figure 3)*			
a. Education expenditure by government as % of GDP	$EDEXP$	100	794
b. Primary and secondary school enrollment ratio	$SCHEN$	101	433
Resource Allocation Processes			
4. *Structure of domestic demand (Figure 4)*			
a. Gross domestic investment as % of GDP	I	93	1,432
b. Private consumption as % of GDP	C	94	1,508
c. Government consumption as % of GDP	G	94	1,508
d. Food consumption as % of GDP	C_f	52	642
5. *Structure of production (Figure 5)*			
a. Primary output as % of GDP	V_p	89	1,325
b. Industry output as % of GDP	V_m	89	1,325
c. Utilities output as % of GDP	V_u	89	1,325
d. Services output as % of GDP	V_s	89	1,325
6. *Structure of trade (Figures 6 and 7)*			
a. Exports as % of GDP	E	93	1,432
b. Primary exports as % of GDP	E_p	88	413
c. Manufactured exports as % of GDP	E_m	88	413
d. Services exports as % of GDP	E_s	88	413
e. Imports as % of GDP	M	93	1,432
Demographic and Distributional Processes			
7. *Labor allocation (Figures 8 and 9)*			
a. Share of primary labor	L_p	72	165
b. Share of industry labor	L_m	72	165
c. Share of service labor	L_s	72	165
8. *Urbanization (Figure 10)*			
Urban % of total population	URB	90	317
9. *Demographic transition (Figure 11)*			
a. Birth rate	BR	83	213
b. Death rate	DR	83	213
10. *Income distribution (Figure 12)*			
a. Share of highest 20%	$DIST$	55	66
b. Share of lowest 40%		55	66

*The variables and sources are defined in the Statistical Appendix.

the relations among development processes in individual countries. In 1950, the beginning of the period considered here, there were only four-teen countries (United States, Canada, Switzerland, Sweden, Australia, United Kingdom, Denmark, Norway, Belgium, France, German Federal Republic, Finland, Netherlands, and Austria) that would be classified as "developed" in respect to all of the ten basic processes. As Kuznets has shown, they constitute a quite homogeneous group in these and other respects. Nine additional countries (New Zealand, Japan, Israel, Puerto Rico, Italy, Czechoslovakia, German Democratic Republic, USSR, and Ireland) have completed the transition in the past twenty years in that they now have structures similar to the first group in almost all of the ten dimensions.[9]

In conventional terminology all other countries are classed as less developed or developing. The identification of separate development pro-cesses provides a differentiated view that focuses on leads and lags from the average patterns of structural change. For policy purposes, the main features of a development strategy can also be described in terms of these processes and the relations among them.

ECONOMETRIC PROCEDURE AND DATA

Since we are concerned with interrelated changes in the structure of the whole economy, the model implicit in our analysis is one of general equilibrium. Simplified versions of such a model have been used for historical analysis of structural change in a number of countries.[10] Although these models are not directly applicable to intercountry analy-sis, they do suggest the nature of the interdependent changes in resource allocation which underlie the major development patterns.

The regression equations proposed in the following paragraphs for the description of development processes can be thought of as reduced forms of a more detailed general equilibrium system. In the simplest case, we can imagine that the observed patterns of resource allocation are pro-duced by only two of the factors suggested above: changes in demand with rising income and differences in trade patterns, resulting from varia-tions in market size as well as changes in factor proportions. On these assumptions, an interindustry model yields solutions for levels of con-sumption, production, and trade by sector as a function of the level of per

---

[9]The criteria on which this judgment is based are given in the next chapter.

[10]Notably in the studies of the United States by Leontief and associates (1953), of Norway by Johansen (1960), of Japan by Chenery, Shishido, and Watanabe (1962) and Kelley and Williamson (1973), and of Israel by Bruno (1962) and Pack (1971).

capita gross domestic product (GDP) and population.[11] Such a model also provides a basis for interpreting the direct and indirect effects of other exogenous variables, such as natural resources and capital inflow.

To deal statistically with the problem of interdependence among processes we will first include as exogenous variables only the income level and population of the country, since these affect virtually all processes. This specification permits a uniform analysis of all aspects of structural change. The resulting descriptions provide a basis for studying the interdependent changes in demand and resource allocation in a consistent framework.

The basic hypothesis underlying this set of statistical estimates is that development processes occur with sufficient uniformity among countries to produce a consistent pattern of change in resource allocation, factor use, and other structural features as the level of per capita income rises. The statistical analysis is designed to explore various aspects of this general hypothesis:

1. The extent of variation in each structural feature with changes in the income level
2. The range of income over which each process shows the most pronounced change
3. The effect on each process of other key variables
4. Differences between time series and intercountry relations
5. The major sources of differences in development patterns and the nature of their effects.[12]

The first three aspects are analyzed in Chapters 2 and 3, which discuss the uniform features of development. Sources of difference are taken up in Chapters 4 and 5.

To make maximum use of intercountry data, the units of analysis and variables used are determined very largely by the uniform accounting systems of the United Nations. The available statistical series cover the period 1950–70 for a maximum of 101 countries. A maximum sample is used for each process. Excluded from this study are most of the communist economies[13] and countries where the population in 1960 was

---

[11]Derivations of such reduced form equations are given in Chenery (1965) and Taylor (1969). They are based on interindustry models in which domestic demand is a function of the level of per capita income, and exports are a function of income and size. In the reduced form the demand equations are eliminated, and the model determines levels of production and factor use as functions of income level and size.

[12]An additional aspect — the relationship between the pattern of development and the rate of growth — is included in Chenery, Elkington, and Sims (1970).

[13]Detailed analyses of patterns of industrialization in communist countries of Eastern Europe are given in Gregory (1970) and Ofer (1973).

TABLE 2. 101 Countries Included in the Study, 1950–70: Samples for Basic Regressions

TO†		Accumulation Processes					Resource Allocation Processes					Demographic and Distributional Processes			
		Investment	Government Revenue	Education		Domestic Demand		Production		Trade	Labor				
		$S\ I\ F$	$GR\ TR$	$EDEXP$	$SCHEN$	$C,\ G$	C_f	$V_p\ V_m\ V_u\ V_s$	E,M	$E_p\ E_m\ E_s$	$L_p\ L_m\ L_s$	URB	$BR,\ DR$	$DIST$
SM	1. Afghanistan		9	6	3							2		
SP	2. Algeria	10	6	6	7	21		21*	10		2	5	2	
SM	3. Angola	11	11	4	2	11		11	11			2		
L	4. Argentina	21*		10	5	20		20*	21	5	1	5	4	1
SP	5. Australia	20*	19	17	5	20	17	19*	20	6	3	4	4	
SM	6. Austria	20*	18*	16	5	20	16	18*	20	5	1	4	4	
SM	7. Belgium	19	16	5	5	19		19*	19	5	4	4	4	
SP	8. Bolivia	13	11	7	11	13		13	13	6	1	3	2	1
L	9. Brazil	20*	20*	9	4	20		19*	20	6	2	4	2	1
L	10. Burma	21*	18*	6	1			21*	21	5	1	5	1	
SP	11. Cambodia (Khmer)	5	5	6	3	7	5	8	5	2	1	1	1	
SM	12. Cameroon			3	2	6			6	1		1	1	
L	13. Canada	19	19*	8	5	19	16	18*	19	5	5	4	4	1
SP	14. Central African Rep.	6	5	5	2	5		6	6	1				3
SP	15. Ceylon (Sri Lanka)	21*	10	8	6	21	17	12	21	6	2	5	4	3
SP	16. Chad	10	7	1	3	11		11	10	2			1	1
SP	17. Chile	20*	19*	7	5	20		19*	20	5	2	4	4	1
SM	18. China (Taiwan)	21*	18	19	7	21	17	20*	21	6	1	5	4	1
L	19. Colombia	20*	20*	9	4	20		20*	20	6	2	4	4	1
SP	20. Congo (Zaire)	15		7	2	16		14	15	2	1	2	1	
SP	21. Costa Rica	21*	19*	7	4	21		18*	21	6	2	5	4	2
SM	22. Dahomey	9	7	2	3	9		5	9	2		1	1	1

TO†	Country													
SM	23. Denmark	20*	19*	13	5	20	17	19*	20	6	3	4	4	2
SP	24. Dominican Rep.	21*	10	6	5	21	12	21*	21	5	1	5	2	
SP	25. Ecuador	20*	18*	10	5	20	12	20*	20	6	2	4	4	
SM	26. El Salvador	12		7	3	12	9	12	12	6	1	2	1	1
L	27. Ethiopia	7	9	9	2	9		9	7	3		1	1	
SM	28. Finland	20*	19*	17	5	20	17	19*	20	6	2	4	4	2
L	29. France	20*	19*	7	5	20	16	20*	20	5	3	4	4	2
L	30. Germany (West)	20*	19*	10	5	20	17	19*	20	5	6	4	4	2
SP	31. Ghana	21*	8	19	5	21	15		21	5	1	5	1	
SM	32. Greece	20*	14	9	5	20	17	20*	20	6	3	4	4	1
SP	33. Guatemala	21*	18*	9	4	21		20*	21	5	2	5	3	
SP	34. Guinea	9	6	6	3	9			9					
SP	35. Haiti	11	3	3	4			12	11	3	2	3	1	
SP	36. Honduras	21*	18*	8	4	21	12	19*	21	6	2	5	2	1
SM	37. Hong Kong	20	7	12	6			21*	20	3	2	5	2	
L	38. India	10	17	8	4	11		10	10	5	2	4	3	1
L	39. Indonesia	13	9	1	2	12		12	13	3	2	3	1	
L	40. Iran	11	6	6	5	12	2	12	11	4	1	3	1	2
SP	41. Iraq		15	10	6	20	4	15			1	4	1	1
SM	42. Ireland	20*	16	11	5	20	17		20	5	3	4	4	
SM	43. Israel	20*	18*	8	5	20	17	17	20	6	5	4	3	1
L	44. Italy	20*	18	9	5	20	17	20*	20	5	6	4	4	
SP	45. Ivory Coast	14	8	9	3	14		11	14	4	1	2	1	1
SP	46. Jamaica	20*	18*	8	4	20	17	20*	20	6	2	4	4	1
L	47. Japan	20*	17	10	5	20	17	20*	20	6	6	4	4	1
SM	48. Jordan	11	10	9	4	11	9	8	11	4	1	2	1	
SM	49. Kenya	6	6	3	2	7		7	6	4		1		
L	50. Korea (South)	18	16	7	6	18	17	18	18	5	4	4	1	1

*Included in compatible (reduced) samples.

†TO (Trade Orientation); L (large); SP (small, primary oriented); SM (small, industry oriented).

TABLE 2 (continued)

TO†		Accumulation Processes					Resource Allocation Processes					Demographic and Distributional Processes			
		Investment	Government Revenue	Education		Domestic Demand	Production		Trade	Labor					
		$S\ I\ F$	$GR\ TR$	$ED\ EXP$	$SCH\ EN$	$C,\ G$	C_f	$V_p V_m V_u V_s$	$E,M\ E_p E_m E_s$	$L_p L_m L_s$	URB	$BR,\ DR$	$DIST$
SM	51. Lebanon	5	9	11	5	5	1	19*	5	1	4		1
SP	52. Liberia		5	4	1			5			1	1	
SP	53. Libya	7	7	6	3	7		7	4	1	1	1	1
SP	54. Malagasy		8	6	3	10		6	5		3		1
SP	55. Malawi	7		2	3	11		7	5		1	1	
SP	56. Malaysia	15	10	7	5	15	7	8	6	2	4	2	1
SP	57. Mali	18	8	5	5	18		13	3		4		
L	58. Mexico	21*	11	10	4	21		21*	6	5	5	4	1
SP	59. Morocco	12	11	10	5	18		18	6	2	3	2	
SP	60. Mozambique	11		4	3	11		11					
SM	61. Netherlands	20*	19*	18	5	20	17	19*	5	1	4	4	1
SP	62. New Zealand	18	18*	18	5	18		9	4	4	4	4	1
SP	63. Nicaragua	12	9	5	3	12	4	11	6	1	3	2	1
SP	64. Niger	11	6	5	3	9	4	5	2	1	2	1	1
L	65. Nigeria	17	17	3	5	17		17	2				1
SM	66. Norway	20*	19*	9	5	20	17	19*	6	6	4	4	1
L	67. Pakistan	10	6	9	4	11		11	5	3	3	2	1
SM	68. Panama	19	19*	9	5	20	16	19*	6	2	4	3	1
SP	69. Papua	7		6	4	7		7	3				
SP	70. Paraguay	20*	7	5	4	20		20*	6	2	4	3	
SM	71. Peru	21*	18	5	4	21	7	19*	5	1	5	4	2
L	72. Philippines	20*	20*	12	5	21	13	21*	6	2	5	1	1
SM	73. Portugal	20*	16	11	5	20		20*	5	2	4	4	
SM	74. Puerto Rico	20*	9	9	5	20	17	20*		3	4	4	1

	Country													
SP	75. Rhodesia		9	5	4	17	5	11	5		3	3		
SP	76. Saudi Arabia	5	7	5	3	5		5	5	3		1	1	1
SM	77. Senegal		7	4	3	10		10	10	4		2	1	1
SP	78. Sierra Leone	6	6	3	2	6	6	6	6	4	1	1	1	1
SM	79. Singapore		10	8	5	11	10	11		2		3	3	
SM	80. Somalia	7	6	6	3	7			7	2		2		
L	81. South Africa	20*	19*	4	3	20	17	20*	20	5	1	4	1	1
L	82. Spain	16	15	8	6	16	14	16	16	5	7	3	4	1
SP	83. Sudan	9	8	6	4	14	3	14	9	5	1	2		
SM	84. Sweden	19	19*	14	3	19	16	18*	19	5	3	4	4	
SM	85. Switzerland	20*	19*	3	5	20	17		20	5	2	4	4	2
SP	86. Syria	8	5	4	3	8		8	8	5	2	2	1	
SP	87. Tanzania	9	7	9	2	9		9	9	4		2		1
L	88. Thailand	21*	10	11	8	21	12	20*	21	6	2	4	2	
SP	89. Togo	13	6	3	3	11	4		13	5			1	
SM	90. Tunisia	11	8	7	6	11		11	11	6		3	1	
L	91. Turkey	21*	5	9	6	21		21*	21	6	3	5	1	
SP	92. Uganda	9	6	5	2	9		9	9	5		1		
L	93. U.A.R. (Egypt)	11		8	7	21	17	15	11	5	1	5	3	
L	94. United Kingdom	20*	19*	14	5	20	16	20*	20	5	2	4	4	1
L	95. U.S.A.	20*	17	17	5	20		19*	20	5	6	4	4	1
SM	96. Upper Volta	15	7	3	4	14			15	1		1	1	1
SP	97. Uruguay	16	15	6	5	16		15	16	6	1	5	4	1
SP	98. Venezuela	21*	9	10	5	21	10	20*	21	5	3	5	4	1
SM	99. Vietnam (South)	10	6	9	5	10	7	6	10	5		1	1	
L	100. Yugoslavia	21*	13	10	6	21	16	21	21	5	2	5	4	2
SP	101. Zambia	5	18*	8	5	19	4	13*	5	4	1	4	1	1
	No. of Obs.	1,432	1,111	794	433	1,508	642	1,325	1,432	413	165	317	213	66‡
	No. of Countries	93	89	100	101	94	52	89	93	88	72	90	83	55

*Included in compatible (reduced) samples.

†TO (Trade Orientation); L (large); SP (small, primary oriented); SM (small, industry oriented).

‡Includes one observation each for Gabon, Guyana, Surinam. These countries do not appear elsewhere in the study.

below one million; the former because of problems of comparability and the latter because of "the erratic character of the production structure of the heavily dependent splinter countries" (Kuznets, 1971, p. 105).

Table 2 lists the 101 countries that form the basis for the analysis and the number of observations on each dependent variable available over the period 1950–70.[14] The cross-country analysis is based primarily on the maximum samples for each variable. In comparing time-series and cross-section results compatible samples are also used, which include only countries having observations for the whole period.

In the first stage of the analysis the most important property of the statistical procedure is that it should apply to a wide variety of countries and processes. The scope for refined econometric specification is quite limited because it greatly reduces the size of the available sample. Once a uniform mapping of the major development phenomena has been completed it is often possible to find better descriptions of a given process by introducing additional variables or dividing the sample.

In addition to using widely available measures, the statistical formulation has to allow for nonlinearities as well as for shifts in cross-country relations over time. In satisfying these requirements the following two specifications have been found to have a wide range of application.[15] Equations (1.1) and (1.2) will be considered as the basic cross-country regressions and used to measure all processes. Equation (1.2) allows for a separate effect of an external resource inflow, while equation (1.1) includes its average effect in the coefficients for Y and N.

$$X = \alpha + \beta_1 lnY + \beta_2(lnY)^2 + \gamma_1 lnN + \gamma_2(lnN)^2 + \Sigma\ \delta_i T_j \qquad (1.1)$$
$$X = \alpha + \beta_1 lnY + \beta_2(lnY)^2 + \gamma_1 lnN + \gamma_2(lnN)^2 + \Sigma\ \delta_i T_j + \epsilon F$$
$$(1.2)$$

where X = dependent variable (see Table 1)

  Y = GNP per capita in 1964 U.S. dollars

  N = population in millions

  F = net resource inflow (imports minus exports of goods and nonfactor services) as a share of total GDP

  T_j = time period (j = 1, 2, 3, 4)[16]

---

[14]The concepts and sources are given in the Statistical Appendix. In cross-section analysis the number of countries is more significant than the number of observations. The country data for 1965 are plotted on the graphs for each variable in Chapters 3 and 4, using the code shown on Table 8.

[15]Equation (1.1) has been developed by testing the usefulness of alternative formulations to a variety of processes. Chenery (1960) used the form $lnX = \alpha + \beta lnY + \gamma lnN$ for the study of production patterns. A nonlinear income term was added in Chenery and Taylor (1968).

[16]In some cases the time variables were not included because of the size of the sample.

Equation (1.3) is used in Chapter 5 to compare time-series and cross-section results. By allowing each country to have a separate intercept, it estimates the average response of the dependent variable to changes in the explanatory variables over time.[17]

$$X = \alpha_i + \beta_1 lnY + \beta_2(lnY)^2 + \Sigma \, \delta_i T_i + \epsilon F \qquad (1.3)$$

where α_i = the constant term for country i.

Although, as suggested above, a logistic curve would provide a more satisfactory representation of many development processes, there are rarely sufficient observations to make it a significant improvement over this simpler form, particularly for the central income range ($100 to $1000) which is of most interest here.

The rationale for these specifications is as follows:

1. *The dependent variable (X)* is usually taken as a ratio to GDP or to its corresponding aggregate for all processes except the demographic transition. This specification leads to consistent estimates of each component of production or other aggregate. To be consistent the sum of all shares must total 100 percent, and the partial effects of each exogenous variable must total zero. These properties hold when the dependent variable is measured as a share or ratio but not when it is put in logarithmic form.

2. *Per capita GNP (Y),* or "income level," serves as an overall index of development as well as a measure of output, although there are difficulties in selecting exchange rates to compare income levels among countries.[18] In time-series analysis the regression coefficients β_1 and β_2 determine a "growth elasticity" that has economic significance in many processes.

3. *The country's population (N)* is introduced as an independent variable to allow for the effects of economies of scale and transport costs on patterns of trade and production.[19] These effects are independent of the income level, since size and level are virtually uncorrelated. Size does,

---

The equations are still identified as (1.1) and (1.2) depending on whether or not the effect of the external resource inflow is allowed for.

The estimated coefficients appear on the statistical tables in the text and appendices in the columns headed by their corresponding variable. The estimated values of α are reported in the column headed "Constant."

[17]By allowing each country to have its own intercept we eliminate all the variation among countries and retain only the variation within each country. This equation is discussed further in Chapter 5.

[18]Since the purpose here is to describe separate development processes, GNP is more useful as an explanatory variable than a broader index of development that would include many of the dependent variables being studied. The effects of the use of exchange rates in cross-country comparisons are discussed in the Technical Appendix.

[19]In Chapter 4, the effect of scale is analyzed more accurately by dividing the sample into large and small countries.

however, affect a surprising number of other development processes either directly or indirectly.

4. *The net resource inflow (F)* also affects directly or indirectly a number of development processes. The next chapter comments on the interaction among the four determinants of F (exports, imports, saving, and investment). Although there is some relationship between the income level and capital inflow, it is rather weak.[20]

5. *Time trends (T).* The assumption in equations (1.1) to (1.3) is that in all countries there are shifts in the structural relationships over time that are independent of income changes within each country.[21] Since a year is too short a unit of time to identify these shifts, five-year periods are used in measuring T which correspond to 1950–54, 1955–59, 1960–64, and 1965–69. In order to test the uniformity of the time trend, each five-year period has its own intercept. The average trend over the twenty-year period can be determined by averaging the values of δ_j.[22]

To avoid difficulties in combining the various results into a consistent analysis, the uniform set of regression equations listed above has been adopted for all processes. Although a better explanation of a given relationship can often be discovered by including additional variables specific to it, the uniform specification has the advantage of being able to compare the effects of given variables on each characteristic and the timing of each type of structural change.

Other explanatory variables suggested in the theoretical literature or significant in statistical studies include indices of resource endowments, the rate of growth, the extent of surplus labor, and the level of exports. Several of these will be utilized in Chapters 2 and 3 in exploring possible refinements of the uniform patterns.

PRESENTATION OF RESULTS

Since this analysis is based on some 20,000 observations, covering about a hundred countries and thirty variables over twenty years, it is

---

[20]Although it is important to investigate the effects of differences in capital inflows on development processes, the treatment of F as an exogenous variable creates statistical difficulties because as equilibrium is reached adjustment takes place in the capital inflow as well as in exports, imports, saving, and investment. The coefficients and standard errors attaching to F are therefore merely measures of partial correlations. To avoid difficulties of interpretation, regressions are in all cases computed with and without F (and other interdependent variables) to test whether the nonexogenous variables substantially affect other coefficients.

[21]While these equations provide an adequate test for the existence of a trend, a more satisfactory analysis can be secured by comparing separate time-series estimates when sufficient data are available.

[22]If only the average trend is desired, it can be determined directly by treating T as a continuous variable and estimating a single value of δ.

useful to get an impression of the overall results before investigating individual sources of variation. The uniform cross-country patterns for the accumulation and allocation processes are therefore summarized in Chapter 2 and the demographic and distributional processes in Chapter 3. These summaries provide a unified view of development measured from a consistent body of data and also a useful starting point for a more detailed study of differences in development patterns in Chapter 4. The relationships between cross-section and time-series estimates of development patterns—which are important for both theory and policy analysis—are discussed in Chapter 5.

To derive uniform cross-section estimates of the structural transformation, the two basic regression equations described above have been applied to the twenty-seven variables chosen to measure the basic processes. The characteristics of each process in relation to the overall structural transformation will be examined as well as its uniformity among countries and the evidence of change over time.

In the first exposition of the empirical results our main purpose is to present the "stylized facts" of development in such a way as to provide an agenda for further theoretical and empirical analysis. In a number of instances cross-country studies have already led to some reformulation of existing theories and attempts to test the consistency of these theories against the growing body of empirical evidence. Apart from a brief reference to the principal explanations of the observed patterns, however, detailed comment on the theoretical implications of these findings will be reserved for later chapters.

By way of introduction, Table 3 provides a composite picture of the development patterns derived by estimating equation (1.1) using values for a country of medium size ($N=10$).[23] These results are also shown graphically in Chapters 2 and 3. Taken together, these processes measure the normal changes in the economic structure that accompany a rise in per capita GNP from \$100 to \$1000.[24] Average values are also given for the countries below \$100 and above \$1000 per capita income;[25] they show that 75 to 80 percent of the total structural change takes place within this range, which has been chosen to represent the transition.

---

[23]A systematic set of solutions for a range of values of N and F is given in Carter and Elkington (1974).

[24]Since the simpler quadratic form of equation (1.1) is used in place of the theoretically more satisfactory logistic function, the results are valid for the middle-income range (\$100 to \$1000) but are not necessarily the best estimates above and below that range (see Chapter 4).

[25]These values are plotted on the graphs and connected by dashed lines to the regression results. For most processes the averages for the rich and poor countries indicate the upper and lower asymptotes; in few of these variables is there much indication of further change beyond \$2000 per capita.

TABLE 3. Normal Variation in Economic Structure with Level of Development

Process	Mean† Under $100	$100	$200	$300	$400	$500	$800	$1,000	Mean‡ Over $1,000	Total Change	Y at Midpoint
				Predicted Values at Different Income Levels*							
Accumulation Processes											
1. *Investment*											
a. Saving	.103	.135	.171	.190	.202	.210	.226	.233	.233	.130	200
b. Investment	.136	.158	.188	.203	.213	.220	.234	.240	.234	.098	200
c. Capital inflow	.032	.023	.016	.012	.010	.009	.006	.006	.001	−.031	200
2. *Government revenue*											
a. Government revenue	.125	.153	.181	.202	.219	.234	.268	.287	.307	.182	380
b. Tax revenue	.106	.129	.153	.173	.189	.203	.236	.254	.282	.176	440
3. *Education*											
a. Education expenditure	.026	.033	.033	.034	.035	.037	.041	.043	.039	.013	300
b. School enrollment ratio	.244	.375	.549	.637	.694	.735	.810	.842	.863	.619	200
Resource Allocation Processes											
4. *Structure of domestic demand*											
a. Private consumption	.779	.720	.686	.667	.654	.645	.625	.617	.624	−.155	
b. Government consumption	.119	.137	.134	.135	.136	.138	.144	.148	.141	.022	
c. Food consumption	.414	.392	.315	.275	.248	.229	.191	.175	.167	−.247	250

5. Structure of production											
a. Primary share	.522	.452	.327	.266	.228	.202	.156	.138	.127	−.395	200
b. Industry share	.125	.149	.215	.251	.276	.294	.331	.347	.379	.254	300
c. Utilities share	.053	.061	.072	.079	.085	.089	.098	.102	.109	.056	300
d. Services share	.300	.338	.385	.403	.411	.415	.416	.413	.386	.086	300
6. Structure of trade											
a. Exports	.172	.195	.218	.230	.238	.244	.255	.260	.249	.077	150
b. Primary exports	.130	.137	.136	.131	.125	.120	.105	.096	.058	−.072	1,000
c. Manufactured exports	.011	.019	.034	.046	.056	.065	.086	.097	.131	.120	600
d. Services exports	.028	.031	.042	.048	.051	.053	.056	.057	.059	.031	250
e. Imports	.205	.218	.234	.243	.249	.254	.263	.267	.250	.045	250

Demographic and Distributional Processes

7. Labor allocation											
a. Primary share	.712	.658	.557	.489	.438	.395	.300	.252	.159	−.553	400
b. Industry share	.078	.091	.164	.206	.235	.258	.303	.325	.368	.290	325
c. Services share	.210	.251	.279	.304	.327	.347	.396	.423	.473	.263	450
8. Urbanization	.128	.220	.362	.439	.490	.527	.601	.634	.658	.530	250
9. Demographic transition											
a. Birth rate	.459	.446	.377	.338	.311	.291	.249	.229	.191	−.268	350
b. Death rate	.209	.186	.135	.114	.103	.097	.091	.090	.097	−.112	150
10. Income distribution											
a. Highest 20%	.502	.541	.557	.554	.547	.538	.511	.494	.458	−.044	
b. Lowest 40%	.158	.140	.129	.127	.128	.130	.138	.143	.153	−.005	

*Predicted values from equation (1.1), Tables 4, 5, and 7. Per capita GNP in US$ 1964. N=10
†Approximately $70. Mean values of countries with per capita GNP under $100 vary slightly according to composition of the sample.
‡Approximately $1,500. Mean values of countries with per capita GNP over $1,000 vary slightly according to composition of the sample.

This uniform framework of analysis is also designed to bring out differences in timing among development processes. Each of the ten processes has a somewhat different relation to the growth of per capita income. Some take place mainly in the early stages of development and are half completed at an income level of $200, while others are typically delayed until income levels of $500 or more are reached. The statistical association of each process with the level of income therefore conceals important differences in timing that differentiate early and late stages of the transition.

To bring out these differences in timing, Table 3 shows the total change between the values for the least developed countries (below $100 per capita income) and the most developed (above $1000). The timing of processes that increase or decrease monotonically (i.e., all except income distribution) can be compared by referring to the income level at which the total change is half completed, which is shown in the last column of Table 3. The average variation in each accumulation and allocation process is also shown in Figures 1 to 6, and the levels at which the transition is 50 percent complete is indicated. Among accumulation processes the range for the midpoint is between $200 and $450, while among allocation processes it is between $150 and $1000.

For all ten processes the average midpoint comes at about $300, and the change is 90 percent complete at a level of $900 to $1000. Individual processes can be classed as early, normal, or late in relation to these averages. Similarly, individual countries can be described as leading or lagging in different aspects of the transition in relation to the average patterns of change.[26]

---

[26]Throughout this book the gross national product and its components are measured at factor cost in U.S. dollars of 1964, converted from local currencies as explained in the Statistical Appendix. GNP at market prices averages about 11 percent higher because of the inclusion of indirect taxes (*World Bank Atlas,* 1973). The following values of the U.S. GNP deflator (with 1964 = 100) can be used to convert to prices of other years: 1968 = 112.4; 1971 = 130.1; 1973 = 141.4).

Chapter 2

ACCUMULATION AND ALLOCATION PROCESSES

THE ACCUMULATION of resources to increase future output and the allocation of resources among different uses have usually been treated separately in empirical studies. However, a number of theoretical systems—balanced growth theories, dual economy models, two-gap models—imply significant interactions between accumulation and allocation that should be taken into account in quantitative analysis. To analyze these relationships, we will first study each set of processes separately and then examine some of their interactions.

ACCUMULATION PROCESSES

Theoretical Background

Accumulation may be defined as the use of resources to increase the productive capacity of an economy.[1] Since formal growth theories concentrate almost exclusively on processes of accumulation as the central phenomena of development, these processes have received a great deal of theoretical and empirical attention. Over the past twenty years there has been a fruitful sequence of *(a)* formulation of theories, *(b)* testing them through cross-section and time-series analysis, and *(c)* reformulating and extending them to include additional variables. Since this sequence of inductive theorizing has probably been pursued further in the study of savings and investment than in any of the other nine processes considered here, the results provide some general methodological insights that are also useful in studying the other processes.[2]

One approach to the analysis of saving in developing economies stems from the Keynesian hypothesis that the marginal propensity to save out of increased income is greater than the average rate of savings. Early tests of this hypothesis in the United States typically showed greater marginal saving propensities in cross-section analysis of different income groups than in time series. Subsequent comparative analyses of developing countries gave similar results: there is a marked intercountry increase in saving

---

[1] Accumulation is conventionally subdivided into increases in physical capital stocks and increases in human capital. Identifiable inputs devoted to improving human capital include formal and informal education, public health, technical assistance, and other public services which augment human productivity.

[2] The theoretical and empirical literature on the savings function in developing countries has been the subject of a very thorough survey by Mikesell and Zinser (1973), which provides a basis for the following summary.

with rising per capita income over the transitional income range (up to $1000), but a less uniform rise in the saving rate over time in individual countries.[3]

To reconcile these findings, a number of authors—Lewis (1954), Kuznets (1960b), Houthakker (1961)—have examined the saving behavior of different groups of income recipients. These studies have shown higher saving rates for entrepreneurs, government, and nonlabor income recipients in general. The econometric results of a number of studies tend to confirm Lewis's original hypothesis that "saving increases relatively to the national income because the incomes of the savers increase relatively to the national income" (1954, p. 417).

This approach can be generalized for the study of other development processes from cross-country data by distinguishing two types of phenomena associated with rising levels of income:

1. Direct effects of increasing income on a particular aspect of economic activity, exemplified by Keynesian aggregate propensities to save or consume or the elasticities of Engel curves for consumer demand
2. Indirect effects stemming from the changes in composition of production, trade, employment, location, and other structural features associated with rising income.

The purpose of the initial cross-country measurements reported in this chapter is to determine only the combined effects of rising income. Attempts to separate direct and indirect effects are deferred to later chapters, except for processes where this has already been done by other authors. In general, the identification of indirect effects reduces the variation attributable to direct effects.[4] For example, several studies indicate that given types of income recipients have a fairly constant saving share, which suggests that all of the income effect on saving may be the result of the change in composition of recipients.

A similar theoretical framework can be applied to the analysis of government revenue and developmental expenditure. An increase in the tax share in GDP with rising income can be broken down into changes in the proportions of different types of taxable income and changes in tax rates applicable to each. As in the case of saving, a substantial proportion of the rise in the overall share of taxes can be shown to result from the changing composition of the tax base, in which international trade, mining, industry, and foreign investors tend to be more readily taxable than

---

[3]Friedman's permanent income hypothesis (1957) provides an alternative explanation for rising savings rates as a function of the rate of growth of GNP. Williamson (1968) in a study of eight Asian countries finds confirmation of the hypothesis that savings out of temporary income should be higher than out of permanent income. This issue is discussed further in Chapter 5.

[4]This need not be the case, since some indirect effects are of opposite sign from the direct effects.

agriculture or services. Much of the literature on variation in the tax share—Hinrichs (1965), Lotz and Morss (1967), Musgrave (1969)—is concerned with the indirect effects of such growth-related structural changes on the government's ability to increase revenue.

As the level of income rises, it is generally assumed that the limitations on the tax base become less important and that the share of government revenue in GDP is determined more by political preferences and the demand for public goods. Even in advanced countries, however, there is a widespread bias against raising taxes above conventionally accepted levels. It is therefore useful to retain the hypothesis that the share of government revenue in GDP is limited more by social and political factors than by the demand for public goods.

Education constitutes the largest element of public expenditure in most developing countries and probably more than half of all investment in human capital. It will therefore be significantly affected by the total budgetary limit as well as by demand. Although there is a substantial body of analysis of the returns from different types of education in individual countries, there is little discussion of how to determine the share of GNP—or of budgetary resources—that should be devoted to increasing the stock of human capital at a given point in time.

The empirical problem is that in most developing countries the volume of resources devoted to education in the early 1950s was much below the optimum on almost any test. The period 1950–70 was one in which countries generally tried to catch up to some educational norm as rapidly as possible. Although the extent of this upward shift can be measured over the twenty-year period, there is no way to determine whether this adjustment process has run its course.

For each of the accumulation processes there are theoretical grounds to predict a period of accelerated structural change, in which direct effects of increasing income are reinforced by indirect effects of change in other structural characteristics, followed by a deceleration as the rate of accumulation approaches the socially desired levels and indirect effects decline in importance. Although there is no basis for interpreting the postwar cross-country results as evidence of an efficient growth path, they can perhaps be thought of as a process of adjustment that is generally in the direction of such a path. Since theory is unable to predict the effects of limitations on sources of revenue or the speed of adjustment, these are matters for empirical investigation.

Statistical Analysis

To describe accumulation processes fully, we would need three types of measures: total stocks, increases in stocks, and resources devoted to producing these increases. The indices that are widely available include two partial measures of increases in stocks (gross investment and school enrollment) and five measures of resource availabilities (domestic saving and capital inflow for physical investment; tax revenue, total government revenue, and educational expenditure for human capital formation). Since a consistent breakdown of government expenditure is lacking, total government revenue is taken as a proxy to indicate the limits to total public development expenditure.[5]

The results of applying the two standard regression equations (1.1) and (1.2) to these seven measures of accumulation are given in Table 4. The normal variation with income level is shown in Table 3 and graphically in Figures 1, 2, and 3.[6] For six of the seven indices there is a substantial increase over the transition, varying from 50 percent of the initial level for educational expenditures and 70 percent for gross investment to 165 percent for tax revenues and 250 percent for school enrollment.[7] For the four measures that show increases of more than 100 percent the proportion of the intercountry variance explained by equation (1.2) (i.e., the value of R^2) is on the order of 60 to 70 percent.

Unlike most other developmental processes there is a significant international time trend in almost all the measures of accumulation. The trends shown in Table 4 for the fifteen-year interval between 1950–54 and 1965–69 amount to an upward shift of about 7 percent of the mean values of saving, investment, and government revenue, 12 percent of school enrollment, and 45 percent of mean educational expenditure.[8]

The other exogenous variables—country size and capital inflow—show a significant relationship to most of the accumulation processes. Capital inflow declines markedly with an increase in the size of country, largely as a result of the smaller share of trade in large countries. The capital inflow (F) partially offsets changes in both saving and government revenue, as shown by the negative coefficients for F in Table 4. In this case, however, the cross-country pattern is not a good guide to predicting changes in individual countries over time because other factors specific to each country

---

[5]Tax revenue, total government revenue, and total government expenditure follow much the same pattern. The first two are both included because taxation has been the subject of an extensive literature based on intercountry data, but total revenue is a better indicator of budgetary resources.

[6]All graphs are based on equation (1.1), in which the effects of the normal decline in capital inflow are incorporated in the total income effect.

[7]The extreme values shown in Table 3 and the figures are the averages for countries below $100 income (mean about $70) and those above $1000 (mean about $1500). The change over the transition is measured from the extreme values and shown in Table 3.

[8]The regression coefficients for T_1, T_2, and T_3 indicate the shift in the estimated relationship for each five-year period compared to the last period (1965–69). For example, the coefficient of $-.012$ for T_1 in the regression for saving (1.2) indicates that there has been an upward shift of 1.2 percentage points since the 1950–54 period.

Figure 1: Investment

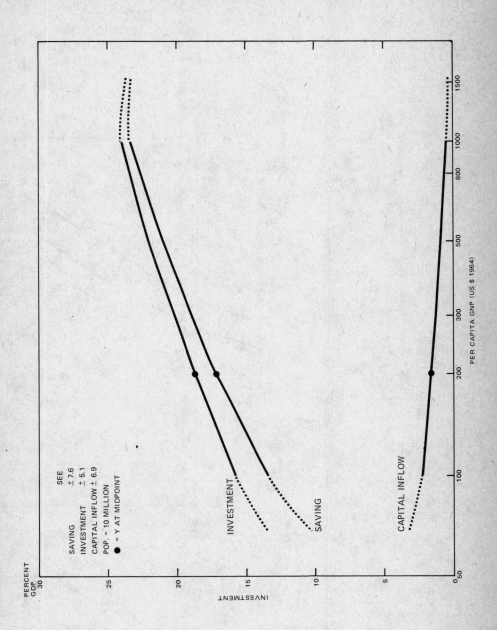

28

Figure 2: Government Revenue

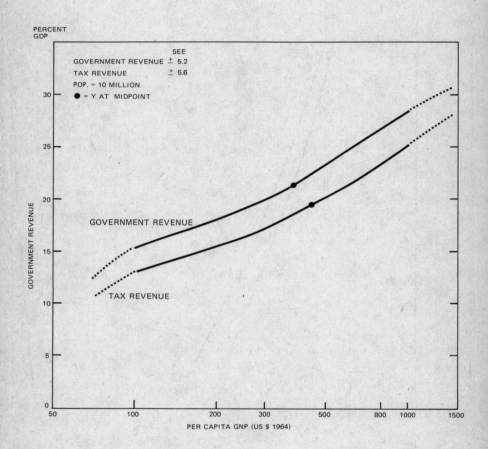

Figure 3: Education

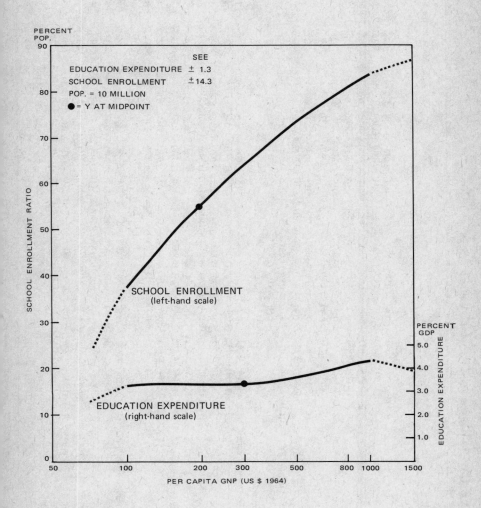

TABLE 4. Basic Regressions: Accumulation Processes

Process	Eqn.	Constant	$\ln Y$	$(\ln Y)^2$	$\ln N$	$(\ln N)^2$	F	T_1	T_2	T_3	R^2	SEE	Y Mean/Range	No. of Obs.
1. Investment														
a. Saving	(1.1)	−.340 (5.814)	.115 (5.674)	−.006 (3.611)	.051 (9.243)	−.007 (6.947)		−.001 (.143)	−.012 (2.190)	−.010 (1.909)	.320	.076	528 34/3615	1432
	(1.2)	−.199 (5.186)	.093 (6.984)	−.005 (4.255)	.020 (5.455)	−.003 (4.555)	−.832 (43.70)	−.012 (3.113)	−.013 (3.559)	−.008 (2.329)	.710	.050	528 34/3615	1432
b. Investment	(1.1)	−.161 (4.116)	.085 (6.259)	−.004 (3.666)	.013 (3.650)	−.002 (3.261)		−.015 (3.842)	−.014 (3.630)	−.008 (2.377)	.373	.051	528 34/3615	1432
	(1.2)	−.188 (4.903)	.089 (6.727)	−.005 (3.995)	.019 (5.278)	−.003 (4.450)	.159 (8.361)	−.013 (3.371)	−.014 (3.676)	−.009 (2.547)	.402	.050	528 34/3615	1432
c. Capital inflow (F)	(1.1)	.170 (3.187)	−.027 (1.460)	.002 (1.094)	−.037 (7.410)	.005 (5.207)		−.014 (2.505)	−.001 (.181)	.002 (.510)	.079	.069	528 34/3615	1432
2. Government revenue														
a. Government revenue	(1.1)	.214 (4.393)	−.073 (4.332)	.011 (7.896)	.024 (6.001)	−.004 (5.704)		−.013 (2.635)	−.008 (1.787)	−.009 (2.334)	.620	.052	536 34/2356	1111
	(1.2)	.251 (5.230)	−.082 (5.005)	.012 (8.604)	.020 (4.974)	−.004 (4.946)	−.148 (7.346)	−.015 (3.187)	−.007 (1.646)	−.007 (1.930)	.638	.050	536 34/2356	1111
b. Tax revenue	(1.1)	.220 (4.164)	−.083 (4.570)	.012 (7.650)	.029 (6.626)	−.005 (6.259)		.000 (.050)	.004 (.726)	−.006 (1.356)	.559	.056	536 34/2356	1111
	(1.2)	.249 (4.735)	−.091 (5.030)	.013 (8.111)	.026 (5.841)	−.005 (5.679)	−.117 (5.273)	−.002 (.305)	.004 (.866)	−.004 (1.044)	.570	.055	536 34/2356	1111
3. Education														
a. Education expenditure	(1.1)	.096 (6.498)	−.028 (5.424)	.003 (6.428)	.004 (3.265)	−.001 (4.065)		−.015 (9.217)	−.010 (5.742)	−.005 (4.801)	.231	.013	556 34/3432	794
	(1.2)	.096 (6.479)	−.028 (5.418)	.003 (6.421)	.004 (3.211)	−.001 (4.028)	−.000 (.064)	−.015 (9.208)	−.010 (5.738)	−.005 (4.796)	.231	.013	556 34/3432	794
b. School enrollment ratio	(1.1)	−1.517 (7.104)	.546 (7.316)	−.030 (4.633)	−.003 (.168)	.004 (.965)		−.083 (3.629)	−.043 (2.010)	−.032 (1.942)	.687	.143	464 35/3201	433
	(1.2)	−1.710 (8.377)	.595 (8.383)	−.034 (5.517)	.019 (1.028)	.000 (.129)	.550 (7.070)	−.067 (3.072)	−.035 (1.743)	−.030 (1.919)	.720	.136	464 35/3201	433

NOTES: *t* ratios in parentheses.

are associated with the variation in capital inflow. When these factors are excluded — as discussed in Chapter 5 — the results of time-series analysis show a much larger proportion of an increase in external resources going into capital formation than the 16 percent shown in Table 4.

Even when allowance is made for differences in external resources, accumulation rates appear to be significantly higher in large countries in all respects except school enrollment. There is no obvious explanation for this finding, which can be noted as a topic for future research.

The Role of Accumulation in the Transition

In relation to the average timing of all ten processes described in Table 3, the changes in the three accumulation processes take place relatively early in the transition. The total increase in saving, investment, and school enrollment is normally half completed at an income of $200 and 90 percent complete at about $700.[9] This characteristic of a rapid rise at low-income levels and subsequent tapering off is shown in Table 4 by large positive coefficients for the lnY term and large negative coefficients for $(lnY)^2$. This interpretation of rising accumulation occurring early in the transition is consistent with the fairly constant rates of investment and school enrollment observed in more advanced countries, where these aspects of the transition have been completed.

Unlike saving and investment, the rise in taxation and government revenue and expenditure is a relatively late process that does not reach its halfway mark until about $400 per capita. The timing becomes more normal, however, if transfer payments are separated from other uses of government revenues. Net transfers are negligible at lower income levels but account for perhaps 25 percent of government revenue at high income levels.[10] If net transfers were deducted other government revenues would rise steadily from 13 percent of GNP at $70 per capita to perhaps 23 percent at $1500 with more normal timing.

One of the largest sources of variation in accumulation processes at low income levels is the inflow of capital. It is typically equal to 25 percent of investment at the lowest levels, declining to 10 percent at $200 and 5 percent at $400, but with substantial variation among countries. Although the relation of capital inflow to income level is quite weak, there is a strong negative correlation with size. The level of capital inflow is an important policy variable which is discussed at length in Chapter 4.

---

[9]If there were measures of the per capita stocks of physical and human capital, however, they would lag behind these proportions. If the stock of human capital is measured by average years of schooling of the labor force, the corresponding increase is from roughly two to twelve years, and the halfway mark is normally reached at above $500 per capita income.

[10]Kuznets (1962), p. 8.

RESOURCE ALLOCATION PROCESSES

Resource allocation processes produce systematic changes in the sectoral composition of domestic demand, international trade, and production as the level of income rises. These patterns result from an interaction between the demand effects of rising income and the supply effects of changes in factor proportions and technology. Except for consumer demand and primary exports, the indirect effects of changes elsewhere in the system make it difficult to decompose the observed patterns of resource allocation into separate processes.

Historically, interest in development patterns has centered on sectoral shifts in consumption and production over time. Engel's law of the declining share of food consumption with rising income levels has been verified in many studies which provide a prototype for empirical and theoretical work on structural change. Looking at the structure of production, Fisher (1939) and Clark (1940) observed a progression in the allocation of labor from primary to secondary to tertiary employment, which Clark described as Petty's law and explained largely on the basis of changes in domestic demand. The subsequent work of Kuznets and other scholars has shown the need for a more comprehensive treatment of both demand and supply factors in seeking to explain allocation patterns.

Theoretical Background

The various theories of balanced and unbalanced growth, which were proposed in rather general terms by Rosenstein-Rodan (1943), Nurkse (1959), Lewis (1955), and Scitovsky (1959), provide a starting point for a systematic analysis of resource allocation processes. These theories are concerned with the relations between the pattern of demand growth on the one hand and the patterns of international trade and domestic production and investment on the other. The argument for balance between production and domestic demand depends critically on two assumptions:
1. That the price elasticity of domestic demand for major commodity groups is relatively low, so that the consumption pattern is determined primarily by the level of income
2. That the levels of exports and imports are not so large as to offset the implied relation between domestic demand and domestic supply of major commodities.

The first assumption has been largely validated in subsequent empirical work[11] and is widely accepted in development theory. The second

---

[11]See Weisskoff (1971) and Lluch (1973).

assumption is shown below to have considerable empirical validity for large countries but only limited applicability to countries of less than 15 million population, in which commodity imports are typically 40 percent or more of the total supply of traded goods.

A second line of analysis of resource allocation processes can be derived from several theories of international trade. The Heckscher-Ohlin theory[12] derives comparative advantage from relative factor proportions. The more rapid growth of capital and human skills, relative to unskilled labor, facilitates the growth of manufactured exports. This shift in export composition is also supported by Linder's (1961) theory of representative demand, according to which a country acquires a comparative advantage in manufactures through producing them first for the domestic market. Through innovation and learning by doing, relative production costs and export patterns are assumed to follow changes in the pattern of domestic demand. These two theories are thus complementary and together predict a shift from primary production and exports to manufacturing in small countries, a group to which the balanced growth argument by contrast has little application.

In summary, theoretical considerations lead to the identification of several direct effects of rising income on resource allocation, which are supplemented by a number of indirect effects of other structural changes. The principal direct effects are: the rise in nonfood consumption predicted by Engel's law; and the change in factor proportions resulting from the growth of physical and human capital in relation to population. The Engel effect can be considered a separate process and measured directly from cross-country data. Changes in the composition of exports can also be measured directly, but the suggested causes cannot be verified from cross-country analysis at this aggregate level.

Although each of these allocation patterns has been studied separately, they have not previously been treated systematically so as to bring out their interdependence. In order to do so we have modified the sector breakdown of production to correspond as closely as possible to the division of trade statistics between primary and manufactured goods. Although strict compatibility with demand can be secured only by means of an input-output analysis that makes explicit provision for intermediate goods, the main Engel effects can be brought out simply by separating demand into food and other items of personal consumption. To conform to available intercountry data on production, consumption, and trade, the following sectoral categories are used in the uniform analysis:

---

[12]For a general exposition of the modern version of this theory, see Bhagwati (1964).

Value Added in Production[13]		(ISIC)[14]	Exports[15]		Consumption	
V_p	Agriculture and mining	(0+1)	E_p	Primary	C_f	Food
V_m	Manufacturing and construction	(2–4)	E_m	Industry		
V_u	Utilities	(5+7)		(nontraded)	C_{nf}	Nonfood
V_s	Services	(6+8–81)	E_s	Services		

Statistical Analysis

Like the three accumulation processes, the three sets of resource allocation processes have a number of common features that can best be brought out by discussing them as a group. The standard regression equations for the three sets of resource allocation processes are given in Table 5. The normal variation with income level is shown in Table 3 and Figures 4, 5, and 6. Taken together, the figures describe the overall transformation of the structure of demand and supply that is implied by a broad use of the term "industrialization."

The interrelations among these three sets of processes are brought out by considering first the Engel effects, which are least dependent on other aspects of structural change. Over the whole transition, per capita food consumption increases only half as much as per capita income.[16] The corresponding drop in the share of food consumption from 41 percent to less than 20 percent of GNP permits a doubling in the share of investment and a 70 percent increase in nonfood consumption. When broken down, these shifts imply a doubling in the share of industrial goods (apart from foodstuffs) in total demand over the transition.

The change in the composition of exports is similar in scope to the reversal in composition of domestic demand, although its timing is usually somewhat later in the transition and largely affected by government policy. Primary exports decline from 13 to 6 percent of GNP, while primary imports rise from 4 to 6 percent over the transition.[17] This reflects

[13]The principal change from Kuznets's classification is that mining is grouped with agriculture in the primary sector, since both are largely determined by natural resource endowments. In addition utilities are treated as a separate sector of production, since power, water, and communications are not traded and are much more capital intensive than other services. Transport exports are a minor element and are included with other service exports.

[14]International Standard Industrial Classification.

[15]The export breakdown follows the United Nations Committee on Trade and Development (UNCTAD) and, as detailed in the Statistical Appendix, includes the first stage of processing for most minerals in primary exports.

[16]The elasticity of food demand with respect to per capita income declines from .70 at $100 to .62 at $1000. Similar results were reported in Lluch and Williams (1973).

[17]Since there is little change in the overall composition of imports with variations in income, this breakdown is not included in the description of trade patterns.

Figure 4: Structure of Domestic Demand

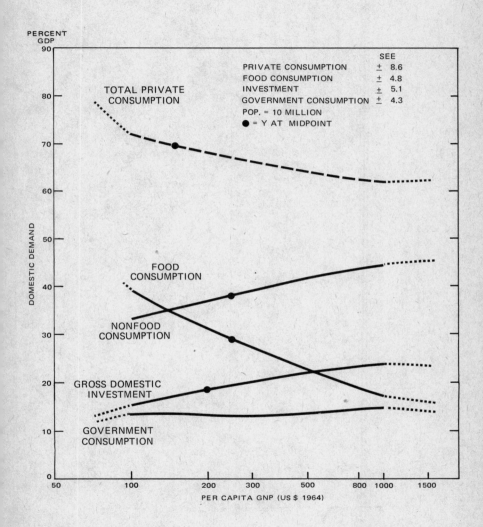

36

Figure 5: Structure of Production (Value Added)

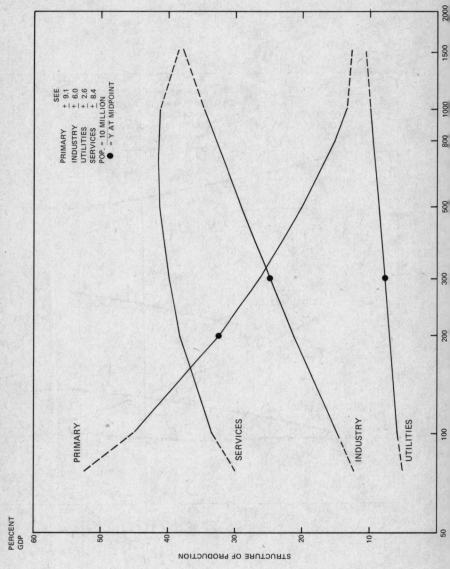

PERCENT
GDP

STRUCTURE OF PRODUCTION

PRIMARY

SERVICES

INDUSTRY

UTILITIES

	SEE
PRIMARY	+ 9.1
INDUSTRY	+|+ 6.0
UTILITIES	+|+ 2.6
SERVICES	+|+ 8.4

POP. = 10 MILLION
● = Y AT MIDPOINT

Figure 6: Structure of Trade

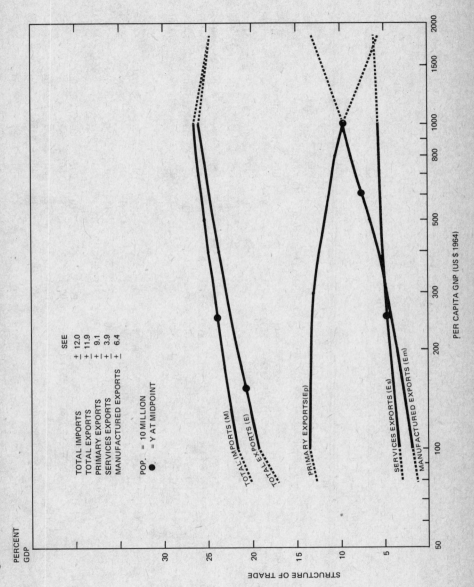

PERCENT
GDP

	SEE
TOTAL IMPORTS	+|+ 12.0
TOTAL EXPORTS	+|+ 11.9
PRIMARY EXPORTS	+|+ 9.1
SERVICES EXPORTS	+|+ 3.9
MANUFACTURED EXPORTS	+|+ 6.4

POP. = 10 MILLION
● = Y AT MIDPOINT

TOTAL IMPORTS (M)

TOTAL EXPORTS (E)

PRIMARY EXPORTS(Ep)

SERVICES EXPORTS (Es)

MANUFACTURED EXPORTS (Em)

STRUCTURE OF TRADE

PER CAPITA GNP (US $ 1964)

TABLE 5. Basic Regressions: Resource Allocation Processes

Process	Eqn.	Constant	lnY	(lnY)²	lnN	(lnN)²	F	T_1	T_2	T_3	R^2	SEE	Y Mean/Range	No. of Obs.
4. Structure of domestic demand														
b. Private consumption	(1.1)	1.098 (16.180)	−.077 (3.265)	.003 (1.354)	−.058 (9.504)	.010 (8.539)		.021 (3.239)	.025 (4.047)	.014 (2.365)	.277	.086	510 35/3615	1,508
	(1.2)	.883 (16.230)	−.021 (1.139)	−.002 (1.028)	−.034 (6.873)	.007 (7.028)	.717 (29.620)	.032 (6.100)	.028 (5.580)	.014 (3.045)	.544	.068	510 35/3615	1,508
c. Government consumption	(1.1)	.283 (8.336)	−.059 (5.054)	.006 (5.537)	.011 (3.669)	−.003 (4.922)		−.022 (6.550)	−.017 (5.513)	−.006 (2.092)	.083	.043	510 35/3615	1,508
	(1.2)	.236 (7.152)	−.047 (4.163)	.005 (4.175)	.016 (5.494)	−.004 (6.351)	.154 (10.510)	−.019 (6.047)	−.017 (5.537)	−.006 (2.143)	.146	.042	510 35/3615	1,508
d. Food consumption	(1.1)	1.199 (13.600)	−.213 (7.364)	.010 (4.378)	−.033 (5.993)	.006 (5.832)		.025 (3.627)	.022 (4.298)	.009 (1.883)	.773	.048	803 73/3551	642
	(1.2)	1.174 (15.080)	−.219 (8.547)	.011 (5.300)	−.017 (3.423)	.004 (4.087)	.340 (12.980)	.028 (4.601)	.022 (5.027)	.011 (2.577)	.820	.042	803 73/3551	642
5. Structure of production														
a. Primary share	(1.1)	1.966 (22.160)	−.449 (14.840)	.027 (10.570)	−.012 (1.712)	.001 (.745)		.015 (1.997)	.006 (.919)	.007 (1.115)	.677	.091	510 47/3551	1,325
	(1.2)	2.025 (26.100)	−.456 (17.230)	.028 (12.270)	−.030 (5.027)	.004 (3.131)	−.588 (20.210)	.012 (1.879)	.011 (1.863)	.010 (1.807)	.754	.079	510 47/3551	1,325
b. Industry share	(1.1)	−.522 (8.989)	.154 (7.776)	−.006 (3.523)	.053 (12.120)	−.007 (8.077)		.010 (2.135)	.005 (1.169)	−.002 (.587)	.692	.060	510 47/3551	1,325
	(1.2)	−.547 (9.759)	.158 (8.260)	−.006 (3.812)	.060 (13.940)	−.008 (9.405)	.213 (10.150)	.011 (2.361)	.003 (.745)	−.004 (.938)	.714	.057	510 47/3551	1,325
c. Utilities share	(1.1)	−.002 (.065)	.006 (.750)	.001 (1.315)	.010 (4.973)	−.002 (4.990)		−.006 (2.750)	−.003 (1.564)	−.001 (.390)	.324	.026	510 47/3551	1,325
	(1.2)	−.004 (.16?)	.007 (.91?)	.001 (1.35?)	.010 (5.1??)	−.002 (5.0??)	.014 (1.52?)	−.006 (2.75?)	−.003 (1.65?)	−.001	.324	.026	510 47/3551	1,325

d. Services share	(1.1)	−.442 (5.413)	.288 (10.350)	−.022 (9.388)	−.051 (8.314)	.008 (6.495)		−.019 (2.825)	−.009 (1.335)	−.004 (.664)	.217	.084	510	47/3551	1,325
	(1.2)	−.473 (6.113)	.291 (11.010)	−.022 (9.945)	−.040 (6.758)	.006 (5.357)	.360 (12.410)	−.018 (2.682)	−.011 (1.855)	−.006 (.969)	.299	.079	510	47/3551	1,325
6. *Structure of trade*															
a. Exports	(1.1)	.038 (.410)	.062 (1.950)	−.003 (1.067)	−.015 (1.758)	−.006 (3.602)		−.002 (.231)	−.014 (1.566)	−.014 (1.706)	.220	.119	528	34/3615	1,432
	(1.2)	.117 (1.324)	.049 (1.661)	−.002 (.799)	−.032 (3.852)	−.004 (2.247)	−.468 (10.680)	−.009 (.947)	−.014 (1.678)	−.013 (1.628)	.278	.115	528	34/3615	1,432
b. Primary exports	(1.1)	−.026 (.187)	.097 (2.040)	−.010 (2.493)	−.032 (2.588)	.000 (.056)					.230	.091	580	35/3551	413
	(1.2)	.359 (3.860)	−.006 (.176)	−.002 (.916)	−.056 (6.956)	.003 (2.224)	−.983 (23.225)				.669	.060	580	35/3551	413
c. Manufactured exports	(1.1)	.073 (.741)	−.053 (1.585)	.008 (2.690)	.025 (2.860)	−.005 (3.247)					.304	.064	580	35/3551	413
	(1.2)	.049 (.493)	−.047 (1.386)	.007 (2.509)	.026 (3.012)	−.005 (3.358)	.060 (1.326)				.307	.064	580	35/3551	413
d. Services exports	(1.1)	−.082 (1.370)	.044 (2.182)	−.003 (1.678)	−.016 (2.991)	.001 (1.088)					.175	.039	580	35/3551	413
	(1.2)	.128 (2.141)	.057 (2.806)	−.004 (2.227)	−.013 (2.465)	.001 (.711)	.116 (4.284)				.211	.038	580	35/3551	413
e. Imports	(1.1)	.213 (2.305)	.033 (1.029)	−.001 (.371)	−.052 (6.007)	−.001 (.572)		−.016 (1.666)	−.015 (1.650)	−.012 (1.409)	.268	.120	528	34/3615	1,432
	(1.2)	.123 (1.391)	.047 (1.548)	−.002 (.741)	−.032 (3.852)	−.004 (2.252)	.532 (12.130)	−.009 (.943)	−.014 (1.675)	−.013 (1.644)	.337	.115	528	34/3615	1,432

t ratios in parentheses.

the shift in domestic demand for primary products and the limited domestic supplies of natural resources as well as the slow growth of total world demand and stability of prices during the period studied. The accumulation of capital and skills, reinforced by the experience of producing for the domestic market and the rapid growth of export markets during this period, leads to an average rise of manufactured exports from 1 to 13 percent of GDP over the transition.

Since the changes in domestic demand and in trade reinforce each other, the total change in the productive structure is more pronounced than in either of its determinants. Value added in primary production falls from 52 percent to 13 percent of GNP over the transition, nearly twice as much as the reduction in food demand, while the rise of industrial output is also much greater than the rise of domestic demand. More detailed studies based on simulation models of the transition show that Engel effects account for only half of the observed rise in the share of industry; the other half is caused in about equal proportions by import substitution and the growth of industrial exports.[18]

The standard regression equations of Table 5 show that the change in composition of demand is the most uniform of these processes, and the change in composition of trade the least uniform. While food consumption, primary exports, and primary production decline with almost equal uniformity, the growth of manufactured exports is less regular. In the overall industrial transformation, however, the allocation processes are as uniform among countries as the accumulation of physical and human capital and other aspects of development.

As will be shown in Chapter 4, two exogenous factors account for the major differences in the structure of production and trade and in the timing of the industrial transformation: the size of the economy and its natural resource endowments. These characteristics influence production primarily through their effects on the volume and structure of trade. The effect of population (and hence of domestic market size) on the levels of imports and exports is also quite pronounced, as shown by the standard equations in Table 5.

Figure 7 illustrates the average effect of market size on total trade at an income level of $300. It shows that when the population size is doubled the share of exports is typically reduced by 3 percent of GNP. Although the average share of exports increases by 8 percent of GDP over the transition (Table 3), this income effect is not as large as the effect of a difference between a population of 50 million and one of 5 million.

There have been several significant intercountry time trends in demand and production over the past twenty years. The following fifteen-

---

[18]See Chenery (1960, 1965) and Taylor (1969).

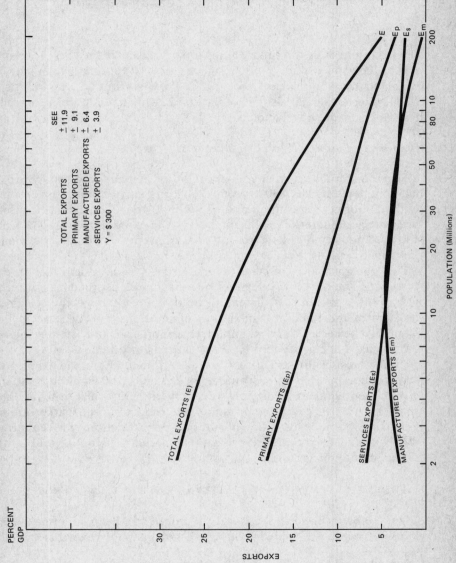

41

Figure 7: Export Variation with Size of Population

PERCENT GDP

TOTAL EXPORTS (E)

PRIMARY EXPORTS (Ep)

SERVICES EXPORTS (Es)

MANUFACTURED EXPORTS (Em)

	SEE
TOTAL EXPORTS	+ 11.9
PRIMARY EXPORTS	+ 9.1
MANUFACTURED EXPORTS	+ 6.4
SERVICES EXPORTS	+ 3.9

Y = $ 300

EXPORTS

POPULATION (Millions)

year shift in the normal pattern of production is indicated by the coefficients of T_1 in Table 5 (the dummy variable for 1950–54):[19]

Primary production	−1.2%
Industry	−1.1%
Utilities	+0.6%
Services	+1.8%

The fall in the share of primary output, over and above the effects of rising income, continues a trend observed over the past century, which may be explained by technological progress and the substitution of industrial products for raw materials. The other trends, while statistically significant, have not been previously noted.[20]

The Role of Resource Allocation in the Transition

The transformation of the composition of demand and production is half completed by the $300 income level. Industrialization, as measured by the fall of primary output and rise of industry, is typical of the structural changes that make up this transition. Above the $300 level, the value added in industry normally exceeds that in primary production, a condition which typifies the later stages of the transition.

The transformation of trade normally takes place much later in the transition. The rise in the share of manufactured exports does not reach its halfway mark until an income level of $600, although there is great variation in the timing of this aspect of the transition. Because of this variability, leads and lags in industrial exports are one of the characteristics used to classify development patterns in Chapter 4.

Unlike most of the structural features considered here, the export pattern is quite sensitive to government policies and provides an index to the development strategy being followed. Governments must bring about a transformation in export composition sufficient to offset market limitations; failure to do this is one of the commonest reasons why countries fail to complete the transition without serious disruptions in other development policies and in the overall rate of growth.

THE INTERACTIONS AMONG EXTERNAL AND INTERNAL PROCESSES

Up to now a uniform statistical procedure has been followed which treats income level, capital inflow, and population as explanatory vari-

---

[19]Since the same sample is used for all four regressions, the time trends are consistent and total zero. The opposite signs in Table 5 reflect the convention of setting T_4 for the most recent period at zero.

[20]These intercountry trends are compared to the average time series trends in Chapter 5.

ables. Both capital inflow and size affect the structure of the economy primarily through adjustments in the volume and composition of external trade. This interaction will now be explored more thoroughly by considering the effects of natural resource endowments and differences in trade policy as well.

Development theory has been concerned with several aspects of the interaction between external policies and internal resource allocation: import substitution and export promotion, the trade-off between aid and trade, and repercussions of· these policies on consumption and investment. Cross-country analysis can contribute to this discussion by providing systematic measures of the average differences in demand, production, saving, and government revenue associated with different trading patterns. This analysis will also provide a basis for identifying alternative development strategies in Chapter 4.

Regression Analysis

The analysis of the level and composition of exports in Table 5 shows a high degree of substitution between primary exports and external resources *(F),* but industry and service exports show little relation to changes in *F* across countries. When *F* is included as an explanatory variable in the regression equation (and exports are not), its regression coefficient therefore includes (mutatis mutandis) the effect of an offsetting reduction in primary exports. Similarly the use of exports alone as an explanatory variable will include the effects of a reduction in *F*. To estimate the effect of each, ceteris paribus, both variables will therefore be included in an augmented regression equation.[21] The results of estimating these regressions for the principal development processes affected by trade are given in the Statistical Appendix, Table S14, and summarized in Table 6.

Since the income and size effects shown in Table 6 are not significantly affected by the addition of the export variables, we can concentrate on the changes in structure associated with different patterns of exports, imports, and capital inflow, with income and size held constant. Under these assumptions the following identities apply to changes in the elements of the national accounts and the balance of payments:

$$\Delta Y = \Delta C + \Delta G + \Delta I + \Delta E - \Delta M = O \qquad (2.1)$$

$$\Delta M = \Sigma \, \Delta M_i = \Delta F + \Delta E_p + \Delta E_m + \Delta E_s, \qquad i = p, m, s \quad (2.2)$$

$$\Delta X_i + \Delta M_i = \Delta D_i + \Delta E_i, \qquad i = p, m, s \quad (2.3)$$

---

[21]The augmented regression adds the shares of GDP of primary exports *(E_p)*, manufactured exports *(E_m)*, and service exports *(E_s)*. Time trends are omitted because the analysis is limited to the 1960–69 period.

Equation (2.1) states that changes in the composition of GNP must total zero; (2.2) defines the trade balance; and (2.3) states that changes in the supply of each group of tradable commodities (Production plus imports) must equal changes in total domestic demand (D_i) plus exports.

The regression coefficients that measure these changes are listed in Table 6.[22] They show the effects of changes in trade patterns under the following alternative assumptions:

Assumption *(a):* A unit increase in capital inflow *(F)* with offsetting changes in exports

Assumption *(b):* A unit increase in one type of exports *(E_i)* with offsetting changes in capital inflow

Assumption *(c):* Unit increases in F or E_i with no change in the other (ceteris paribus).

Since each type of export has a different relation to the structure of production, Table 6 lists four cases in which primary, manufactured, and service exports are varied separately. For each case it shows the structural changes that normally accompany incremental differences in trade and aid patterns.

TABLE 6. Effects of a Unit Increase in Exports and External Capital

Assumption of a Unit Increase in	Case 1 F		Case 2 E_p		Case 3 E_m		Case 4 E_s	
	(a)	(c)	(b)	(c)	(b)	(c)	(b)	(c)
Exports	−.47	0	1.0	1.0	1.0	1.0	1.0	1.0
Imports	+.53	1.0	.39	1.0	.75	1.0	1.07	1.0
Capital inflow (F)	1.0	1.0	−.61	0	−.25	0	.07	0
Primary production	−.59	−.14	.56	.47	−.24	−.25	−.30	−.31
Industry production	.21	−.03	−.30	−.32	.32	.32	.09	.09
Utilities and services	.38	.17	−.26	−.15	−.08	−.07	.21	.22
Private consumption	.72	.46	−.65	−.37	−.41	−.31	−.27	−.30
Government consumption	.15	.25	−.02	.13	−.03	.03	.22	.20
Investment	.16	.29	.06	.24	.22	.28	.12	.10
Saving	−.83	−.73	.64	.21	.20	.06	.32	.21
Government revenue	−.15	−.05	.15	.12	.15	.15	.05	.05

SOURCE: For (a), equation (1.2) in Tables 4 and 5; for (b) and (c), Table S14 in the Statistical Appendix.

The relevant equations are:

(a) $X = \alpha + \beta_1 lnY + \beta_2 (lnY)^2 + \gamma_1 lnN + \gamma_2 (lnN)^2 + \epsilon F + \Sigma \delta_i T_i$

(b) $X = \alpha + \beta_1 lnY + \beta_2 (lnY)^2 + \gamma_1 lnN + \gamma_2 (lnN)^2 + \epsilon \mu_k E_k$

(c) $X = \alpha + \beta_1 lnY + \beta_2 (lnY)^2 + \gamma_1 lnN + \gamma_2 (lnN)^2 + \epsilon F + \epsilon \mu_k E_k$

where X stands for the dependent variable and E_k for exports of the k component (p, m, s).

_____
[22]The equations are not satisfied exactly because of minor differences in the country samples.

Shifts in Production and Trade

The first part of Table 6 shows the magnitude of the adjustments in the structure of production that are associated with unit changes in the elements of equation (2.2). Under assumption *(c)*, an added dollar of primary exports (Case 2) results in a shift of 47 cents of value added to primary production from industry and services. The shift toward industry [Case 3*(c)*] or services [Case 4*(c)*] that is caused by a unit increase in exports is only 32 or 22 cents respectively. These differences are of the magnitude that would be expected from solutions to an input-output system under these assumptions. They reflect the fact that primary products have a higher proportion of value added than do manufactured goods.[23]

The provision of additional imports through borrowing without a corresponding increase in exports also causes a shift in the composition of production. In this case it is a movement of resources from tradables to nontradables. When exports are held constant [Case 1*(c)*], the magnitude of this shift is substantially less than the amounts indicated by the compensated coefficients of Case 1*(a)*. The total shift to nontradables in Case 1*(c)* is 17 cents per dollar of increase in capital inflow, as shown by the coefficient for utilities and services.

Shifts in Accumulation and Demand

Although different ways of acquiring foreign exchange have quite predictable effects on the structure of production, their effects on patterns of resource use are less easily foreseen. It is not clear on a priori grounds that the composition of demand in a more open economy would differ from that of an economy of the same size and income level but with less trade. Since external resources are supplied to countries for a variety of reasons—to offset production shortfalls as well as to increase investment—their average effects are also hard to predict on theoretical grounds.

The average shifts in the composition of resource use associated with unit changes in exports and external capital are shown in the lower part of Table 6. Most notable is the fact that each type of export increase is accompanied by a reduction in private consumption of 30 percent or so, which is offset by increases in investment and government consumption. The main explanation that has been suggested for this phenomenon is the greater ease of taxing trade, although the increase in government revenue is considerably less than the total shift of resource use.[24]

---

[23]The largest item of service exports is the purchase of goods as well as services by tourists, which helps to explain the smaller increase in services.

[24]Hinrichs (1966) obtained similar results for the increase in government revenue with an increased level of trade.

The regressions for F in Case 1 (c) show that about half of any increase in external resources goes into private consumption and only 29 percent into investment. Although the estimated investment share is larger than the uncompensated estimate (16 percent), it is considerably smaller than the time-series estimates of 35 percent to 45 percent that are described in Chapter 5.

Table 6 also shows that external resources are provided as much to offset a shortfall in exports—especially primary exports—as to increase the level of imports above normal levels. These and other trade effects are examined in further detail in Chapter 4, where they are made the basis for a classification of alternative development patterns.

Chapter 3

DEMOGRAPHIC AND DISTRIBUTIONAL PROCESSES

NOW THAT ACCELERATED growth has been achieved in a number of countries, the attention of both theorists and policy makers is increasingly shifting to the distribution of its benefits. The distribution of income is affected by several of the processes studied above: the level of education, the structure of production, and the availability of government revenue for redistribution. It is also affected by several socioeconomic processes — mortality, fertility, urbanization — that are themselves highly correlated with the level of income. Although it is impossible to unravel the complex set of interactions among these factors by using the present statistical methods, our approach can show the general relationship between these processes and the more strictly economic aspects of development and thus provide a basis for further research.

Although comprehensive models of income distribution remain to be tested, many of the relations that should be included in such models are clear. In schematic terms the distribution of income in developing countries is determined largely by: *(a)* the relative growth of different sectors and of modes of production (modern, traditional) within each; *(b)* the growth in numbers, education, and sectoral distribution of the labor force; *(c)* the ownership of assets and the relative rates of savings of different groups; and *(d)* the extent of political opposition to or support for the equilibrating mechanisms (factor substitution, education, asset redistribution) that would tend to equalize factor returns.[1] In the spirit of the preceding analysis of accumulation and resource allocation, we will identify a few aspects of this set of interactions that can be measured on a comparable basis and apply our standard regression equations to them.

The preceding chapter described the changes in the composition of production which, together with the available technology, determine changes in the demand for labor. Factors affecting the supply of labor include the growth of population, its distribution between rural and urban areas, and levels of education. The most widely available measures of those factors that affect the labor supply are birth and death rates, urbanization, and school enrollment. The interaction between supply and demand determines the observed allocation of labor by sector as well as differences among sectors in labor productivity and income.

For analytical convenience the observed sectoral allocation of labor will be discussed first, together with the implications of the differences in

---

[1] A review of theoretical and empirical work on distribution in developing countries is given by Cline (1973) and Chenery and associates (1974).

labor productivity among sectors. We then take up urbanization, population growth, and income distribution.

EMPLOYMENT BY SECTOR

If all sectors had the same production functions, factor prices, and entry conditions, the changes in the pattern of employment would be expected to follow closely the pattern of structural change in output. What we observe, however, are systematic differences between the two patterns that reflect the following factors:

1. Demand for labor grows more rapidly in urban areas, whereas the greater part of the increase in supply is from rural areas.
2. Equalization of factor returns is hampered by immobility and unequal access to capital, land, and other complementary factors.
3. Investment and technological advance have been concentrated in the modern branches of each sector, primarily in industry and public utilities.
4. The unprecedented growth of the labor force in recent years has greatly exceeded the growth of demand in the organized sectors of most economies.

The effects of these factors would show up more sharply if each of the main sectors could be subdivided into a modern, large-scale component and a traditional, small-scale component, as suggested by dual-economy theories. Although this has not yet been done for any significant number of countries, some conclusions can be drawn from the aggregate data.

The regression results for the allocation of the labor force are shown in Table 7. In overall terms the standard equations provide as good an explanation of the intercountry variation in labor allocation as that shown above for sectoral output, and the coefficients for income and size are comparable. Time trends are omitted because the sample pertains mainly to the 1960s.

The normal variation of labor allocation with the level of income is shown in Table 3 and Figure 8. Although there is the same general pattern of a rapidly declining primary share and a rising industrial share, there are also significant differences from the production pattern that reflect the lag in the adjustment process. At the lowest income levels the primary sectors produce 52 percent of total output and provide 71 percent of employment. As income rises, the fall in the share of primary output is more rapid than the fall in primary employment, reflecting the concentration of investment and technological progress in industry and the accumulation of surplus labor in agriculture.

This trend is brought out more clearly in Figure 9, which shows changes in labor productivity (relative to average national productivity) for

TABLE 7. Basic Regressions: Demographic and Distributional Processes

Process	Eqn.	Constant	$\ln Y$	$(\ln Y)^2$	$\ln N$	$(\ln N)^2$	F	T_1	T_2	T_3	R^2	SEE	Y Mean/Range	No. of Obs.
7. Labor allocation														
a. Primary share	(1.1)	.858 (2.439)	.041 (.348)	−.019 (1.957)	.005 (.226)	−.000 (.045)					.741	.118	734 / 41/3551	165
	(1.2)	.821 (2.351)	.058 (.501)	−.020 (2.123)	.000 (.014)	.000 (.098)	−.292 (2.014)				.748	.116	734 / 41/3551	165
b. Industry share	(1.1)	−.519 (2.697)	.136 (2.119)	−.003 (.566)	−.031 (2.360)	−.005 (1.958)					.732	.064	734 / 41/3551	165
	(1.2)	−.500 (2.613)	.127 (1.988)	−.002 (.423)	.034 (2.570)	−.005 (2.106)	.153 (1.921)				.738	.064	734 / 41/3551	165
c. Services share	(1.1)	.664 (2.478)	−.178 (1.996)	.022 (2.993)	−.036 (1.950)	.005 (1.423)					.539	.090	734 / 41/3551	165
	(1.2)	.682 (2.543)	−.187 (2.084)	.023 (3.081)	−.034 (1.813)	.005 (1.335)	.135 (1.213)				.543	.089	734 / 41/3551	165
8. Urbanization	(1.1)	−1.154 (4.854)	.365 (4.475)	−.016 (2.308)	.019 (1.003)	−.002 (.487)		−.017 (.803)	−.019 (.968)	−.006 (.306)	.666	.127	494 / 34/3201	317
	(1.2)	−1.155 (4.863)	.363 (4.454)	−.016 (2.291)	.023 (1.217)	−.002 (.663)	.122 (1.311)	−.013 (.634)	−.018 (.900)	−.006 (.325)	.668	.127	494 / 34/3201	317
9. Demographic transition														
a. Birth rate	(1.1)	1.091 (5.857)	−.137 (2.214)	.004 (.731)	−.057 (4.407)	.007 (3.114)					.667	.071	721 / 48/3551	213
	(1.2)	1.109 (6.070)	−.139 (2.283)	.004 (.751)	−.061 (4.773)	.008 (3.343)	−.228 (3.022)				.681	.070	721 / 48/3551	213
b. Death rate	(1.1)	1.010 (12.080)	−.268 (9.656)	.020 (8.643)	−.002 (.343)	−.000 (.423)					.550	.031	721 / 48/3551	213
	(1.2)	1.022 (12.720)	−.269 (10.100)	.020 (9.010)	−.004 (.790)	−.000 (.191)	−.143 (4.322)				.587	.031	721 / 48/3551	213
10. Income distribution														
a. Highest 20%	(1.1)	−.228 (.747)	.292 (2.836)	−.027 (3.188)							.291	.071	622 / 67/3387	66
b. Lowest 40%	(1.1)	.466 (2.978)	−.119 (2.256)	.010 (2.400)							.116	.037	622 / 67/3387	66

t ratios in parentheses.

50

Figure 8: Labor Allocation

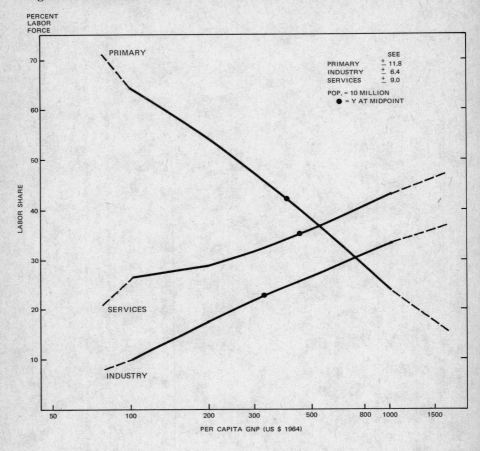

TABLE 8. Key to Graphs

Country	Code	Country	Code
1. Afghanistan	AF	51. Lebanon	LE
2. Algeria	AL	52. Liberia	LBR
3. Angola	AN	53. Libya	LBY
4. Argentina	AR	54. Malagasy	MAG
5. Australia	AU	55. Malawi	MAI
6. Austria	AUA	56. Malaysia	MA
7. Belgium	BE	57. Mali	MLI
8. Bolivia	BO	58. Mexico	ME
9. Brazil	BR	59. Morocco	MOR
10. Burma	BA	60. Mozambique	MOZ
11. Cambodia (Khmer)	CB	61. Netherlands	NE
12. Cameroon	CM	62. New Zealand	NZ
13. Canada	CAN	63. Nicaragua	NI
14. Central African Republic	CA	64. Niger	NIR
15. Ceylon (Sri Lanka)	CE	65. Nigeria	NGA
16. Chad	CD	66. Norway	NO
17. Chile	CH	67. Pakistan	PAK
18. China (Taiwan)	CHA	68. Panama	PAN
19. Colombia	CO	69. Papua	PNG
20. Congo (Zaire)	CON	70. Paraguay	PA
21. Costa Rica	CR	71. Peru	PE
22. Dahomey	DA	72. Philippines	PH
23. Denmark	DE	73. Portugal	PO
24. Dominican Republic	DO	74. Puerto Rico	PR
25. Ecuador	EC	75. Rhodesia	RHO
26. El Salvador	ES	76. Saudi Arabia	SAU
27. Ethiopia	ET	77. Senegal	SE
28. Finland	FI	78. Sierra Leone	SL
29. France	FR	79. Singapore	SI
30. Germany (West)	GE	80. Somalia	SO
31. Ghana	GH	81. South Africa	SA
32. Greece	GR	82. Spain	SP
33. Guatemala	GU	83. Sudan	SU
34. Guinea	GUI	84. Sweden	SWE
35. Haiti	HA	85. Switzerland	SWI
36. Honduras	HO	86. Syria	SYR
37. Hong Kong	HK	87. Tanzania	TA
38. India	IN	88. Thailand	TH
39. Indonesia	IND	89. Togo	TO
40. Iran	IRN	90. Tunisia	TUN
41. Iraq	IRQ	91. Turkey	TU
42. Ireland	IRE	92. Uganda	UG
43. Israel	IS	93. U.A.R. (Egypt)	UAR
44. Italy	IT	94. United Kingdom	UK
45. Ivory Coast	IVC	95. U.S.A.	USA
46. Jamaica	JM	96. Upper Volta	UV
47. Japan	JA	97. Uruguay	UR
48. Jordan	JO	98. Venezuela	VE
49. Kenya	KE	99. Vietnam (South)	VN
50. Korea (South)	KO	100. Yugoslavia	YU
		101. Zambia	ZA

52

Figure 9: Labor Productivity Indices
Scatter for Primary Sector of 39 Countries, 1965

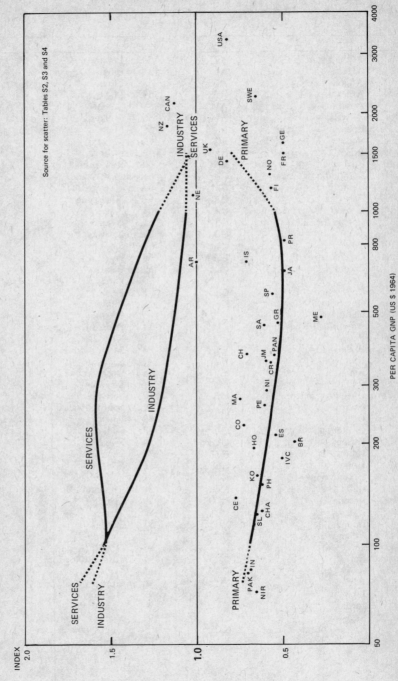

Source for scatter: Tables S2, S3 and S4

PER CAPITA GNP (US $ 1964)

each of the three sectors and the values of labor productivity in the primary sector for each country observed.[2] Relative labor productivity in the primary sector falls from about 70 percent to 50 percent at an income level of $500 and then gradually rises as agricultural technology is modernized and the surplus agricultural labor is absorbed by the rest of the economy.[3] The productivity gap between primary production on the one hand and industry and services on the other is greatest in the middle income range ($200 to $500), which is also the range of greatest inequality of income, as shown in Figure 12.

Once the $1500 income level has been reached, the primary labor share has fallen to 15 percent, and migration has reduced the labor productivity differential quite substantially, then the shares of industry and services in the labor force are much larger and become very close to their shares in production. The relative labor productivity in the primary sector, however, still lags in a number of the advanced countries.

At income levels above $1500 the patterns of production and labor use tend to diverge in the opposite direction, with services requiring a larger share of the labor force than their contribution to GNP. This phenomenon reflects the greater difficulty of substituting capital for labor and the lower rates of technological improvements in the service sectors as compared to commodity production.[4]

The relatively low productivity of labor in agriculture in poor countries is thus attributable to the time needed to acquire technical knowledge and the immobility of productive factors rather than to any inherent properties of agricultural production. It is not found in the earlier history of some of the newly settled areas such as New Zealand, Canada, or Argentina, nor in some of the fully developed economies.

In summary, Figure 9 provides a striking illustration of the disequilibrium in factor returns that characterizes the transition and the convergence to greater equality as the transition is completed. The consequences of this pattern for income distribution are noted below.

URBANIZATION

In an economy continuously in equilibrium, urbanization[5] might appear as the net result of a causative chain of events, beginning with changes in

---

[2] A key to the country abbreviations is given in Table 8.

[3] This phenomenon has been analyzed in detail by Kuznets (1971, ch. 5), who shows that it must be attributed to low productivity of all factors in agriculture rather than to the substitution of labor for capital.

[4] This is the conclusion reached by Fuchs (1969) as a result of extensive studies of the service sectors in advanced countries.

[5] The definition of "urban" used here is that of the United Nations. It is based on economic and administrative characteristics rather than a fixed size. "Rural" is defined as nonurban.

demand and trade which lead to industrialization and result in a steady movement of the labor force from rural to urban occupations. However, the growth of national output in the past two decades has rarely been sufficiently rapid to keep up with accelerating population growth and prevent a rise in rural underemployment. As a consequence, migration from rural to urban locations has taken place ahead of the growth of demand for labor and has been determined increasingly by expected income rather than current wages.[6] It is therefore necessary to treat urbanization as a somewhat separate developmental process that is affected by the expectation of future income and employment, the distribution of government expenditure, and a variety of social factors, as well as the changing structure of production.

The process of urbanization is measured by the standard regression equations in Table 7 and Figure 10. Its relationship to the level of development is shown to be about as uniform and stable as that of most other processes. Contrary to the popular impression that migration to cities has been accelerating recently, the regression shows no significant time trend.

Since the share of urban population is closely related to the sectoral composition of employment, there is a strong resemblance between Figures 8 and 10.[7] The population typically becomes predominantly urban above $500 per capita income, and the labor force employed in industry typically exceeds that in primary production above $700. It is only after the level of income has passed $2000, however, that these transitional processes have been completed. In world experience up to now the urban share then has tended to stabilize at some 75 percent of the population.

The leads and lags in urbanization shown in Figure 10 are associated to a large extent with the differences in patterns of production and trade derived in the next chapter. The relatively highly urbanized countries— Austria, United Kingdom, Israel, Argentina, Uruguay, Chile, Taiwan, Colombia, Brazil—have development patterns classified as either "industry oriented" or "import substitution." Similarly, most of the countries that are less urbanized than predicted are classed as either "primary oriented" or "balanced."[8]

---

[6]Harris and Todaro (1968); Todaro (1969).

[7]If a breakdown of the service sector between rural and urban occupations were available, the relations between these two patterns could be specified. A comparison of the two figures implies that in the middle-income range service employment is about two-thirds urban.

[8]There are also several cases of countries with decentralized industry, such as Switzerland and Portugal, which are both industry oriented and less urbanized than predicted. Differences in definitions prevent more detailed analysis of these differences in the present statistical framework.

Figure 10: Urbanization
Scatter for 90 Countries, 1965

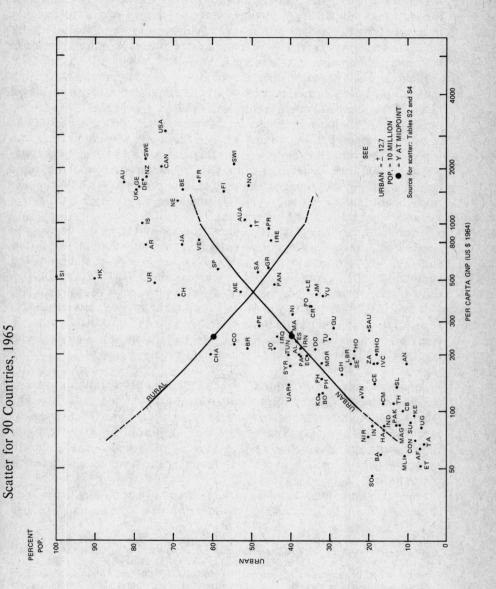

PERCENT POP.

URBAN

SEE

URBAN = $\pm$ 12.7
POP. = 10 MILLION
● = Y AT MIDPOINT

Source for scatter: Tables S2 and S4

PER CAPITA GNP (US $ 1964)

DEMOGRAPHIC TRANSITION

Given the crucial impact of population growth on the level of per capita income, it is important to show the extent to which the two are related and to indicate the linkages between them. Although these relations are the subject of active research by demographers and economists, there are wide areas of disagreement as to the nature and relative importance of the various factors involved. This discussion is therefore limited to presenting the results of our standard regression analysis and analyzing the effects on birth rates of some of the other processes already studied.

Demographers have described the historical fall in birth and death rates as "the demographic transition," which is conceived in much the same terms as the other development processes discussed here.[9] While the causes of the worldwide fall in death rates are well understood, the inter-relations among the socioeconomic processes related to fertility—educa-tion, health, urbanization, mobility, etc.—are still subjects of active debate.

Although the relations between income levels and birth and death rates are indirect, they are nevertheless quite uniform. Our standard regression equations give a reasonably accurate cross-country representation of the demographic transition, as shown in Table 7 and Figure 11. The unifor-mity of these processes, as measured by standard errors of estimate and values of R^2, is as great as the other structural changes described above. Figure 11 shows that on the basis of the data for 1950–70 the income-re-lated fall in the birth rate exceeds the fall in the death rate above income levels of $200, giving maximum rates of population growth early in the transition.

Since the explanatory value of the income level is largely indirect, its effects can be clarified by introducing some of the related socioeconomic factors into the regression equations. This has been done at a less aggreg-ated level by a number of authors in studying fertility.[10] On the basis of their results and our own experiments, we have selected school enroll-ment and urbanization as exogenous variables and have added the infant mortality rate.

Many demographic influences vary in importance according to the level of development. Where birth rates are high, greater education will lead

----

[9]Bogue (1969, p. 55) summarizes the relationship as follows: "As public health and medi-cal technology bring about a fall in the death rate the population begins to grow more rapidly, because birth rates lag behind and remain at their former high level. Eventually, by the process of demographic regulation...the birth rate is lowered and again brought into bal-ance with the death rate."

[10]For example, Adelman (1963), Heer (1966), Friedlander and Silver (1967), Phillips, Votey, and Maxwell (1969), and Willis (1973).

Figure 11: Demographic Transition
Scatter for Birth Rate in 76 Countries, 1965

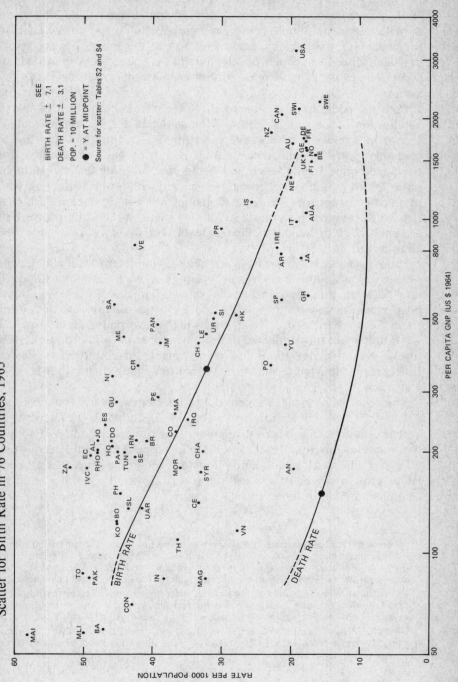

BIRTH RATE ± 7.1   SEE

DEATH RATE ± 3.1

POP. = 10 MILLION

● = Y AT MIDPOINT

Source for scatter: Tables S2 and S4

RATE PER 1000 POPULATION

PER CAPITA GNP (US $ 1964)

people to try to reduce them, but this need not be true at higher-income levels where birth rates are already low. In such cases it is no longer valid to make the assumption of multiple regression analysis that the effects of the explanatory variables are additive. To test this possibility the sample has been divided between developed and less developed countries, and separate regressions have been run for each group as well as for the total sample.[11]

Both the addition of two of the three socioeconomic variables and the subdivision of the sample improve the statistical results considerably, as shown in Table 9.[12] Perhaps the most important finding is that the explanatory variables affect developing countries quite differently from developed ones. In the less developed group, both higher education and lower infant mortality are strongly associated with lower birth rates, while in advanced countries these relationships are not significant. Urbanization, however, does not show a significant effect on the birth rate once the separate effects of education, income level, and infant mortality have been allowed for.

Some evidence of the lag between changes in income level and the consequent effects on birth rates is provided by an examination of the deviation between predicted and actual values. Large positive deviations in birth rates are shown in Figure 11 by countries such as Mexico, Venezuela, South Africa, and Nicaragua, which have had a rapid growth of GNP that is not fully reflected in their present social and economic structures.[13] Negative deviations are most notable in countries in Eastern Europe and the Mediterranean area that have long had higher levels of education.

The regression results are generally consistent with the conclusions of Adelman (1963), Friedlander and Silver (1967), and Rich (1973), who suggest the nature of the causal relations that underlie them. We support their conclusions that development policy should take into account the effects of education, health, and other socioeconomic processes on population growth rather than continuing to treat the birth rate as an exogenous variable in development plans.

---

[11]Adelman (1963) demonstrated the usefulness of this procedure. We conducted a similar set of experiments for the death rate. In poor countries education showed a substantial negative relation, but none of the other variables was significant. For birth rates the regression equations for the two subgroups are significantly different at a one percent confidence level.

[12]The capital inflow remained highly significant for both groups of countries despite the addition of other variables, although it has the opposite sign between less developed and developed countries. One can only speculate as to the causal nature of this association.

[13]Rich (1973) has suggested that fertility rates are more closely associated with the income levels of the lowest income groups. The relatively unequal distribution of income in Mexico, Peru, and South Africa would help to explain the high birth rates in those countries.

TABLE 9. Augmented Regressions: Birth Rates

	Constant	$\ln Y$	$(\ln Y)^2$	$\ln N$	$(\ln N)^2$	$SCHEN$	IMR*	R^2	SEE	Y Mean/Range	No. of Obs.
All countries											
	.8506 (3.377)	-.0560 (.674)	-.0028 (.406)	-.0667 (4.004)	.0096 (3.084)			.634	.073	694 44/3045	146
	.5361 (2.179)	.0253 (.314)	-.0063 (.979)	-.0718 (4.578)	.0102 (3.468)	-.0011 (2.446)	.0007 (2.834)	.682	.068	694 44/3045	146
Less developed countries (Y less than $800)											
	.2038 (.420)	1.814 (1.034)	-.0243 (1.537)	-.0549 (2.685)	.0063 (1.570)			.405	.080	319 44/955	101
	.0237 (.051)	.2158 (1.316)	-.0237 (1.598)	-.0599 (3.139)	.0067 (1.788)	-.0012 (2.151)	.0064 (2.438)	.494	.074	319 44/955	101
Developed countries (Y greater than $800)											
	1.6160 (.480)	-.3841 (.415)	.0271 (.427)	-.0484 (1.970)	.0078 (1.725)			.172	.035	1537 843/3045	45
	.9917 (.278)	-.2641 (.270)	.0206 (.309)	-.0422 (1.628)	.0058 (1.184)	.0066 (1.000)	.0014 (1.288)	.218	.035	1537 843/3045	45

t ratios in parentheses.

*Infant mortality rate (deaths per thousand live births).

INCOME DISTRIBUTION

Only in the past several years has sufficient information on income distribution become available to support a statistical analysis of the present type, and income distribution is still subject to many more qualifications than are the other processes.[14] Nevertheless a preliminary analysis of the existing material is presented because of the great importance of the subject matter.

The principal hypotheses as to the nature and causes of the variation in income distribution in the course of development were formulated by Kuznets (1955, 1963) and Myrdal (1957). They asserted that the processes of industrialization and urbanization lead to a worsening of income distribution in developing countries because in the early stages growth is concentrated in the modern sectors. It is only at relatively high levels of income that technological progress affects the bulk of the economy and that redistribution through income transfers becomes significant.

Kuznets (1963) bases much of his analysis on the difference between factor productivity in agricultural and nonagricultural activities, which has been discussed above. Incomes in industry and services are not only higher but also more unequally distributed. In the earlier stages of development both these factors contribute to the increasing inequality of income distribution. Weisskoff (1970) has traced the interaction of these factors in Puerto Rico, Argentina, and Mexico and generally confirms Kuznets's hypotheses.

Another approach to comparative analysis stresses the importance of other factors such as economic dualism, the availability of natural resources, the extent of education, and social mobility. Adelman and Morris (1973) demonstrate by an analysis of hierarchical interactions that a large proportion of the intercountry variance in income distribution can be associated with these and other socioeconomic variables. They also confirm the cross-country version of the Kuznets-Myrdal hypothesis that distribution worsens between the poorest and middle-income countries and then improves in the advanced countries.

These results are taken as a starting point for the application of our basic regressions. To achieve the greatest degree of comparability, income recipients have been divided into three groups: the top 20 percent, the

---

[14]The most comprehensive tabulation is that of Jain and Tiemann (1973), which gives data for sixty-six countries. From these fifty-five have been selected for which national estimates could be made on a reasonably comparable basis. The sample includes two observations on eleven countries for which there was significant growth of per capita income over the intervening period. Ten years ago Kuznets could base his pioneering study on only twenty countries.

middle 40 percent, and the lowest 40 percent.[15] The results of applying the basic regression to the shares of income received by the top and bottom groups are shown in Table 7.[16]

The predicted values are given in Table 3 and Figure 12. For both income groups the curvature is quite significant and of the shape predicted by the Kuznets-Myrdal hypothesis. The share of the lowest 40 percent of income recipients in GNP declines from 15.8 percent for the group with the lowest per capita income to 12.7 percent for the group at the middle-income level of $300 per capita; the share of the top 20 percent rises from 50.2 to 55.4 percent for the equivalent groups. At higher incomes this trend is reversed; the average income distribution of the richest countries is more equal than that of the poorest.[17]

Although income distribution worsens significantly during the transition, the level of income does not explain a large part of the intercountry variation. Proxy variables were therefore tested for several of the factors that are thought to have some effect on income distribution: education (measured by school enrollment), dualism (measured crudely by the share of primary exports), and the extent of the agricultural sector (measured by the share of primary production). The results of adding these variables to the basic equation is a notable improvement in the regression results, as shown below:[18]

| | Regression Coefficients | | | | |
	School Enrollment	Primary Export Share	Primary Production	R^2	SEE
Highest 20%	−.223 (3.08)	.286 (2.99)	−.329 (2.14)	.52	.058
Middle 40%	.155 (3.31)	−.160 (2.58)	.172 (1.72)	.55	.038
Lowest 40%	.068 (1.56)	−.126 (2.18)	.157 (1.69)	.24	.035

[15]These are aggregated from the finer size classes in Jain and Tiemann (1973).

[16]Since population was not significant, it is omitted from these results.

[17]This analysis is based on income distributions before taxes, since few countries have information on incomes received after taxes and transfers. Meerman's study (1972) of the available evidence indicates that there is little difference among developing countries between the two distributions.

[18]Data availability on the additional variables reduces the sample size to fifty observations. The coefficients for the standard regression variables $(lnY$ and $(lnY)^2)$ are only slightly changed from those in Table 7. t ratios are in parentheses.

62

Figure 12: Income Distribution
Scatter for 55 Countries, 1965

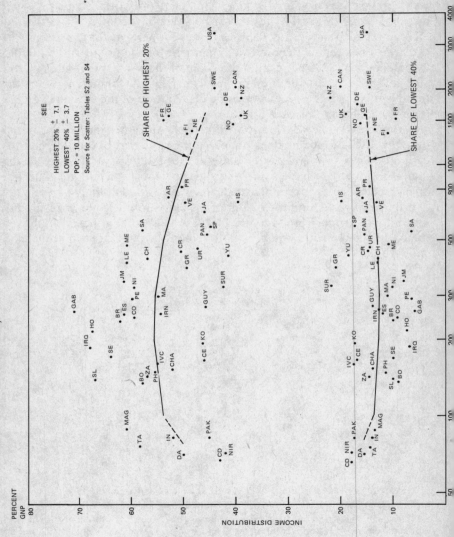

The principal findings from this extension of the basic regression equations are:

1. All three variables have a significant relation to the share of income received by the top group. Since the samples are the same, the coefficients for each variable add to zero, and together they show how income shifts among the three groups in association with changes in each variable.

2. Primary exports are related to both economic dualism and external investment. Notable examples of the increase in the income of the top 20 percent associated with high primary exports are shown in Figure 12 for Iraq, South Africa, Bolivia, and Sierra Leone.[19]

3. High levels of education are associated with a shift of income away from the top 20 percent, with a larger proportion going to the bottom 40 percent than would otherwise be its share. This pattern is shown in Costa Rica, Korea, and Ceylon, although in each case a number of other factors is also present.[20]

4. At a given level of income higher shares of primary production are associated with a more equal distribution of income, which is consistent with Kuznets's observation that agriculture usually has a more equal distribution than nonagricultural sectors.[21]

For lack of data it is not yet possible to carry out a comparable analysis of changes in income distribution over time, which would be necessary to verify these speculations as to the effects of such changes in the economic structures. When taken together with the preceding analysis of labor productivity and population growth, however, these results confirm the tendency for income distribution to worsen in the early part of the transition, when population growth is at its highest and the modern sector is too small to absorb a substantial proportion of the growth of the labor force. They also demonstrate the advantages of studying structural change in an integrated analytical framework in which the changes in each process can be related to the others.[22]

---

[19]Exports based on smallholder agriculture would not show this association.

[20]Fishlow (1972) found that educational levels explain a substantial part of the interregional differences in income distribution in Brazil.

[21]Primary production and primary exports are not highly correlated when allowance is made for the level of income.

[22]The links among processes have been tested on only a partial basis here because of the differences in the samples for each process. In the future, however, a more general statistical treatment of the interdependence of the several processes should become feasible.

Chapter 4

ALTERNATIVE PATTERNS OF DEVELOPMENT

ANALYSIS OF THE UNIFORMITY of development patterns constitutes a first step toward identifying the sources of diversity. Although it is useful to know the average variation in economic structures with rising income, it is of greater value for development policy to investigate systematic differences in these patterns and to associate them with country characteristics such as resource endowments or differences in development strategy. This chapter summarizes some of the results of ongoing research directed to this objective.

Much of development theory implies a classification of countries according to either their structural characteristics (surplus labor economies, primary exporters) or their development strategies (import substituting, outward looking, aid supported). Although this type of theory is useful in analyzing particular features of development, it needs to be combined with a broader empirical assessment of structural change in order to evaluate development policies.

From an empirical standpoint it is very difficult to separate the effects of development policies from the underlying structural characteristics that condition them. In extreme cases — such as the existence of rich mineral resources — the structure dictates the policy to a large extent. Virtually all countries with rich mineral deposits have used them as a basis for exports, which consequently affects their patterns of trade, production, and imports. Even in this case, however, the policymaker must decide how long to pursue a policy of extreme specialization and when to shift to other patterns of production and trade. In the other extreme case — that of the resource-poor, surplus labor economy — the structural factors are somewhat less compelling, although there is a common incentive to make use of labor-intensive techniques for both domestic production and exports if policies can be devised for this purpose.

With the statistical methodology of the present study it is possible to test the relationship between any identifiable characteristic — whether deriving from a country's basic structure or its policy choices — and the intercountry patterns of resource allocation that have been measured. Up to now we have treated the effects of structural characteristics as being independent, on the assumption that the influence of each is additive to the others. The analysis of interactions among internal and external factors in Chapter 2, however, has demonstrated the limitations to this procedure. An approach is therefore needed that can identify alternative patterns associated with different combinations of structural factors.

If we were not restricted by the limited number of developing countries and the short period of observation, one obvious solution to this problem would be to classify countries according to several significant structural differences and then to estimate separate patterns for each group. On the basis of tests already made, countries might be divided according to whether they were large or small, more or less developed in 1950, resource rich or poor, and perhaps according to the extent of their access to foreign capital. Even a two-way split for each of these four characteristics, however, would produce sixteen groups of countries, while a three-way division would lead to a potential of eighty-one categories. It is therefore clear that subdivision of the country sample can be used only to a limited extent before its advantages are offset by the small samples of countries that result.

These statistical limitations have led us to focus on one set of development processes for which policy-oriented theory is fairly well developed: the interaction among trade, domestic resource allocation, production, and factor use. In this area existing theories can be combined with the results of the uniform regressions in Chapter 2 to test several alternative classifications of country development patterns. The groups are chosen so as to bring together countries following similar strategies and to allow for the major qualitative differences that have been identified in the timing and sequence of development processes.

In this procedure the major choice is between a typology based primarily on factors related to the level of development and one based primarily on participation in the international economy. The second option has produced results that are more interesting for the analysis of alternative development strategies and is therefore developed in this chapter. However, the subdivision by levels of income (or levels of development) also yields some significant refinements in the interpretation of the results of the uniform regressions; these are summarized at the end of the chapter.

CLASSIFICATION OF TRADE PATTERNS

The effects of the exogenous variables which were analyzed in Chapter 2 reflect differences in the country's participation in the international economy. The size of the domestic market, the nature of resources, and the inflow of capital affect the sectoral allocation of capital and labor primarily through their impact on the pattern of trade, although there are indirect effects on the choice of techniques, relative prices, and demand patterns. In seeking to classify countries into more homogeneous groups, therefore, our main objective has been to group together countries that show a similar evolution of their trade patterns.

The other criteria for classification are essentially statistical: the proxy variables that are available, the extent to which the effects of each variable are independent, and the quantitative importance of the results achieved. The methodological alternatives can be clarified by comparing the results of multiple regression analysis presented in Chapter 2 with the more general hypotheses that can be explored by first classifying countries. This discussion leads to the identification of a set of country groupings for use in the rest of the chapter.

Classification vs. Regression Analysis

Multiple regression is an efficient technique for testing whether a given exogenous factor has a significant effect on a particular dependent variable. Apart from the infrequent cases in which hypotheses can be specified on theoretical grounds with some precision, however, the nature of a given relationship can be determined only by testing alternative statistical formulations.

Theoretical analysis of development processes suggests several reasons for expecting systematic deviations from the additivity assumption that is the basis for the multiple regression formulation. For example, the convergence hypothesis advanced in Chapter 2 suggests that development patterns have a similar starting point in a status of underdevelopment (U) and converge toward a similar structure, defined as developed (D). The different paths connecting U and D cannot be accurately represented by an additive system because a marked increase over one income range implies a smaller increase at a subsequent stage. For example, if large countries industrialize early, size will have a stronger positive effect on the level of industrial output in the middle income range than at low or high levels. Conversely, a late start implies more rapid change at a later stage.[1]

A second type of phenomenon that is poorly represented in the multiple regression formulation is the difference in timing made possible by substitution within the productive system. To cite two extreme cases, development based on the initial exploitation of primary exports requires an initial inflow of capital, which is subsequently replaced as a source of foreign exchange by the expansion of primary exports; thus there is typically a capital outflow during much of the transition. In the absence of such resources, the initial inflow is less but may extend much later in the transition until it can be replaced by manufactured exports. The regres-

---

[1] It may be noted that this type of behavior is also characteristic of "turnpike" solutions to optimal growth models, although there is no reason to assume that observed cross-country patterns are reflections of such behavior.

sion analysis of Chapter 2 shows a significant degree of substitution between capital inflow and primary exports, but it cannot differentiate between different sequences.

Finally, there is little reason to expect a given behavioral relation to apply with equal force throughout the transition. The arguments supporting
the Keynesian consumption function and rising savings rates seem to be
relatively stronger for poor countries, while the assumptions leading to
the permanent income hypothesis and constant savings rates may gain in
validity as the level of affluence rises.

These qualifications apply to some extent to all of the exogenous variables of concern here: scale, resource endowment, and capital inflow. To
determine their quantitative significance, preliminary tests were made of
country classifications based on each factor separately.[2] These tests
showed that better measurements of scale and resource effects are obtained when the sample is divided between large and small countries and
according to an index reflecting the resource endowment and trade policy.
Once these factors are allowed for, the other exogenous variables—income level and capital inflow—are adequately represented in the multiple
regression formulation.[3]

On the basis of these experiments the sample will be divided by indices
of scale and trade orientation and separate regressions will be computed
for the resulting groups.

The Scale Index

Although most of the effects of scale depend on the economic size of
the domestic market, the total GNP is a less useful measure of market size
than its two components, population (N) and income level (Y). For commodities in which the income elasticity is greater than unity, such as industrial goods, an increase in Y has a greater effect on total demand than
an increase in N, whereas the opposite is true for foodstuffs. In the
uniform regressions the elasticities with respect to Y and N are therefore
measured separately; the two regression coefficients for each variable can
be combined to give an average income elasticity or an average size
elasticity, each of which measures one dimension of market size.

Countries are here classified on the basis of population rather than total
income in order to derive patterns that are applicable to the same group of
countries over time. The dividing line between large and small countries

---

[2]These preliminary results are discussed in Chenery and Taylor (1968), Chenery,
Elkington, and Sims (1970), and Chenery (1970).

[3]As discussed in the Technical Appendix, the validity of aggregating can be tested by the
significance of the F test of the regressions based on the subsamples. The regression coefficient estimated for the capital inflow is relatively stable in alternative formulations.

was set at 15 million people in 1960 after testing alternatives from 10 to 20 million (Chenery and Taylor, 1968). On this basis there were thirty-four large countries in the world in 1960, of which twenty-six are included in these samples.[4] Raising the cutoff point to 20 million would shift four countries (Canada, Yugoslavia, Colombia, and South Africa) but would not significantly affect the regression results.

The Trade Orientation Index

The trade pattern has both a static and a dynamic effect on other aspects of development. In a static analysis higher primary exports imply higher levels of production and factor use in primary sectors at a given income level, as was demonstrated in Chapter 2. In a dynamic analysis the ability to maintain a given pattern of trade and the timing of the shift to other patterns is also important.

Although the immediate purpose of this analysis is to classify countries into groups having more homogeneous patterns of resource allocation, these groups can also be used to compare time-series and cross-section patterns in which the dynamic effects are important. The index proposed for classifying countries is therefore based on a compromise between these two purposes.

Both the level and composition of exports (as well as imports) have some effect on other aspects of the development pattern. Since primary exports depend to a high degree on natural resource endowments, they can be considered largely exogenous. While the desirability of developing other exports (manufactures and services) depends on what level of primary exports can be achieved, a country's success in developing nonprimary exports is largely a result of government policy. When these export levels are treated as exogenous factors, therefore, elements of both natural endowments and policy reactions to them are combined.[5]

Since the level and composition of exports are affected by different policies and have different implications for other development processes, it is useful to treat them separately in classifying countries. The level of exports is readily measured by the ratio of the actual export level in the country (E) to the value predicted for the country's size and income level $(\hat{E})$. The effect of the capital inflow is indicated by its share in GDP. Both sets of measures are given in Tables 10 to 13.

---

[4]Omitted are five communist countries (China, USSR, Poland, North Vietnam, and Romania) for which data are not sufficiently comparable.

[5]Chenery (1964) tested alternative classifications based on both imports and exports and compared them to a classification based on arable land per capita plus mineral exports. This and subsequent tests by Chenery, Elkington, and Sims (1970) show that the resulting classification is relatively insensitive to the particular trade or resource index used.

A separate index of the composition of exports can be developed by comparing the actual and predicted levels of primary exports (E_p) and industrial exports (E_m).[6] Chapter 2 indicates that there is a normal shift in the composition of exports as the level of income rises, as shown below:[7]

Per Capita Income Level ($)	Normal Exports $\hat{E}$ ($)	Normal Primary Exports $\hat{E}_p$ ($)	Normal Manuf. Exports $\hat{E}_m$ ($)	Normal Trade Bias $\hat{T}$
50	8.5	6.4	.5	.69
200	43.6	27.1	6.8	.47
500	121.9	59.8	32.5	.22
1000	260.3	96.2	96.9	.00
1500	403.1	117.1	178.4	−.15

From this average pattern a normal trade bias can be defined as: $\hat{T} = \dfrac{\hat{E}_p - \hat{E}_m}{\hat{E}}$. Deviations from this average composition can be measured by the difference between the actual trade bias and the normal bias. This leads to the definition of the following trade orientation index (TO):

$$TO = \left(\frac{E_p - E_m}{E}\right) - \left(\frac{\hat{E}_p - \hat{E}_m}{\hat{E}}\right) = T - \hat{T} \qquad (4.1)$$

where the predicted values of $\hat{E}_p$, $\hat{E}_m$, and $\hat{E}$ are determined from equation (1.1) in Chapter 1.[8]

Although export level and capital inflow also have a significant relation to patterns of resource allocation, the division of countries according to values of the trade orientation index, when combined with the division between small and large countries indicated above, has proved to be the most useful. For purposes of policy analysis, countries will be classified as primary oriented (high values of TO), normal, and industry oriented (significantly negative values of TO). The basic data for eighty-six countries for 1965 are listed in Tables 10 to 13 on this basis.

Application to Regression Analysis

The classification of countries by scale and trade orientation shown in Tables 10 to 13 was used as a basis for computing separate regressions for the principal allocation and accumulation processes. The original division

---

[6]Service exports are omitted for simplicity although they affect $\hat{E}$.

[7]All values are per capita based on a population of 10 million.

[8]An alternative measure of the absolute trade bias was used by Chenery and Taylor (1968) in their earlier work on this subject. There is little difference between the two classifications when export levels are close to normal, but otherwise the relative measure is more closely related to policy differences. The characteristics of the trade orientation index are discussed further in the Technical Appendix.

TABLE 10. Classification of Trade Patterns (1965): Large Countries

Code	Country	N	Y (US$ 1964)	Export Level	T	$\hat{T}$	$T - \hat{T} = TO*$	F
				High Export Levels				
NGA	Nigeria	48.7	87.8	1.57	.89	.75	.14	.021
TH	Thailand	31.0	110.4	1.31	.46	.62	−.16	.013
				Normal Export Levels				
ET	Ethiopia	22.7	51.6	.94	.73	.77	−.04	.019
BA	Burma	24.7	59.1	1.10	.82	.76	.07	.043
IND	Indonesia	104.9	83.8	.84	.89	1.14	−.25	.005
PAK	Pakistan	113.9	84.3	1.04	.23	1.22	−.99	.057
UAR	U.A.R. (Egypt)	29.4	137.7	1.23	.36	.55	−.20	.025
PH	Philippines	31.8	149.3	1.07	.55	.53	.02	.009
IRN	Iran	24.8	217.9	1.20	.84	.42	.42	−.059
YU	Yugoslavia	19.5	414.9	1.10	−.32	.23	−.55	.007
SA	South Africa	17.9	552.2	1.24	.25	.14	.11	.000
JA	Japan	98.0	780.4	.81	−.79	−.20	−.59	−.015
IT	Italy	51.6	989.1	.97	−.44	−.23	−.22	−.026
UK	United Kingdom	54.4	1,534.4	1.05	−.53	−.47	−.05	.009
GE	Germany (West)	59.0	1,613.7	1.11	−.64	−.52	−.12	−.001
FR	France	48.8	1,705.7	.75	−.41	−.51	.10	−.009
CAN	Canada	19.6	2,056.7	.85	−.09	−.42	.32	−.004
				Low Export Levels				
KO	Korea (South)	28.4	123.4	.58	−.19	.58	−.77	.076
BR	Brazil	81.3	216.3	.79	.64	.48	.16	−.026
CO	Colombia	18.0	227.9	.60	.70	.42	.29	−.010
TU	Turkey	31.1	244.3	.37	.58	.38	.20	.014
ME	Mexico	42.7	434.2	.58	.37	.16	.21	−.001
SP	Spain	31.6	572.2	.59	−.01	.08	−.09	.039
AR	Argentina	21.7	786.6	.40	.73	−.01	.74	−.014

SOURCE: Equation (1.1), Table 5.

NOTE: India and the United States are not classified because predicted values have large margins of error.

*$T - \hat{T}$ may not equal TO due to rounding.

TABLE 11. Classification of Trade Patterns (1965): Small, Primary-oriented Countries

Code	Country	N	Y (US$ 1964)	Export Level	T	T̂	T - T̂ = TO*	F
			High Export Levels					
UG	Uganda	8.7	82.9	1.29	.91	.67	.24	-.011
CE	Ceylon	11.2	141.8	1.32	.90	.55	.34	-.004
ZA	Zambia	3.7	178.8	2.31	.97	.59	.39	-.170
MA	Malaysia	9.4	258.1	2.06	.74	.42	.32	-.046
SAU	Saudi Arabia	6.8	270.8	2.44	.91	.44	.48	-.425
LBY	Libya	1.6	695.0	1.85	.95	.35	.60	-.219
			Normal Export Levels					
CD	Chad	3.3	58.5	.77	.94	.79	.15	.078
SU	Sudan	13.7	87.8	1.08	.87	.65	.22	.044
CA	Central African Rep.	1.4	96.7	.79	.91	.81	.10	.066
BO	Bolivia	4.3	124.0	.92	.87	.64	.22	.060
SL	Sierra Leone	2.4	134.9	1.15	.87	.69	.18	.040
HO	Honduras	2.2	207.4	1.00	.70	.61	.09	-.003
NI	Nicaragua	1.7	330.3	.97	.71	.54	.17	.024
VE	Venezuela	8.7	829.5	1.21	.96	.80	.88	-.096
			Low Export Levels					
NIR	Niger	3.5	72.9	.70	.95	.75	.20	.005
CB	Cambodia (Khmer)	6.5	101.8	.59	.85	.65	.20	.010
PNG	Papua	2.2	168.0	.63	.75	.65	.10	.161
EC	Ecuador	5.2	195.3	.74	.89	.54	.36	-.002
PA	Paraguay	2.0	200.1	.56	.77	.63	.15	.008
DO	Dominican Rep.	3.5	215.4	.60	.80	.55	.25	.023
GU	Guatemala	4.4	277.9	.67	.59	.47	.13	.028
CH	Chile	8.7	418.7	.59	.62	.30	.32	-.008
UR	Uruguay	2.7	497.5	.64	.66	.37	.28	-.060
AU	Australia	11.4	1,680.4	.60	.52	-.23	.75	.025
NZ	New Zealand	2.6	1,806.4	.71	.82	-.03	.85	.026

SOURCE: Equation (1.1), Table 5.

*T - T̂ may not equal TO due to rounding.

TABLE 12. Classification of Trade Patterns (1965): Small, Balanced Countries

Code	Country	N	Y (US$ 1964)	Export Level	T	$\hat{T}$	$T - \hat{T}$ = TO*	F
				High Export Levels				
TA	Tanzania (P)	11.7	67.1	1.57	.77	.70	.07	−.038
IVC	Ivory Coast (P)	4.3	178.7	1.35	.56	.57	−.01	−.034
NE	Netherlands (M)	12.3	1,335.4	1.83	−.21	−.14	−.07	.006
				Normal Export Levels				
UV	Upper Volta (M)	4.9	35.1	.64	.88	.82	.06	.094
MAI	Malawi (P)	3.9	57.5	.92	.75	.78	−.03	.120
TO	Togo (P)	1.6	86.8	.86	.80	.81	.00	.062
SYR	Syria (P)	5.2	173.6	.89	.55	.56	−.01	.004
MOR	Morocco (P)	13.3	179.1	1.04	.50	.49	.00	−.015
ES	El Salvador (M)	2.9	240.5	1.01	.56	.54	.02	.024
PE	Peru (M)	11.7	288.7	.83	.34	.38	−.04	.014
CR	Costa Rica (P)	1.5	360.7	.77	.57	.53	.04	.104
JM	Jamaica (P)	1.8	419.7	1.23	.44	.47	−.03	.020
PAN	Panama (M)	1.3	474.4	1.20	.39	.49	−.09	.020
IRE	Ireland (M)	2.9	815.1	1.09	.14	.23	−.08	.089
DE	Denmark (M)	4.8	1,727.1	1.04	−.16	−.10	−.06	.013
				Low Export Levels				
MLI	Mali (P)	4.5	57.0	.65	.80	.77	.03	.108
GH	Ghana (P)	7.6	155.6	.73	.60	.56	.04	.077
GR	Greece (M)	8.6	585.0	.38	.16	.20	−.04	.127

SOURCE: Equation (1.1), Table 5.

NOTE: In regressions, countries are classified as primary (P) or industry oriented (M), as indicated.

*$T - \hat{T}$ may not equal TO due to rounding.

TABLE 13. Classification of Trade Patterns (1965): Small, Industry-oriented Countries

Code	Country	N	Y (US$ 1964)	Export Level	T	$\hat{T}$	$T - \hat{T}$ $= TO^*$	F
				High Export Levels				
SO	Somalia	2.5	45.9	1.14	.68	.85	−.17	.140
KE	Kenya	9.6	95.5	1.79	.45	.64	−.19	−.010
HK	Hong Kong	3.6	511.8	2.39	−.71	.33	−1.05	.004
BE	Belgium	9.5	1,538.0	1.41	−.50	−.16	−.34	−.002
NO	Norway	3.7	1,608.9	1.37	−.23	−.04	−.19	.002
				Normal Export Levels				
TUN	Tunisia	4.4	198.0	.82	.28	.55	−.27	.143
CHA	China (Taiwan)	12.4	201.0	.91	−.07	.47	−.54	.033
PO	Portugal	9.2	361.1	1.11	−.35	.33	−.68	.050
AUA	Austria	7.3	1,052.3	.98	−.52	.02	−.54	.010
FI	Finland	4.6	1,485.9	.75	−.67	−.04	−.62	.019
SWI	Switzerland	6.0	2,112.8	1.10	−.65	−.22	−.43	.001
SWE	Sweden	7.7	2,242.7	.86	−.60	−.29	−.31	.012
				Low Export Levels				
DA	Dahomey	2.4	72.3	.59	.51	.79	−.28	.112
VN	Vietnam (South)	16.1	117.7	.49	.20	.59	−.39	.117
JO	Jordan	2.0	216.7	.63	.19	.61	−.42	.209
LE	Lebanon	2.4	446.4	.67	.12	.42	−.30	.208
IS	Israel	2.6	1,126.2	.63	−.20	.14	−.34	.130

SOURCE: Equation (1.1), Table 5.
*$T - \hat{T}$ may not equal TO due to rounding.

into five groups was then consolidated into the following three in order to obtain larger samples: large *(L);* small, primary oriented *(SP);* and small, industry oriented *(SM).*[9] A comparison of the statistical results of these three groups showed that the three-way division provided a significant improvement over the pooled regressions of Chapter 2 for most of the allocation processes, as indicated in the following discussion. The further subdivision of the large countries by the trade index was of little statistical benefit because of the relative uniformity of this group. Similarly, the three-way subdivision of the small countries shown in Tables 11 to 13 did not significantly improve on the two-way division.

Since the principal effects of the trade classification are captured by this subdivision into three groups *(L, SP, SM),* the results are presented in these categories. The separate regressions for the allocation and accumulation processes are given in the Statistical Appendix, Tables S5 through S12. The differences in the predicted variation with the income level are shown in Tables 14 and 15 and in the figures for each process, which also show the observed values for each country in order to indicate the nature of the intercountry variation.

SCALE EFFECTS: THE LARGE-COUNTRY PATTERNS

The most obvious effect of scale is on the volume of trade. At each income level, large countries normally have less than half the volume of imports and exports that small countries do. Given the larger size of the economy, there is also less specialization in either primary or industrial exports. Among the twenty-four large countries listed in Table 10 only Nigeria has a level of exports more than a third above its predicted value, while a dozen small countries are highly specialized on this measure. Similarly, only two large countries, Korea and Pakistan, were heavily dependent on external capital in the 1960s, while there were a dozen small countries of this type. Specialization is also less extreme in export patterns, as shown by comparing Figure 13 for large countries with Figure 14 for small.

Beyond these external aspects, the most obvious effects of large scale are on the pattern of production. The more closed, less specialized trade pattern has its counterpart in a more balanced, less variable pattern of domestic production. In addition, large countries have with few exceptions adopted more inward-looking development policies which have repercussions on other aspects of accumulation and resource allocation.

---

[9]The terminology is taken from Chenery and Taylor (1968) although the trade index used is somewhat different. A division of the large countries into two groups (*LP* and *LM*) was included in the initial tests.

TABLE 14. Comparison of Large and Small Country Patterns

	Y = $200		Y = $500		Y = $800		R²		SEE	
	Large	Small	Large	Small	Large	Small	Large	Small	Large	Small
Accumulation processes										
Saving	.181	.144	.218	.186	.228	.208	.537	.776	.050	.047
Investment	.201	.168	.231	.204	.237	.225	.425	.461	.050	.047
Government revenue	.158	.194	.215	.245	.255	.275	.676	.649	.053	.047
Resource allocation and trade processes										
Exports	.123	.250	.131	.285	.140	.296	.380	.154	.052	.131
Primary exports	.063	.166	.049	.151	.043	.130	.633	.642	.028	.067
Manufactured exports	.028	.034	.049	.072	.061	.096	.451	.332	.033	.072
Primary production	.320	.323	.187	.204	.139	.160	.886	.693	.057	.087
Industry production	.250	.192	.328	.272	.357	.315	.731	.699	.056	.057
Private consumption	.708	.701	.651	.665	.633	.645	.481	.607	.070	.065

SOURCE: Tables S5, S6, S9, and S10. NOTE: The effect of *F* has been removed from predicted values.

TABLE 15. Comparison of Small Country Patterns: Primary and Industry-oriented

	Y = $200		Y = $500		Y = $800		R²		SEE	
	Primary	Industry	Primary	Industry	Primary	Industry	Primary	Industry	Primary	Industry
Accumulation processes										
Saving	.163	.094	.207	.151	.229	.184	.728	.859	.048	.040
Investment	.154	.195	.191	.230	.219	.245	.414	.568	.048	.040
Government revenue	.198	.181	.243	.237	.268	.272	.511	.729	.047	.046
Resource allocation and trade processes										
Exports	.239	.266	.247	.321	.239	.337	.421	.232	.081	.154
Primary exports	.203	.098	.210	.086	.200	.077	.632	.466	.074	.039
Manufactured exports	.016	.088	.021	.135	.023	.157	.225	.379	.014	.093
Primary production	.358	.235	.249	.146	.207	.116	.656	.589	.086	.067
Industry production	.177	.216	.241	.310	.278	.347	.672	.688	.043	.063
Private consumption	.686	.746	.645	.696	.625	.665	.563	.717	.071	.052

SOURCE: Tables S7, S8, S11, and S12. NOTE: The effect of *F* has been removed from predicted values.

Figure 13: Comparison of Trade Patterns: Large Countries
Scatter for 26 Countries, 1965

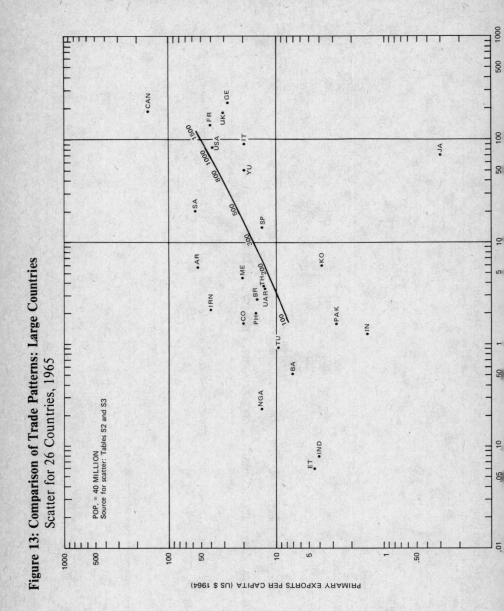

POP. = 40 MILLION
Source for scatter: Tables S2 and S3

PRIMARY EXPORTS PER CAPITA (US $ 1964)

Figure 14: Comparison of Trade Patterns: Small Countries Scatter for 60 Countries, 1965

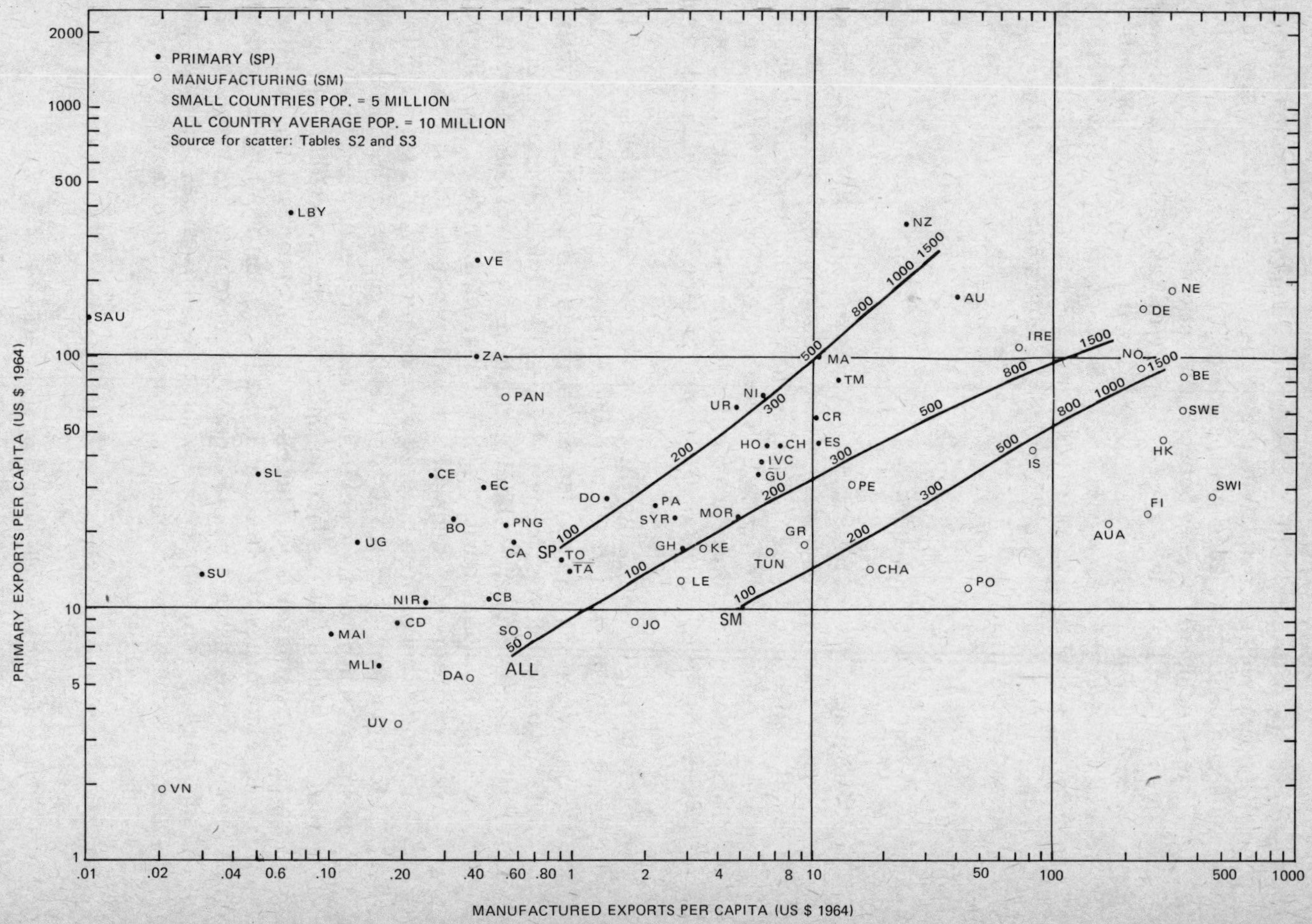

Since there has been no systematic exploration—neither theoretical nor statistical—of these indirect effects, the standard regression equations have been applied separately to the large- and small-country samples for all accumulation and allocation processes.

The principal differences between the patterns of structural change for large and small countries are summarized in Table 14, which shows the difference in predicted values of the accumulation and allocation processes at selected income levels and also contains the standard errors of estimate for both groups of countries. Predicted values are shown graphically in Figures 15 to 23, which also indicate the actual values for all the large countries.[10]

Scale and Resource Allocation

The major effect of large scale and low exports on resource allocation is to require countries to transform their economic structures at an earlier point in their development. The productive structures of large and small countries do not differ significantly at the lowest income levels, and they also appear to converge at the highest income levels. In between, however, several aspects of the transformation are accelerated in large countries.

It is for this reason that splitting the country samples by size produces significantly different regression equations for many processes.[11] Large scale is associated with accelerated change in production and investment at lower-income levels, followed by a deceleration at higher levels as the small countries catch up. Although the introduction of population into the regression equations measures the average magnitude of this effect, it is understated at middle-income levels and overstated at the two extremes.

The most pronounced effect of scale on production is shown in Figure 23 for industry. Between $200 and $800 per capita GNP, the share of industry is 5 to 6 percentage points higher in large countries. Put differently, the large country has as large an industrial share at $200 as the average small country has at $400. This phenomenon of the early industrialization of large countries has been analyzed in greater detail by Chenery and Taylor (1968), using a similar country breakdown. They show that the difference is concentrated in industries such as basic metals, paper, chemicals, and rubber products, which have important economies of scale.

---

[10]Observations for the small countries are plotted in Figures 24 to 32.

[11]Tests of significance are discussed in the Technical Appendix.

79

Figure 15: Total Exports
Scatter for 26 Large Countries, 1965

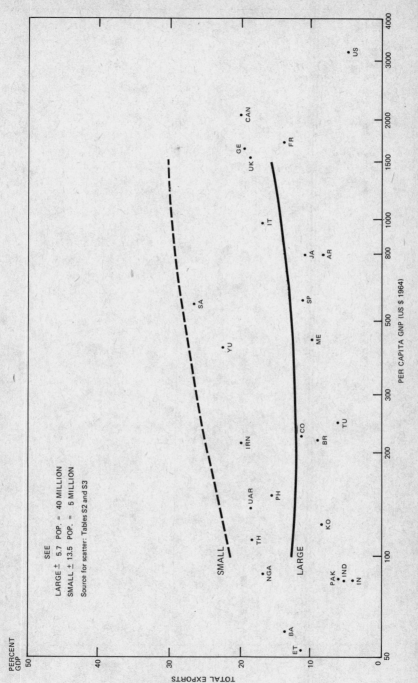

PERCENT
GDP

TOTAL EXPORTS

SEE

LARGE ± 5.7 POP. = 40 MILLION
SMALL ± 13.5 POP. = 5 MILLION

Source for scatter: Tables S2 and S3

PER CAPITA GNP (US $ 1964)

Figure 16: Primary Exports
Scatter for 26 Large Countries, 1965

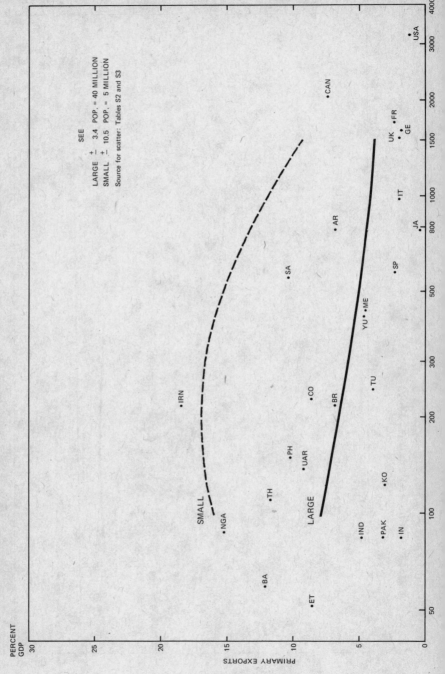

Figure 17. Manufactured Exports

Scatter for 26 Large Countries, 1965

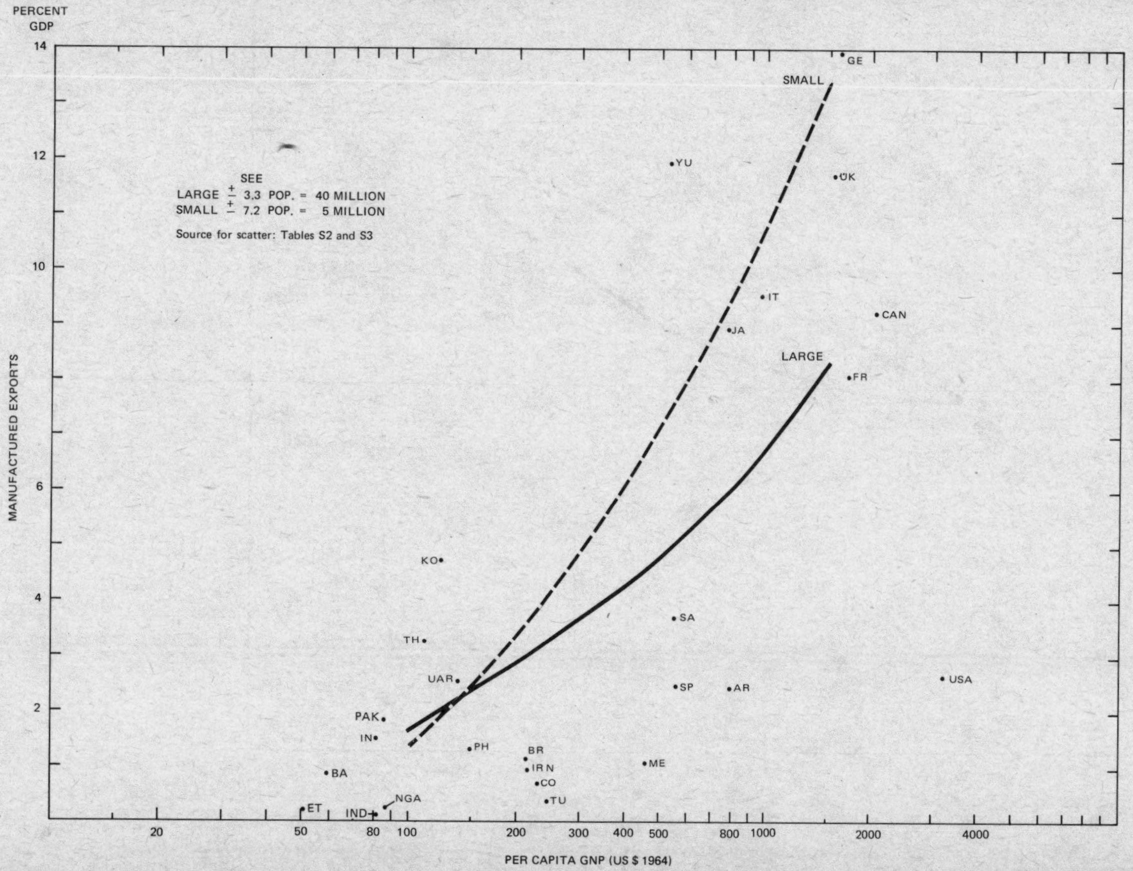

LARGE ÷ 3.3 POP. = 40 MILLION
SMALL ÷ 7.2 POP. = 5 MILLION

Source for scatter: Tables S2 and S3

Figure 18: Saving
Scatter for 26 Large Countries, 1965

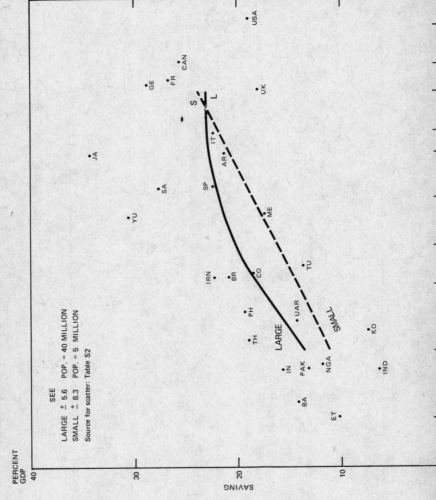

PERCENT
GDP

SEE
LARGE ± 5.6   POP. = 40 MILLION
SMALL ± 8.3   POP. = 5 MILLION
Source for scatter: Table S2

83

Scatter for 26 Large Countries, 1965

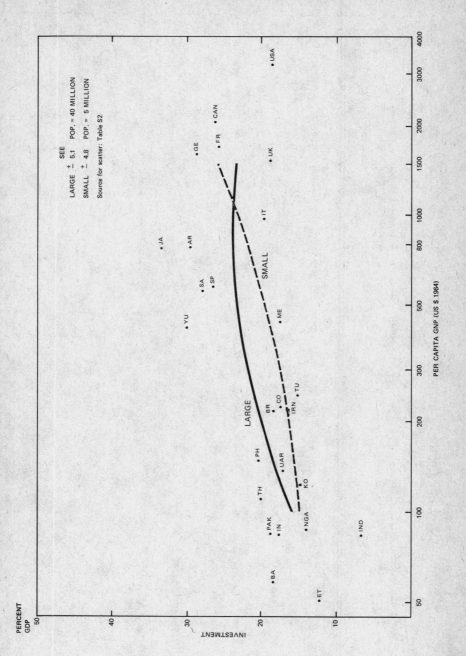

Figure 20: Private Consumption
Scatter for 25 Large Countries, 1965

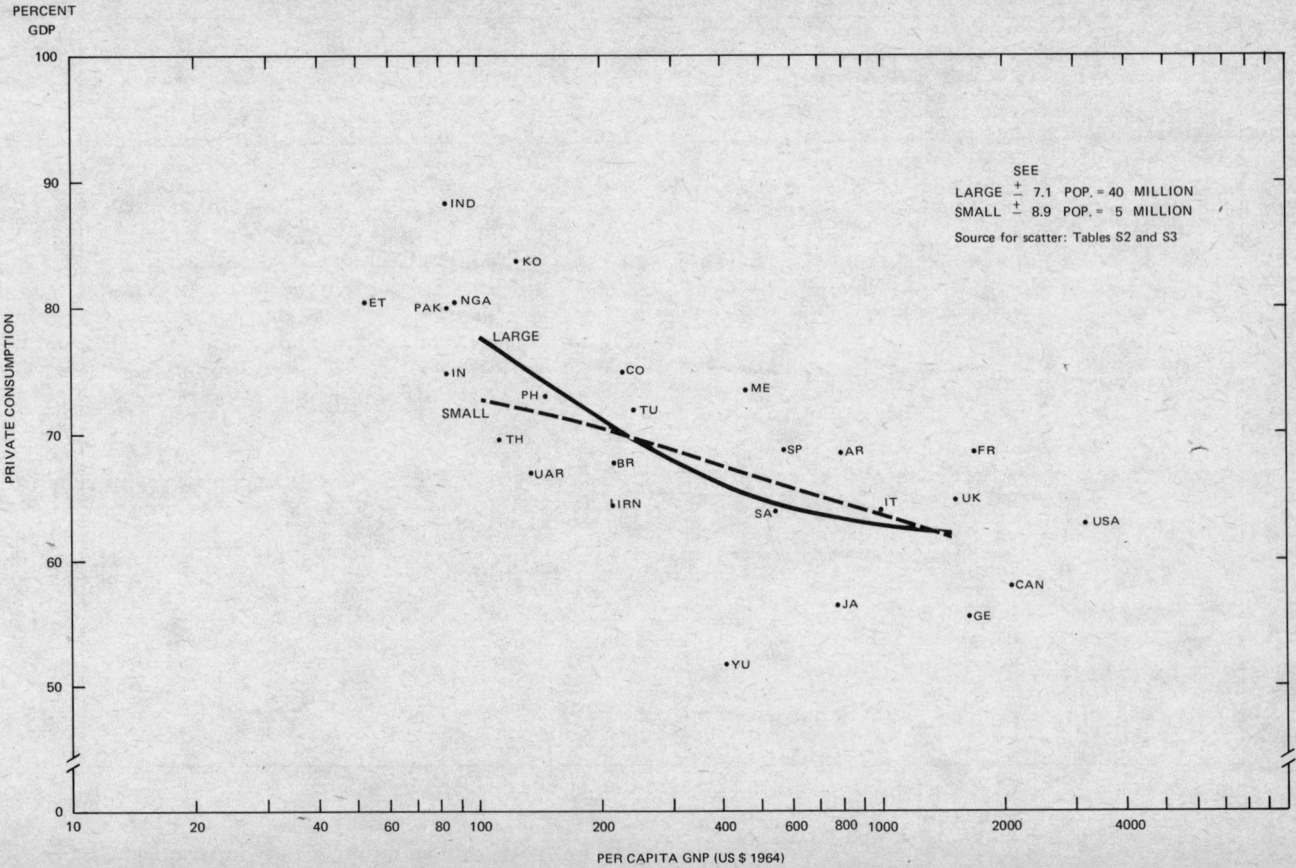

PERCENT GDP

PRIVATE CONSUMPTION

PER CAPITA GNP (US $ 1964)

SEE

LARGE ± 7.1 POP. = 40 MILLION
SMALL ± 8.9 POP. = 5 MILLION

Source for scatter: Tables S2 and S3

Scatter for 23 Large Countries, 1965

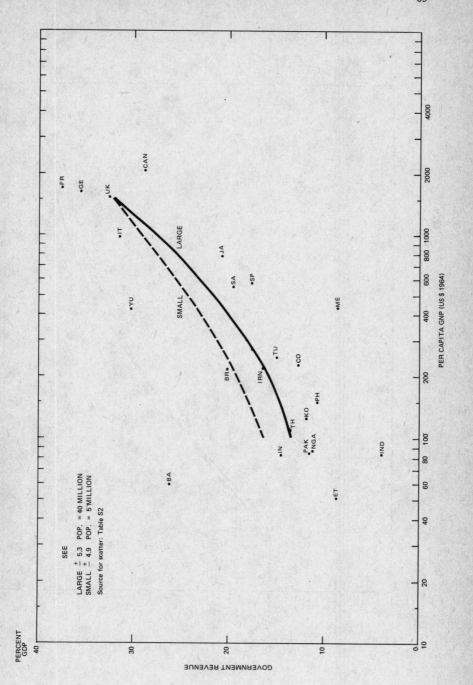

86

Figure 22: Primary Share of Production
Scatter for 25 Large Countries, 1965

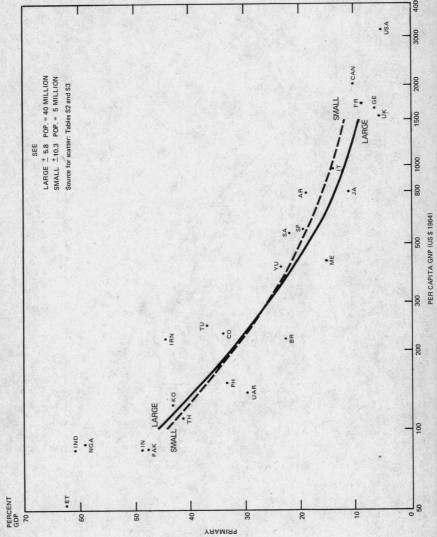

PERCENT GDP

SEE

LARGE ± 5.8   POP. = 40 MILLION
SMALL ±10.3   POP. = 5 MILLION

Source for scatter: Tables S2 and S3

PER CAPITA GNP (US $ 1964)

PRIMARY

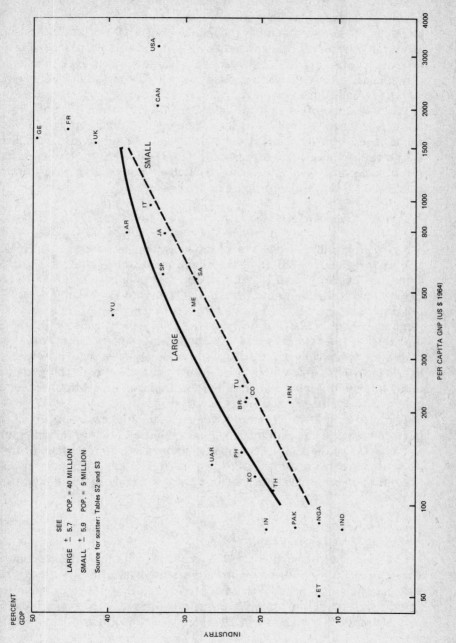

Scatter for 25 Large Countries, 1965

As a result of the early industrialization of large countries, the difference in export levels is concentrated in primary exports. For example, Table 14 shows that at an income level of $500 primary exports account for two-thirds of the difference in commodity exports per capita between large and small countries. In large countries exports are systematically biased toward industry at all income levels as compared with the small country average.

Table 14 also shows that the allocation processes are generally more uniform among the large countries, which justifies their being treated as a single group while the small countries are further subdivided. ie standard errors for the trade processes of large countries are less than half those of the small ones, which have a much greater variation in the timing of the shift from primary to industrial exports.

Scale and Accumulation

A less predictable result of this analysis is that large countries have significantly higher levels of investment and saving during the transition, as shown in Figures 18 and 19. Although higher savings are partly offset by lower levels of capital inflow, investment levels are 15 percent higher. We can only speculate on the reasons for these differences. Although there is some evidence that large countries have grown slightly faster than small ones over the past twenty years,[12] the higher investment rates shown here may also indicate larger capital requirements. These can plausibly be associated with a greater need for infrastructure and with the predominant strategy of import-substituting industrialization that has been more extensively pursued in the larger countries.

The collection of government revenue is the only process in which the large countries lag behind the small ones (Figure 21). Here the difference is explained by the fact that in smaller countries the larger share of trade leads to higher tax revenues, as shown in Chapter 2. This greater tax base does not appear to produce a higher level of saving in small countries, however.

Other Effects of Scale

The greater preoccupation of large countries with internal problems of development has produced an inward-oriented set of policies that have wide ramifications. Some of these are reflected in the statistical measures summarized here. For example, the effects of excessive import substitution and neglect of exports (in 1965) are shown in the low export ratios

---

[12]Chenery, Elkington, and Sims (1970).

and primary export bias of Argentina, Brazil, Colombia, Mexico, and Turkey. These policy effects are discussed in the concluding section.

As a result of early industrialization large countries have a larger industrial labor force, somewhat greater urbanization, and marginally higher levels of education than small ones. But even though most of the economic factors measured here seem to favor large countries, they may be offset by greater political and administrative difficulties.[13] It is therefore not possible to establish any clear advantage for the larger economic units in the development process.

RESOURCE EFFECTS: THE SMALL-COUNTRY PATTERNS

Just as the development patterns of large countries reflect their concern with the internal market, those of small countries are more influenced by external markets and capital flows. Few small countries are able to sustain satisfactory rates of growth with import levels of less than 20 percent of GNP, and the norm varies from 20 percent to 30 percent for the smallest units. Since over the 1950–70 period primary exports (excluding petroleum) expanded at only about 3 percent per year (in both quantity and value terms), most developing countries must at some point shift toward nonprimary exports if they are to continue to expand.[14]

Variability of the Transformation

The average expansion path of primary and industrial exports measured for small countries is shown in Figure 14. As the income level rises from $100 to $500, primary exports typically expand from $16 to $60 per capita and manufactured exports grow from $2 to $30.[15] Beyond the $500 income level, however, manufactured exports normally provide the bulk of the increase.

There is great variation in the timing of this shift in the composition of exports. This phenomenon is taken as the basis for dividing small countries in Tables 11 to 13 into three groups having different trade patterns. At one extreme countries like New Zealand, Venezuela, and Libya have reached relatively high levels of income with little reduction in the primary bias of their exports. At the other extreme countries such as Israel, Greece, Taiwan, and Tunisia have sufficient primary exports to support a

---

[13]The political and administrative advantages of small countries are stressed by Kuznets (1960a).

[14]Current projections of the growth of primary (nonoil) exports for the decade of the 1970s are on the order of 4 percent in real terms.

[15]Services are shown in Figures 6 and 7 but are omitted here.

per capita GNP of only $150 or less and have had to develop other exports at an early stage in their development in order to raise their income above this level.

The lead or lag in changing the composition of exports in relation to the normal small-country pattern is measured by the trade orientation index described above. A positive value of this index shows that the country's primary exports make up a higher proportion of its total commodity exports than the norms shown for each income level in Figure 14.[16] High values of primary exports usually reflect a rich natural-resource base, which dominates the trade orientation at low-income levels. Failure to develop other exports when primary exports cease to grow will leave a country with a primary bias and an inadequate base for further expansion, as with Chile and Uruguay. A low level of total exports distinguishes these cases in Table 11 from countries with more adequate specialization on primary exports.

Although there are significant policy and structural differences associated with the level of exports as well as with their composition, the latter bears a closer relation to production and other development processes and has therefore been used as the principal basis for classifying the small countries. Separate regressions for primary-oriented and industry-oriented groups are given in the Statistical Appendix, Tables S7, S8, S11, and S12.[17] The differences in the predicted values for the accumulation and resource allocation processes are summarized in Tables 14 and 15 and in Figures 24 to 32.

Effects of Primary Orientation

Primary orientation of exports reflects a lag from the average transformation of the productive structure. In many cases the rich resources that favor this lag also lead to relatively high levels of total exports from poor countries. Apart from the oil-exporting nations, countries that maintain this pattern at higher-income levels typically lag behind in export growth, and the export share in GNP tends to decline. This is true of the richest countries — New Zealand and Australia — that have maintained a primary trade bias, as well as of middle-income countries such as Chile and Uruguay.

---

[16]This statement must be qualified for the level of exports, as explained in the Technical Appendix.

[17]Experiments were done with regressions for the three groups shown in Tables 11 to 13. Only the two-way split is presented since the balanced group is almost as well explained by either regression. The allocation of the poorest countries between the two groups is fairly arbitrary but has little effect on the results. (See discussion in the Technical Appendix.)

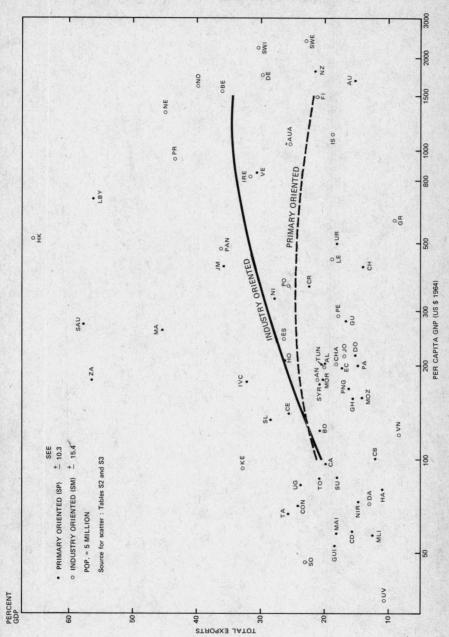

Figure 24. Total Exports, Small Countries
Scatter for 67 Countries, 1965

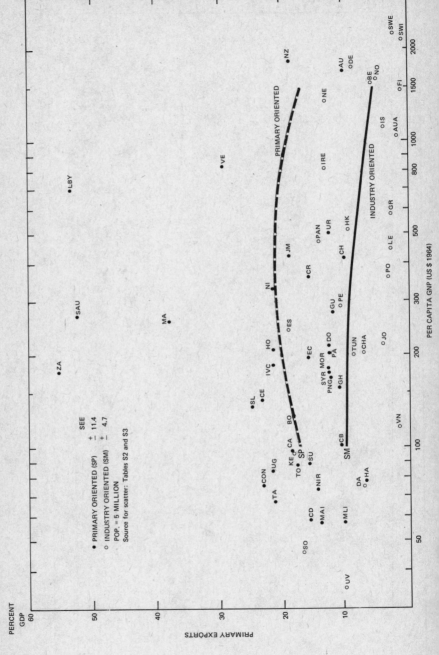

Figure 25: Primary Exports: Small Countries
Scatter for 62 Countries, 1965

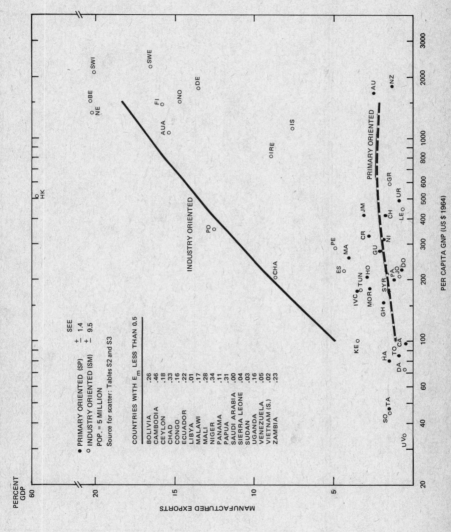

Figure 26: Manufactured Exports: Small Countries
Scatter for 62 Countries, 1965

94

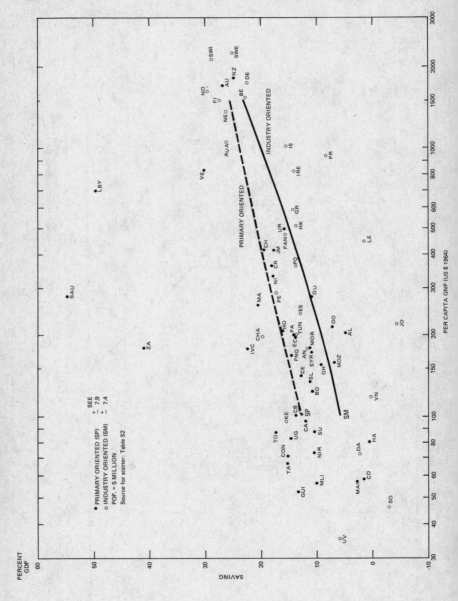

Figure 27: Saving: Small Countries
Scatter for 67 Countries, 1965

Figure 28: Investment: Small Countries
Scatter for 67 Countries, 1965

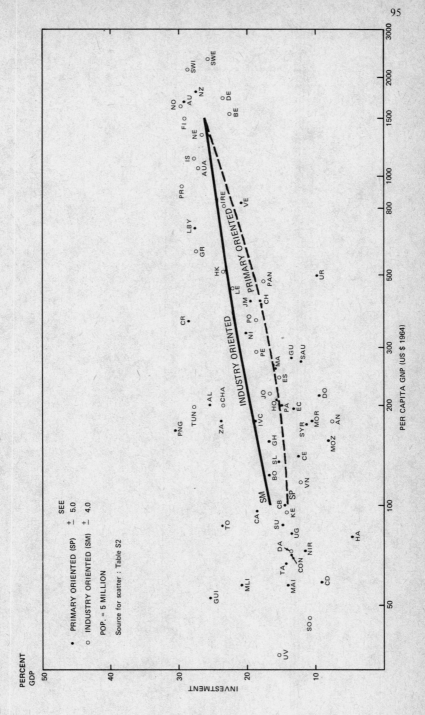

PERCENT
GDP

PRIMARY ORIENTED (SP)   SEE
                         +/- 5.0
INDUSTRY ORIENTED (SM)   +/- 4.0

POP. = 5 MILLION

Source for scatter : Table S2

PER CAPITA GNP (US $ 1964)

INVESTMENT

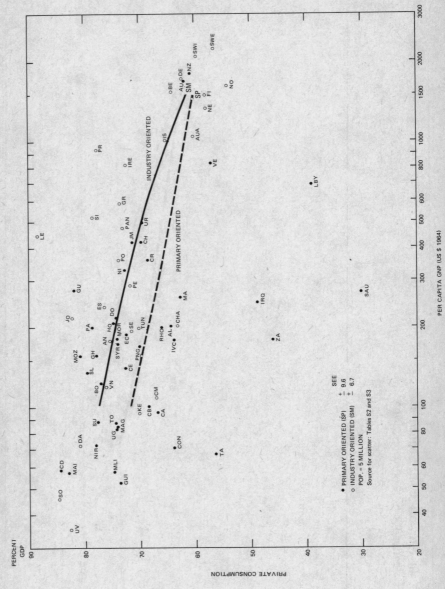

Figure 29: Private Consumption: Small Countries
Scatter for 71 Countries, 1965

Scatter for 66 Countries, 1965

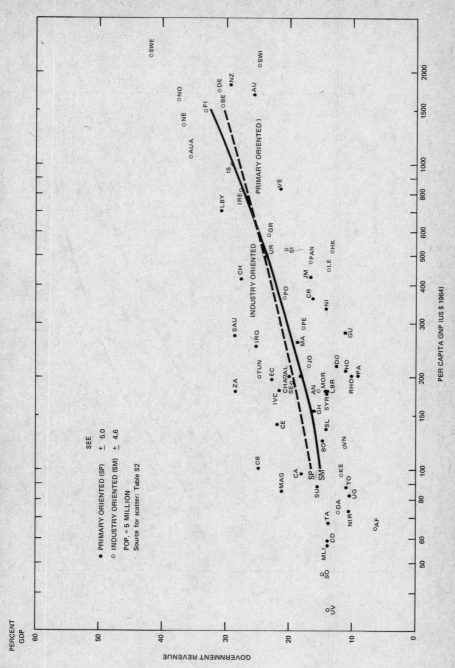

PERCENT
GDP

GOVERNMENT REVENUE

PER CAPITA GNP (US $ 1964)

	SEE
● PRIMARY ORIENTED (SP)	± 5.0
○ INDUSTRY ORIENTED (SM)	± 4.6

POP. = 5 MILLION
Source for scatter: Table S2

PRIMARY ORIENTED)

INDUSTRY ORIENTED

98

Figure 31: Primary Share of Production: Small Countries
Scatter for 64 Countries, 1965

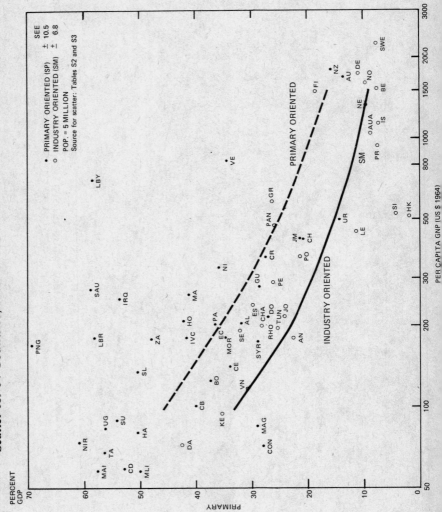

Scatter for 64 Countries, 1965

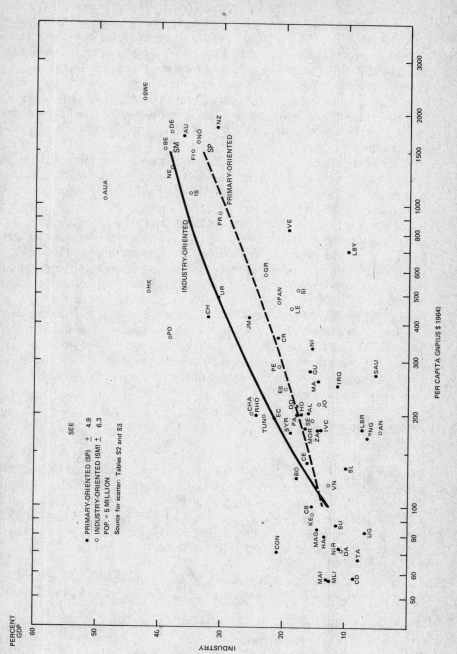

The average extent of the lag in transformation is indicated by the relation between the primary-oriented curve and the normal curve for small countries in Figure 14. For example, the threshold level of $10 per capita of manufactured exports is reached by the typical small, primary-oriented country *(SP)* only at $500 per capita income, compared to the average level of $250, and the small, manufacturing-oriented country *(SM)* level of $150. These differences in export patterns carry over to the composition of commodity production, as shown in Figures 31 and 32. Here the lag in the average transformation for *SP* countries is almost as great as with exports.

The statistical argument for dividing the sample according to the trade orientation is quite similar to the case for dividing it by size. The effects of rich primary resources vary with the level of income. In poor countries they lead to relatively high exports and rapid growth. At higher-income levels a primary export bias is more often associated with a slow growth of exports and GNP and low trade levels (always excepting the oil exporters). Even though the values of the coefficient of determination (R^2) are not significantly increased by splitting the sample (since the variance is reduced), the errors of estimate are substantially reduced for the allocation processes.[18]

Unlike the scale effects, the effects of the trade bias do not carry over to accumulation and other processes to any significant degree. Although early industrialization is associated with higher savings and investment in both cases, the other development processes are not affected. (Figures 27 to 30 for these processes are included to show the relative structures of individual small countries.)

Effects of Industry Orientation

Industry orientation arises in most cases because of a lack of natural resources to provide an export base. The countries for which this pattern is most typical—Hong Kong, Israel, Greece, Portugal, Lebanon, Tunisia, Taiwan—have only developed primary exports of $40 or less per capita, which would support only a per capita income of $150 on the normal trade pattern. To compensate for this limitation the successful countries have developed high levels of either manufactured exports or services, or both.[19]

A second characteristic of virtually all the countries that have followed this pattern successfully has been an abnormally high inflow of external

---

[18]The significance of these divisions is discussed in the Technical Appendix.

[19]Since service exports play an important role in most of these countries, their trade orientation would be more accurately described as nonprimary. Inasmuch as the more important structural effects are associated with industrial exports that designation is retained.

capital. In the early stage of development this is largely public capital, but once growth is established the private component increases. The two large, low-income countries that have a significant industry orientation—Pakistan and Korea—have also had volumes of external assistance abnormally large in relation to their size. The availability of external capital replaces primary exports and enables countries to continue growing while they are developing the capability of exporting manufactures.

The early development of industrial and service exports is associated with a pattern of resource allocation which more closely resembles that of large countries than that of the other small countries. For example, Table 15 shows that at an income level of $500 the *SM* country derives 31 percent of its GNP from industry—7 percentage points more than the *SP* country but 2 percent less than the large country. The primary share is also low, however, as a result of the substantial capital inflow which permits some replacement of primary production by imports.[20]

The pattern of early industrialization has also led to relatively high rates of growth for most of the small countries that have been able to carry out the required transformation of both their productive structures and their exports. Apart from the communist countries of Eastern Europe, however, all countries following this pattern have required large amounts of external capital over a period of ten years or more. It is only after considerable development has taken place in domestic industry that the shift to manufactured exports becomes significant and export expansion makes it possible to replace external borrowing as a source of foreign exchange.

A TYPOLOGY OF DEVELOPMENT PATTERNS

The preceding analysis has extended the search for uniformity in development experience by subdividing countries into more homogeneous groups, based on their size and trade patterns. In summarizing the implications of these results for the study of development policy it is useful to organize them in a typology that focuses on the extent of individual deviations from the average relationships. Examination of the nature of a given country's departures from the average patterns for its group may be more instructive than the analysis of the average changes that may be expected.

Criteria for Classification

The typology proposed here[21] is based on a comparison of the deviations from the average patterns of trade and production. Under the

---

[20]This effect was discussed in Chapter 2.

[21]This section is based on Chenery (1973).

simplifying assumptions as to the nature of demand and comparative advantage that were outlined in Chapter 2, there are predictable relations among the level and composition of exports, the level of capital inflow, and the sectoral composition of production. A classification of countries based on these factors therefore gives some indication as to the validity of these underlying assumptions. It also provides a basis for associating identifiable development strategies, such as import substitution or export-based growth, with characteristic deviations from the average patterns of structural change.

Since our primary interest in this volume is in the transitional developing countries, the least developed, the fully developed, and the transitional countries in which growth has been seriously disrupted during the decade of the sixties will be omitted. The sample is thus reduced in stages to fifty countries that meet four criteria: *(a)* those which had reached $80 per capita GNP by 1965 (or the equivalent level of industrialization for larger countries) but were not yet fully developed; *(b)* those for which the required statistical measures can be estimated; *(c)* those which are large enough to be representative (a minimum of 1.5 million people); and *(d)* those whose economies were not too disrupted by wars and political disturbances to achieve significant growth.

The first three criteria yield a sample of 62 countries having over 1.5 million population and income levels in the transitional range of $100 to $1000 for at least part of the decade 1960–70. From this group six politically disturbed countries with low growth in this decade[22] and six small, unrepresentative countries[23] have been deleted, leaving the sample of fifty given in Table 16. An effort has been made to include the larger countries — on a provisional basis if necessary — so that only eight transitional countries of over 5 million population[24] have been excluded.

As a basis for this typology the two measures of deviations in export level and export composition from Tables 10 to 13 were recomputed using the separate regressions for large and small countries (Tables S9 and S10). The production pattern is summarized by the following index of production orientation *(PO)*, which is analogous to the trade orientation:[25]

$$PO = P - \hat{P} = (V_p - V_m) - (\hat{V}_p - \hat{V}_m) \qquad (4.2)$$

where $\hat{P}$ is the normal production bias and P is the actual bias. As in the

---

[22]South Vietnam, Cambodia, Dominican Republic, Haiti, Nigeria, Indonesia.

[23]Honduras, Paraguay, Jordan, Papua New Guinea, Libya, Panama.

[24]Cameroon, Mozambique, Malagasy Republic, Algeria, South Vietnam, Cambodia, Nigeria, and Indonesia.

[25]It is not necessary to correct for the variation in production levels, since the total of primary and industrial production shows only a limited variation as a share of GNP. The index can therefore be stated as $(V_p - \hat{V}_p) - (V_m - \hat{V}_m)$ or $(\delta V_p - \delta V_m)$. It is also computed from the separate regressions for large and small countries.

TABLE 16. A Classification of Allocation Patterns

Pattern	Country	1965 Population (mil.)	1965 Per Capita GNP ($)	1960–70 Growth of Per Capita GNP (%)	Rel. Export Level*	Trade Orient. $(TO)*$	Prod. Orient. $(PO)*$	Capital Inflow (%)	Income Shares† Upper 20% (%)	Income Shares† Lower 40% (%)	Gini†
1. PRIMARY SPECIALIZATION‡	Tanzania	12	67	3.0	1.52	.05*	.06*	−.04	57.0	14.0	.48
	Uganda	9	83	2.2	1.28	.21	.14	−.01	47.1	17.1	.38
	Sudan	14	88	0.5	.96*	.19	.08	.04	50.3	14.2	.43
	Ceylon	11	142	2.3	1.19	.32	−.04*	.00	46.0	17.0	.37
	Sierra Leone	2	135	−0.5	1.23	.11*	.14	.04			
	Zambia	4	179	4.6	2.36	.36	.16	−.17	57.0	14.6	.49
	Ivory Coast	4	179	4.8	1.37	−.04*	.11	−.03	55.0	17.5	.43
	Iran	25	218	5.7	1.39	.48	.22	−.06			
	Iraq	8	249	2.6			.34	−.04	68.0	6.8	.61
	Malaysia	9	258	3.7	1.86	.31	.20	−.05	43.9	17.7	.36
	Saudi Arabia	7	271	6.3	2.30	.47	.47	−.42			
	Nicaragua	2	330	3.2	.99*	.12	.12	.02			
	Venezuela	9	830	2.5	1.09	.90	.31	−.10	58.0	9.7	.52
Total for 13 countries		116									
2. BALANCED Normal capital inflow§	Thailand	31	110	4.5	1.40*	−.06	−.03	.01	57.7	12.9	.50
	Philippines	32	149	2.7	1.21	.13*	−.05	.01	55.4	11.6	.50
	Syria	5	174	5.4	.89	−.03	−.07	.00			
	Morocco	13	179	1.5	.89	−.03	.02	−.01			
	El Salvador	3	240	1.8	1.03	−.01	−.01	.02	52.0	12.7	.45
	Guatemala	4	278	1.9	.65*	.12*	.07	.03			
	Peru	12	289	1.7	.72	−.06	.01	.01	60.0	6.5	.57
	Jamaica	2	420	2.7	1.24	−.06	−.07	.02	61.5	8.2	.56
	South Africa	18	552	3.4	1.46*	.06	.05	.00	58.0	6.2	.56
High capital inflow	Ghana	8	155	0.3	.70	.03		.08			
	Costa Rica	2	360	3.1	.78	−.01	−.00	.10	50.6	14.7	.43
	Spain	32	572	6.4	.73	−.05	.02	.04	45.2	17.0	.38
	Greece	9	585	6.2	.34	−.03	.13*	.13	49.5	21.0	.37
	Ireland	3	815	3.2	1.07	−.04		.09			
Total for 14 countries		174									
3. IMPORT SUBSTITUTION	India	481	84	1.3				.02	54.0	14.0	.46
	Bolivia	4	124	2.3	.95*	.19	−.06	.06			
	Ecuador	5	195	1.7	.73	.34	.01	0	73.5	6.4	.66
	Brazil	81	216	2.2	.94	.54	−.03	−.03	66.7	6.5	.61
	Colombia	18	228	1.8	.68	.29	.04	−.01	59.5	9.4	.54
	Turkey	31	244	3.3	.44	.30	.12*	.01			
	Chile	9	419	1.4	.53	.32	−.08	−.01	56.8	13.0	.49
	Mexico	43	434	3.5	.73	.35	−.02	0	65.8	10.2	.58
	Uruguay	3	497	−0.3	.64	.28	−.13	−.06	47.4	14.3	.42
	Argentina	22	787	1.6	.48	.67	−.01	−.01	52.0	17.3	.42
Total for 10 countries		697									
4. INDUSTRIAL SPECIALIZATION Normal capital inflow	Kenya	10	95	3.4	1.72	−.21	−.12	−.01			
	Egypt	29	138	1.6	1.37	−.10	−.16	.02			
	China (Taiwan)	12	201	6.3	.78	−.57	−.11	.03	40.1	20.4	.32
	Yugoslavia	20	415	4.5	1.30	−.56	−.09	.01	41.5	18.5	.33
	Hong Kong	4	512	8.7	2.34	−1.03	−.34	0			
	Singapore	2	522	5.5			−.11	.04			
High capital inflow	Pakistan	114	84	2.9	.88	−.31	−.00*	.06	45.0	17.5	.37
	South Korea	28	123	6.4	.64	−.69	−.00*	.08	45.0	18.0	.36
	Tunisia	4	198	1.9	.82	−.30	−.12	.14	55.0	10.5	.50
	Portugal	9	361	5.2	.99	−.70	−.17	.05			
	Lebanon	2	446	1.3	.67	−.31	−.06*	.21	61.0	13.0	.52
	Puerto Rico	2	936	5.9	1.97		−.08	.21	50.6	13.7	.44
	Israel	3	1,126	5.1	.62	−.28	−.10	.13	39.4	20.2	.30
Total for 13 countries		239									

SOURCE: Chenery (1973).
*Deviations from large- and small-country regressions.
†SOURCE: Chenery et al (1974).
‡Additional Group 1 countries in 1970: Nigeria, Indonesia, Mozambique.
§Additional Group 2 countries in 1970: Malagasy Republic, Cameroon.
*Features that deviate from the criteria for each pattern.

case of the trade orientation, positive values indicate a bias toward primary production or a lag in industrialization.

Since the classification of countries is based on their departure from the average patterns of production and trade, it is convenient to define a normal range for each of the three measures and to classify countries as high, low, or normal for each dimension. The width of the normal range has been chosen to include roughly 40 percent of the observations for each measure.[26] The level and orientation of exports and the orientation of production will be taken as the basic criteria for the typology; the level of the capital inflow is used to subdivide the categories where it is important.

On this basis four main patterns can be identified, defined by the following values of the indices. The resulting classification is given in Table 16.

1. *Primary specialization*
    a. Primary-oriented exports (*TO* greater than .10)
    b. Primary-oriented production (*PO* greater than .07)
    c. Export level usually above normal

This group corresponds to the established concept of an export-led growth pattern based on favorable primary resources. In the 1960s it included thirteen transitional countries having a total population in 1965 of 116 million (plus Nigeria, which was temporarily disrupted by civil war).

2. *Balanced production and trade*
    a. Normal export orientation (*TO* −.10 to +.10)
    b. Normal production orientation (*PO* −.07 to +.07)

This group of fourteen countries can be subdivided into nine having normal levels of capital inflow and exports and five with high capital inflow (*F* equal to or greater than .04). The total population for the whole group was 174 million.

3. *Import substitution*
    a. Primary export orientation (*TO* greater than .10)
    b. Low total exports (exports below .75 of normal levels)
    c. Production not primary oriented (*PO* less than +.07)

This group includes nine countries having a total population of 216 million plus India, which will be treated as a special case because of its exceptional size.

4. *Industrial specialization*
    a. Industrial export orientation (*TO* less than −.10)
    b. Industrial production orientation (*PO* less than −.07)

This category can also be usefully subdivided into seven countries with a

---

[26]For the capital inflow a distinction is made between high (over 4 percent), normal (0 percent to 4 percent), and negative values.

high capital inflow (F more than .04) and six with more normal levels of F. The total population for the whole group was 240 million in 1965.[27]

Once these four basic allocation patterns had been identified, all but six of the fifty countries could be assigned to them without difficulty on the basis of data for 1965. Consideration of other years between 1960 and 1970 showed that in most cases the apparent conflicts were temporary phenomena, and the remaining countries could reasonably be classified in one of the four groups.[28] Since the primary objective is to describe the characteristics of the predominant development strategies followed in the recent past, these results are quite sufficient to indicate the representative examples for each pattern.

In summary, the four indices lead to the identification of four major patterns of resource allocation, each of which applies (in 1970) to 200 million to 300 million people in transitional countries. In addition, India may be classed in the import substitution group on the basis of its development policies and their effect in limiting exports.

Applications

To assess the usefulness of this typology it must first be asked whether the patterns observed in Table 16 represent the working out of similar strategies of development or whether other factors may be responsible for some of these uniformities. The most direct approach to this question is to compare a country's results with its intentions, as represented by its development programs. A preliminary assessment indicates that two of the main features observed reflect policy failures more than intended results. For example, virtually all the countries classified as having import-substitution patterns (Group 3) had planned to increase manufactured exports in the past decade and in some cases had taken extensive measures to do so. If these measures had succeeded in producing an average level of industrial exports, both the total export level and the trade bias would have become normal, and the country would be classed in Group 2.[29] It therefore appears that countries in Groups 2 and 3 have attempted a balanced allocation strategy. Nevertheless the distinctive features of the im-

---

[27] As of now Bangladesh would be separated from Pakistan and the 1965 population reduced to 180 million.

[28] Features that do not fit the criteria stated above are shown by stars (*) in Table 16. For example, Turkey still had a primary production orientation in 1965, but by 1969 it fell within the normal range characteristic of the import-substitution pattern. In borderline cases such as this the country has been classified on the basis of the policies followed and other structural characteristics. India has been classified in this way because of its large size, which renders its deviations not statistically significant.

[29] As of 1973 this would be true of Mexico and Brazil.

port-substitution strategy are sufficiently widespread to warrant its treatment as a separate allocation pattern, even though in the longer run it may appear as a transitory phase in most countries.

Another transitory feature that can be identified from comparison with development plans is excessive reliance on external capital. Although external borrowing is a normal feature of the development strategies of many countries, it also constitutes a safety valve that can offset a decline in export markets as well as production failures and other mistakes in implementation. Few countries, however, can sustain borrowing much in excess of 4 percent of GNP over long periods of time; capital inflow much above this level must therefore be considered a transitory phenomenon in most of the twelve countries where it occurs in Table 16.

Our general conclusion is that the four basic patterns observed here have their counterparts in the development plans and policies of the transitional countries. While there are sometimes large differences between intended and actual resource allocation, the experience of the more successful countries in each of the four groups indicates the opportunities as well as the problems that characterize each type of strategy.

The value of this classification of development patterns can be determined only in the course of subsequent research. The work done so far, however, suggests that this typology provides a useful basis for comparative studies of development strategy, extensions of development theory, and the evaluation of country performance. The nature of these applications can be briefly indicated.[30]

Comparative country studies are often undertaken to illustrate the effects of different types of policies. The ability to generalize from them is enhanced by relating the limited sample of countries studied to the full range of developing economies. For example, two of the most comprehensive recent studies of trade policies and resource allocation — those of Little, Scitovsky, and Scott (1970) and Balassa (1971) — are largely concentrated on the group of countries following policies of import substitution. These studies provide a detailed interpretation of the sources of the distortions in resource allocation that are reflected in the indices for countries in Group 3, as well as comparisons with a few countries in Group 2 and Group 4.

Development theory has tended to concentrate on a few of the problems that characterize some transitional countries and to neglect others that are equally important. Although the pattern of primary specialization was one of the first to be identified, the policies of countries that have continued to follow it have been relatively neglected because of the

---

[30]An application of the typology to the evaluation of alternative strategies is given in Chenery (1973).

greater interest in the process of industrialization. The recent improvement in the export markets for primary commodities should lead to a revival of interest in this development strategy as well as to greater theoretical attention to the employment and distributional problems that are raised by delayed industrialization.

Although the typology proposed here is based on patterns of resource allocation, there are numerous hypotheses relating these patterns to rates of growth as well as to inequality of income distribution. For the benefit of researchers who wish to pursue these relations, the available information on both is summarized in Table 16.[31] There is some evidence of more equal distribution of income in countries in Group 4 (industrial specialization) and less equality in Group 1 (primary specialization), but the nature of the causal relations remains to be explored.

Finally, this classification of development patterns may provide a basis for evaluating development performance. The strategies corresponding to each pattern require a different sequence of structural changes and are not likely to permit growth at a steady rate during each phase. A comparison among countries faced with similar problems—of increasing industrial exports or reducing aid, for example—is likely to be more valid than the application of general indicators to all developing countries.

PATTERNS FOR DEVELOPED COUNTRIES

A number of scholars have suggested that since the economic structures of developed countries reflect factors other than their level of income, the results of cross-country regressions that include these countries must be heavily qualified. In this section the results of dividing the sample into two or three groups are presented in order to test the assumption that the same basic regression equations fit both poor and rich countries. As in the case of size, some statistical improvements would be expected in the estimates of almost all processes by splitting the sample in this way. The main objective, however, is to identify processes for which the overall cross-country relation is significantly changed by this division and where the pooled regression is therefore misleading.

There are several reasons why for some processes it may be more valid to preserve the now traditional dichotomy between developing and developed countries rather than to treat them as a homogeneous group. First, different lags in development processes are omitted in a pure cross-country analysis. The best illustration of such a lag is fertility, which appears to have a much longer adjustment period than any of the other processes examined here. When only current income is considered in

---

[31]The relation to growth rates is analyzed by Chenery and Taylor (1968) and Chenery (1971). Income distribution relations are analyzed by Adelman and Morris (1971).

measuring the level of development, the fact that countries have been growing at different rates is ignored. If fertility responds with a lag of several decades to the socioeconomic changes associated with income growth, the cross-section results will overestimate the predicted fall in fertility rates in rapidly growing countries—a phenomenon that was noted in Chapter 3.

A second reason for treating developed countries separately has to do with their historical position as political and economic leaders. The approximately fourteen countries considered as developed in 1950 had certain political and social characteristics that may or may not be duplicated by the next group of transitional countries to achieve the same income levels. For example, the developed countries in 1950 were also leaders in trade and technological change and had already completed the demographic transition. By 1970 there were some thirty countries with per capita incomes above $1000, but they had less homogeneous social and political characteristics.

For reasons such as these, several authors have found it misleading to draw conclusions about structural change from cross-country regressions that include the developed countries. Musgrave (1969, p. 123), for example, found that the positive association of the tax ratio with the level of per capita GNP disappears when the sample examined is divided into low and high-income groups. Although Kuznets cautions against the use of cross-country regression techniques because they tend to obscure the unquantifiable factors, he also stresses the general similarities between the historical experience of the advanced countries and the relations derived by intercountry comparisons (1966, 1971).

Within the general framework of the present study it is possible to test the nature of the transition from less-developed to developed status in two ways. First, the sample is divided by income level into two or three groups and separate regressions are estimated for each, as was done for scale in the preceding section. Second, in Chapter 5 the time series for individual countries are compared with the cross-country results.

As will be shown, both of these tests support the general validity of cross-country analysis applied to the full sample of countries. They also, however, provide a significant improvement in the description of the transition for certain processes. The present analysis focuses on the most important cases.

Effects of Income Level on Accumulation Processes

Since there is no satisfactory basis for an a priori classification of countries by level of development, two alternative groupings have been tested: a two-way split of countries above and below a per capita income of $500

Figure 33: Saving: Three Income Groups

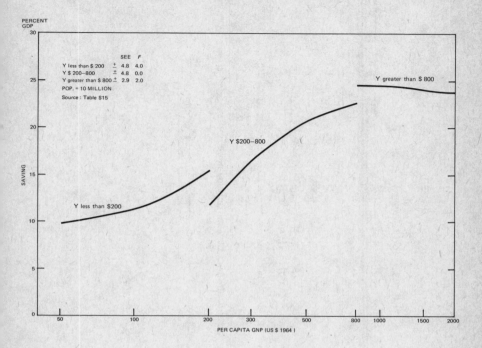

PERCENT
GDP

SAVING

	SEE	F
Y less than $ 200	± 4.8	4.0
Y $ 200–800	± 4.8	0.0
Y greater than $ 800	± 2.9	2.0

POP. = 10 MILLION

Source : Table S15

Y greater than $ 800

Y $200–800

Y less than $200

PER CAPITA GNP (US $ 1964)

in 1960; a three-way split of below $200, $200 to $800, and above $800 in 1960. The finer subdivision was used only when the first split indicated a significant difference between the two groups.

Results of applying the basic regression equations to the two income groups for three accumulation processes are given in Tables 17 and 18. In each case there is a significant acceleration in the rate of change with income level in the lower group, followed by a deceleration in the upper group. These results support the hypothesis that the underlying relationship is best described by an **s**-shaped function. To avoid the arbitrary division at $500 the three-way split has been used to derive a more precise measure of the saving-income relation.[32] The results shown in Figure 33 resemble a logistic function in having upper and lower asymptotes.

---

[32]For greater homogeneity, these results are based on the post-1960 data only, which gives a more constant sample of countries in each year.

TABLE 17. Accumulation Processes: Richer Countries with per Capita Income Greater than $500 in 1960

Process	Constant	$\ln Y$	$(\ln Y)^2$	$\ln N$	$(\ln N)^2$	F	T_1	T_2	T_3	R^2	SEE	Y Mean/Range	No. of Obs.
Saving	−.301 (.664)	.146 (1.102)	−.010 (1.062)	.016 (1.499)	−.003 (1.449)	−.857 (18.830)	−.020 (2.891)	−.017 (2.528)	−.001 (.112)	.590	.050	1228 250/3614	453
Investment	−.293 (.645)	.144 (1.083)	−.010 (1.043)	.016 (1.491)	−.003 (1.445)	.141 (3.102)	−.020 (2.840)	−.017 (2.472)	−.000 (.052)	.066	.050	1228 250/3614	453
Government revenue	−1.502 (2.733)	.476 (2.958)	−.031 (2.679)	.019 (1.399)	−.003 (1.120)	.010 (.164)	−.031 (3.919)	−.029 (3.844)	−.020 (2.825)	.271	.045	1240 282/2356	336

Normal Variation in Economic Structure with Level of Development*
Per Capita Income (US$ 1964)

	$500	$800	$1,000	$1,500
Saving	.219	.226	.228	.228
Investment	.240	.247	.249	.250
Government revenue	.273	.307	.318	.330

t ratios in parentheses.
*$N = 10$; $F = .02$.

TABLE 18. Accumulation Processes: Poorer Countries with per Capita Income Less than $500 in 1960

Process	Constant	$\ln Y$	$(\ln Y)^2$	$\ln N$	$(\ln N)^2$	F	T_1	T_2	T_3	R^2	SEE	Y Mean/Range	No. of Obs.
Saving	.178 (2.341)	−.060 (1.986)	.010 (3.452)	.019 (4.686)	−.003 (3.214)	−.836 (39.270)	−.009 (1.802)	−.011 (2.559)	−.010 (2.590)	.699	.049	204 34/1089	979
Investment	.179 (2.364)	−.059 (1.949)	.010 (3.386)	.018 (4.510)	−.002 (3.139)	.153 (7.195)	−.011 (2.275)	−.012 (2.802)	−.012 (2.937)	.300	.049	204 34/1089	979
Government revenue	.372 (4.522)	−.124 (3.914)	.016 (5.103)	.022 (5.192)	−.004 (5.488)	−.185 (8.601)	−.024 (3.986)	−.006 (1.161)	−.006 (1.470)	.336	.050	231 34/1141	775

Normal Variation in Economic Structure with Level of Development*
Per Capita Income (US$ 1964)

	$100	$200	$300	$400	$500
Saving	.132	.161	.182	.198	.214
Investment	.153	.182	.204	.219	.235
Government revenue	.152	.172	.191	.207	.222

t ratios in parentheses.
*N = 10; F = .02.

The subdivision of the sample also makes it possible to determine whether scale effects and time trends are similar in rich and poor countries (which is assumed when the two samples are pooled). The results show that while the time trends are uniformly upward for both groups, they are somewhat larger for the upper-income countries.

The more detailed analysis of the interaction between income level and scale (given in Table 19) shows that the positive relation between size and saving rate noted in Chapter 2 is concentrated in the middle-income group. There is no significant relationship to size in either rich or poor countries.

TABLE 19. Size Effects for Saving and Exports: Three-way Income Split

| | Coefficient of: | | Slope at |
	lnN	$(lnN)^2$	$N = 10$*
Saving			
Y less than $200	−.00076	.00038	.001
Y $200 to $800	−.02899	.00884	.012
Y greater than $800	.01308	−.00447	−.007
Exports			
Y less than $200	−.02248	−.00267	−.035
Y $200 to $800	−.05354	−.00356	−.070
Y greater than $800	−.00880	−.00681	−.040

SOURCE: Table S15.

*The slope is equal to $\gamma_1 + 2\gamma_2 lnN$ where γ_1 and γ_2 are the coefficients of lnN and $(lnN)^2$ respectively and N equals 10.

Effects of Income Level on Allocation Processes

The subdivision of the sample by income level leads to a similar refinement in the description of allocation processes but suggests no major modification in the uniform patterns of Chapter 2. The basic regression equations for five allocation processes and two income groups are given in Tables 20 and 21. The most significant improvement from a statistical point of view is in the description of exports, which is shown graphically in Figure 34. As in the case of saving, both income terms in the regression are more significant for the split than for the pooled regression, and together the regressions suggest a logistic form for the underlying relationship. The income effects in the other four processes are adequately represented by the pooled regressions already described.[33]

---

[33]For exports the interaction between income and size is similar to that already described for saving. When the sample is divided into three income groups, the negative relation between size and export level is most pronounced in the middle-income group, although it is also significant in the other two.

TABLE 20. Resource Allocation and Trade Processes: Richer Countries with Per Capita Income Greater than $500 in 1960

Process	Constant	$\ln Y$	$(\ln Y)^2$	$\ln N$	$(\ln N)^2$	F	T_1	T_2	T_3	R^2	SEE	Y Mean/Range	No. of Obs.
Private consumption	1.046 (2.274)	−.091 (.678)	.004 (.442)	−.001 (.088)	−.000 (.042)	.724 (15.680)	.033 (4.541)	.030 (4.385)	.011 (1.679)	.556	.050	1229 251/3615	452
Government consumption	.142 (.621)	−.020 (.294)	.003 (.675)	−.022 (3.910)	.004 (4.013)	.123 (5.354)	−.010 (2.905)	−.011 (3.306)	−.011 (3.366)	.331	.025	1229 251/3615	452
Primary production	1.990 (4.517)	−.450 (3.474)	.027 (2.911)	−.022 (2.006)	.000 (.129)	−.561 (12.780)	.046 (6.609)	.025 (3.654)	.011 (1.618)	.611	.045	1205 250/3551	387
Industry production	−2.912 (5.418)	.855 (5.415)	−.058 (5.086)	.100 (7.448)	−.014 (5.810)	.269 (5.018)	.007 (.821)	.002 (.228)	.003 (.337)	.394	.055	1205 250/3551	387
Total exports	−2.317 (2.822)	.716 (2.979)	−.049 (2.836)	.028 (1.415)	−.014 (3.831)	.091 (1.099)	.001 (.096)	−.004 (.355)	−.005 (.446)	.391	.090	1228 251/3615	453

Normal Variation in Economic Structure with Level of Development*

	Per Capita Income (US$ 1964)			
	$500	$800	$1,000	$1,500
Private consumption	.656	.640	.632	.620
Government consumption	.120	.131	.136	.147
Primary production	.189	.143	.126	.101
Industry production	.314	.363	.377	.388
Total exports	.225	.263	.273	.279

t ratios in parentheses.
*$N = 10$; $F = .02$

**TABLE 21. Resource Allocation and Trade Processes:
Poorer Countries with per Capita Income Less than $500 in 1960**

Process	Constant	$\ln Y$	$(\ln Y)^2$	$\ln N$	$(\ln N)^2$	F	T_1	T_2	T_3	R^2	SEE	Y Mean/Range	No. of Obs.
Private consumption	1.101 (9.228)	−.115 (2.432)	.008 (1.765)	−.039 (6.721)	.008 (7.150)	.733 (24.690)	.041 (5.599)	.032 (4.943)	.018 (3.073)	.464	.074	203 35/1089	1,056
Government consumption	−.236 (3.284)	.145 (5.095)	−.015 (5.261)	.023 (6.611)	−.006 (8.238)	.157 (8.815)				.186	.045	203 35/1089	1,056
Primary production	2.098 (12.080)	−.483 (7.171)	.030 (4.652)	−.036 (4.954)	.006 (3.952)	−.608 (16.880)	−.005 (.542)	.008 (.996)	.011 (1.544)	.627	.089	223 47/1089	938
Industry production	−.483 (4.427)	.149 (3.516)	−.006 (1.533)	.046 (9.987)	−.005 (5.544)	.216 (9.538)	.006 (1.154)	−.002 (.334)	−.010 (2.085)	.492	.056	223 47/1089	938
Total exports	.728 (3.869)	−.198 (2.633)	.023 (3.064)	−.042 (4.281)	−.001 (.405)	−.606 (11.480)	−.008 (.674)	−.013 (1.157)	−.012 (1.253)	.279	.121	206 35/1089	979

Normal Variation in Economic Structure with Level of Development*

	Per Capita Income (US$ 1964)				
	$100	$200	$300	$400	$500
Private consumption	.712	.688	.678	.673	.669
Government consumption	.148	.148	.141	.134	.126
Primary production	.448	.320	.259	.221	.195
Industry production	.152	.213	.245	.267	.283
Total exports	.186	.205	.226	.245	.263

t ratios in parentheses.
*$N = 10$; $F = .02$

Figure 34: Total Exports: Two Income Groups

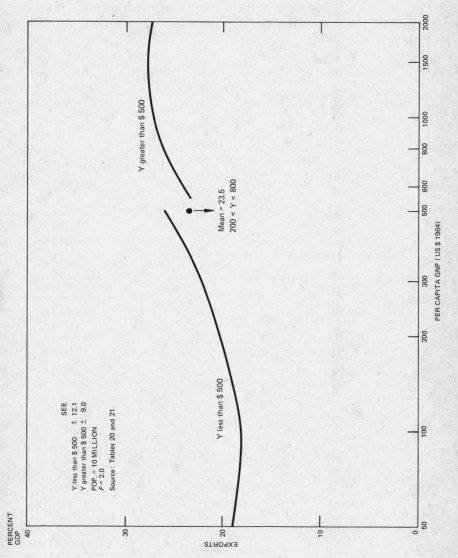

PERCENT
GDP

EXPORTS

PER CAPITA GNP (US $ 1964)

Y greater than $ 500

Mean = 23.5
200 < Y < 800

Y less than $ 500

SEE
Y less than $ 500   ± 12.1
Y greater than $ 500 ± 9.0
POP. = 10 MILLION
F = 2.0
Source : Tables 20 and 21

The other notable result of this set of experiments is the distinction be-tween the time trends in poor and rich countries. The downward shift in the share of primary production (and the corresponding rise in services) is shown to be characteristic of the upper income group only; there are no significant time trends in the composition of production among the lower-income countries.

Chapter 5

TIME-SERIES VS. CROSS-SECTION PATTERNS

THE STUDY OF ECONOMIC and social development raises basic questions as to the way in which the economy adjusts to changes in the underlying technological and behavioral relations. While this problem is virtually ignored in general equilibrium theory, it arises in almost every attempt to estimate the basic relationships that are posited in empirical versions of theoretical models. Although the initial discrepancies between time-series and cross-section estimates of demand functions, production functions, and savings functions have often been puzzling, attempts to solve these puzzles have turned out to be among the most fruitful sources of new theoretical developments.

While the present study is based on a minimum of explicit theory, it has impinged at some points on fields in which competing theories have different empirical implications. In other cases uniformities have been uncovered that could provide a basis for further theoretical analysis. For both these purposes it is important to determine the relationship between the cross-section patterns that have been measured and their time-series counterparts.

The availability of time-series data for a large number of countries over much of the past twenty years makes possible an exploration of the relation between time-series and cross-section patterns on a more extensive basis than has previously been possible. The main objective of such a comparison has been to determine the general nature of the relationships between the two rather than to make detailed tests of alternative hypotheses. However, we will point out the relationship of our findings to other results in the same areas.

The history of attempts to reconcile cross-section and time-series estimates of consumption and production functions suggests some of the problems in this field.[1] A large part of the discrepancy between the two types of estimates is due to the fact that some factors (relative prices, social objectives) omitted from the model vary systematically across countries or households, while other omitted factors (technology, new products) vary systematically over time. A judicious combination of the two types of estimation makes it possible, however, to explore a wider range of variables than would be possible from either one separately.[2]

---

[1]The present authors' more detailed experience has been in the analysis of production relations: Arrow, Chenery, Minhas, and Solow (1961), Chenery and Taylor (1968), Syrquin (1970).

[2]Since the variation in both income levels and relative factor prices is much greater among countries than in available time series, it is possible to get an idea of the nature of structural relations over a wide range of income and prices only from cross-country data.

TIME-SERIES ESTIMATION

To compare the time-series patterns with cross-section patterns in a systematic way a procedure was followed that can be applied to the relations already studied. The principal measures of accumulation and allocation are analyzed, and for most of these measures there are other time-series studies which can be compared with our results.

Average Time-series Relations

The notion of a uniform or universal structural relation, such as Engel's law, implies some similarity in the parameters of the same structural equation estimated from time series for different countries. There are several ways of determining such similarities. The most direct approach is to make separate estimates of the same equation for a number of countries and then summarize the results in the form of averages or ranges.[3] Since the main interest here is to determine the average value of the time-series relations, however, this can be done more efficiently by estimating a single time-series equation for the whole sample, allowing for intercountry variation by the use of dummy variables, one for each country.[4]

Although our objective is to estimate average time-series relations that are comparable to the standard cross-section patterns of Chapter 2, the limited range of variation for any single country requires a simpler formulation. In time-series analysis any uniform change such as the growth of population is indistinguishable from a time trend, and therefore N is omitted from the time-series regressions. As indicated in Chapter 1, the standard equation for time-series analysis takes the following form:

$$X = \alpha_i + \beta_1 lnY + \beta_2(lnY)^2 + \Sigma \, \delta_i T_i + \epsilon F \tag{1.3}$$

where $\alpha_i =$ the constant (dummy variable) for country i.
The difference from the cross-country model is that by letting each country have its own intercept the variation *between* countries is eliminated and only the *within* country component of the total variation is considered.

In the cross-country model the effects of omitted factors associated with income and the other exogenous variables were reflected through their estimated coefficients. Two types of such omitted variables can be distinguished: those whose association with income and the other variables

---

[3]This was the procedure followed in Houthakker's 1957 estimates of the average values of the Engel function and in the comparison of time-series to cross-section production relations by Chenery and Taylor (1968). It is particularly useful in testing for the effects of country characteristics that have been omitted.

[4]The estimation procedure is discussed in the Technical Appendix. The effect of scale is included in this dummy variable and can be estimated only in a cross-section framework.

is a common feature of the development process and therefore is expected to continue into the future; and others where the systematic relation with the exogenous variables reflects some historical or geographical accident not likely to be repeated. Long-run trends for individual countries, such as the ones presented in Kuznets (1971) and in Chenery and Taylor (1968), reflect the first type of interactions but not the second.

A further difference between the time-series equation (1.3) and the cross-country pattern stems from the dynamic nature of some of the relations. Adjustment mechanisms are seldom instantaneous and are sometimes spread over long periods of time. Little evidence is available on the nature of the lag structures. Most existing work relates to the processes of investment and consumption and almost invariably refers to advanced countries.[5] The lagged response in consumption to variations in income postulated by the permanent income theory, for example, would imply larger saving propensities in the short run than in the long run, an expectation confirmed by our results.

Estimation of equation (1.3) from a set of time series for n countries gives an average value of the income effects (β_1, β_2), the capital inflow effect (ϵ), and the time trends (δ_j) within these countries.[6] These average time-series results concentrate in the country dummy (α_j) the effects of omitted variables having little change over time as well as any lag in the reaction to past income changes, while the exogenous variables act no longer as proxies for these effects.[7] This procedure has notable advantages in cases where the excluded variables clearly influence the cross-country relationship, as in the case of capital inflows.

The Samples

Equation (1.3) is estimated for two different samples. The full or maximal sample is the one used in the corresponding cross-section study and contains a minimum of five annual observations for each country. This sample has the advantage of including all the available information, but it is biased by the fact that additional countries become available over time. To overcome this difficulty a second, reduced sample has been used consisting of the forty or so countries with data for the full period.[8]

---

[5] There are some exceptions such as Behrman's investment study for Chile (1972) and various empirical studies on the demand for money.

[6] The nature of the implied weights and other characteristics of this procedure are described in the Technical Appendix.

[7] This assumes that the omitted factors enter the correctly specified equation in an additive form (or in a multiplicative form in the case of a logarithmic equation).

[8] The number of countries and period of observation vary somewhat by variable and are given in the Statistical Appendix.

These compatible (reduced) samples have the disadvantage of under-representing the countries at low levels of income. But when the same number of observations is used for all countries, the estimated short-run patterns are more comparable to the corresponding cross-section results[9] and are easier to relate to the individual time series within the countries.

The high correlation between income and time presents a serious problem when the attempt is made to allocate the total change in a process to an income effect and to an exogenous time shift.[10] To identify the relative importance of the two effects it is necessary to have within the sample a large variation in the growth of income over time in order to reduce the overall association of the two variables. The full samples approximate this condition better but at the cost of having to average a much wider range of time-series behavior.[11]

Nature of the Results

Estimates of equation (1.3) for the principal accumulation and allocation variables are given for both sets of samples in Table S16 in the Statistical Appendix. The results are summarized in Table 22, which also compares them with the corresponding cross-country patterns of Chapter 2. Income elasticities are given at three levels of income.[12]

The short-run elasticities are in most cases significantly different from those derived from the long-run patterns, but not always in the same direction. The differences in the income elasticities are usually accompanied by compensating time trends. These time trends are larger than those found in cross-country analysis.

In interpreting these average results there are two cases that must be distinguished: one where the time-series behavior within countries is not too different from that among countries; and a second case where the average values of both income effects and time trends conceal different tendencies across countries. The division of the total effects between the income and the time variables is less valid in this second case, although the total effect is still a good indicator of the average time-series experience. In the discussion of the results an attempt will be made to distinguish between the two cases.

---

[9]The equality in the number of observations per country does not imply that all countries have the same weight in the within-country regressions. As explained in the Technical Appendix, the weights are related to the within-country variance of the explanatory variables, and therefore they assign more importance to the time-series experience of the richer and faster-growing countries.

[10]The time trend is analyzed further in the Technical Appendix.

[11]Including all the countries in the maximal samples adds to the range of variation but makes the resulting average less representative of any one country. It also incorporates very slow-growing countries where no growth process can be discerned.

[12]The elasticities are calculated letting the predicted values equal their cross-section value for the corresponding level of income as given in Table 3.

TABLE 22. Comparison of Long-run and Short-run Patterns

Process	Long Run Sample	Long Run No. of Obs.	Short Run Sample	Short Run No. of Obs.	Income Elasticities* 200	500	800	Effect of Capital Inflow (ε)	Time Trend†
Saving	Full	1,432	Full	1,432	.25	.16	.13	−.82	.004
			Reduced	820	.50	.38	.34	−.65	—
					.67	.51	.46	−.56	−.006
Investment	Full	1,432	Full	1,432	.22	.15	.12	.16	.004
			Reduced	820	.45	.35	.31	.34	—
					.62	.48	.43	.45	−.006
Exports	Full	1,432	Full	1,432‡	.12	.09	.08	−.47	.002
			Reduced	820	.40	.36	.35	−.57	−.010
Government revenue	Full	1,111	Full	1,111	.25	.29	.29	−.15	.005
			Reduced	468	.16	.21	.23	.04	.009
					.33	.32	.31	.11	.006
Primary production	Full	1,325	Full	1,325	−.50	−.57	−.57	−.59	−.004
			Reduced	756	−.14	−.21	−.25	−.24	−.020
					−.20	−.34	−.46	−.10	−.011
Industry production	Full	1,325	Full	1,325	.43	.28	.23	.21	−.004
			Reduced	756	.28	.15	.10	.11	.006
					.32	.18	.13	.14	.002
Services production	Full	1,325	Full	1,325	.16	.04	−.01	.36	.006
			Reduced	756	−.07	−.01	.01	.11	.010
					−.11	−.01	.04	−.03	.008

*Income elasticities computed as: Elasticity = $(\delta X/\delta \ln Y)(1/\hat{X})$, where X stands for the seven dependent variables and $\hat{X}$, the predicted values, are taken from Table 3.

†The values given are five-year shifts. They represent the average of the five-year shifts implied by the coefficients of the time dummies (δ_t) in the regressions with signs reversed.

‡Income coefficients are not significant because of the erratic export performance of the poorer countries not in the reduced sample.

ACCUMULATION

Dynamic theories of the process of accumulation almost always conclude that reactions to changes in exogenous variables will not be instantaneous but spread over time. The cross-country description of accumulation incorporates the total adjustment to such changes. In addition, the transformation over the transition does not distinguish the direct effects of rising levels of income from the indirect effects of structural changes associated with income. The changing distribution of income among recipients having different saving propensities and the changing composition of the tax base are two processes that influence the rates of accumulation in the long run but are relatively absent from the short-run effects of rising income.

The effect of differences in income effects and time trends can be illustrated by comparing the main estimates in Table S16 over a specified period of time. In order to combine income and time effects, we assume the current rate of growth of per capita income of 2.5 percent, which implies that the transition from $100 to $1000 per capita income will be completed in a century. Table 23 shows the total change in the accumulation measures predicted by the time-series and cross-country results over twenty years as income rises from $300 to about $500.

Saving and Investment

In the overall description of the total transformation provided by the two methods, the relative increases in saving and investment are fairly similar and quantitatively important. The direct income effect implied by the short-run patterns is considerably larger than the total income effect suggested by the cross section, but the final prediction is not very different in view of the compensating time trends. These results are in accord with predictions from permanent-income and life-cycle theories of saving behavior and are similar to Houthakker's 1965 results for personal saving.[13] This pattern of a delayed adjustment in private consumption to an increase in income has also been described for government saving by Please (1967). While there are thus theoretical reasons to expect a larger short-run saving propensity and a delayed increase in private and public consumption when income rises (implying a negative time shift for saving), the estimates have to be evaluated for individual countries.

---

[13]The Mikesell and Zinser (1973) survey of the saving function in developing countries summarizes the results of various theoretical and empirical studies, including tests of the permanent-income and life-cycle theories of saving behavior. Their suggestion that, as a general trend, cross-sectional income propensities tend to be higher than time-series income propensities (p. 8) is not confirmed here. Unlike the studies compared in the survey, the present one estimates both the cross-section and time-series patterns, using a consistent methodology on the most comprehensive cross-country sample so far available.

The time-series coefficients of saving regressions for each of the forty-one countries in the reduced sample are given in Table S13 in the Statistical Appendix.[14] The main finding of positive income effects is confirmed by about three-fourths of the time-series regressions, but in the rest the estimated income coefficient is negative. In the cross-country results the variation across countries is large enough to dwarf the few within-country negative income elasticities.

When taken together with the cross-section results, the time-series evidence does not support the implication of several theories that the saving ratio should be constant. The significant average increase in saving and investment rates since 1950 cannot be explained as merely temporary effects of an increase in transitory income. This conclusion is strengthened by the wide coverage of our sample both across countries and over time.

Kuznets's finding of the long-run constancy of the saving rate in the United States, which led to subsequent developments in the theory of consumption and saving, cannot be generalized for either the less developed or the developed countries as a group. However, the constancy of the ratio in a high-income country such as the United States could be incorporated within a logistic-type pattern which could cover the whole range of variation.

An earlier study of the saving function in a group of Latin American countries (Landau, 1971)[15] concluded that both the cross-section and the time-series evidence revealed a significant association of saving rates with income levels, although the relation seemed to taper off for the most developed countries within the group. Our results, based on a larger number of countries over a longer period of time, are in accord with Landau's conclusions.

Foreign Capital Inflow

In the past several years there has been considerable debate over the interpretation to be given to the observed relations among saving, investment, and capital inflow. Earlier models of the effects of aid on growth had assumed that all or a substantial part of any increase in external resources would be translated into increased investment. Subsequent cross-country and time-series analyses have suggested that more than half of the increase in external resources has typically gone into increased consumption and less than half into investment. Since saving is defined in the na-

---

[14]The functional form estimated was $S = \alpha + \beta \ln Y + \epsilon F$. Within a country over a twenty-year period there is not enough curvature to warrant a nonlinear income term. The time variables were also omitted.

[15]The 1971 paper was based on Landau (1969) where the literature and the evidence on the alleged constancy of the saving rate are reviewed.

TABLE 23. Comparison of Accumulation Estimates

Accumulation	Initial Value at $300*	Cross-country Regressions				Time-series Regressions†			
		Income Effect	Time Trend	Total Change	% Change‡	Income Effect	Time Trend	Total Change	% Change‡
Saving	.190	.017	.012	.029	15	.055	−.019	.036	19
Investment	.203	.015	.013	.028	14	.055	−.018	.037	19
Capital inflow	.013	−.002	.014	.012	100	−.024	.030	.006	50
Government revenue	.202	.030	.015	.045	23	.037	.026	.063	32

* From Table 3. Per capita income is assumed to rise at 2.5 percent per year for twenty years.

† Reduced samples.

‡ Total change over initial value.

TABLE 24. Comparison of Allocation Estimates

Allocation	Initial Value at $300*	Cross-country Regressions				Time-series Regressions†			
		Income Effect	Time Trend	Total Change	% Change‡	Income Effect	Time Trend	Total Change	% Change‡
Primary production	.266	−.061	−.012	−.073	−27	−.036	−.040	−.076	−29
Industry production	.251	.043	−.011	.033	13	.025	.008	.033	13
Services	.403	.015	.018	.033	8	−.005	.029	.024	6
Exports	.230	.013	.009	.022	10	.044	−.032	.012	5

* From Table 3. Per capita income is assumed to rise at 2.5 percent per year for twenty years.

† Reduced samples

‡ Total change over initial value.

tional accounts as investment minus capital inflow, there is a corresponding negative effect on the ratio of saving to GNP.

Statistical analysis of this set of relations is complicated by the fact that the distribution of public capital flows is systematically related to the saving level.[16] The net effect of the political and economic criteria that determine the allocation of foreign aid is to provide higher amounts to a number of countries that have lower saving rates. This factor has a significant impact on the cross-country regression results and makes them an inappropriate basis for determining the average effect of increasing capital inflow to a given country.[17]

Table 22 gives two estimates of the average effect of changes in capital inflow over time on saving and investment. For the maximal sample of ninety-three countries, the average short-run impact of a unit increase in external capital is that investment increases by .34 and total consumption by .65, implying a drop in saving by .65. However (as demonstrated in the Technical Appendix), these results are affected by the addition of countries to the sample over the period. The estimate of the reduced sample for the forty-one countries having data for the whole period is therefore more relevant to policy analysis. It suggests that on the average 45 percent of an increase in external resources is translated into a net increase in investment. If we consider this result as a measure of the propensity to save out of external resources, it is considerably higher than the average saving ratio from domestic income although much below the value of 100 percent implied by earlier models. This estimate is also close to that estimated for Latin America (47 percent) by Landau (1971), who suggested that a value of less than 100 percent can be explained by the existence of a predominant trade constraint in most Latin American countries over the period studied.[18]

The finding that on the average an increase of external resources is only partially translated into investment does not demonstrate that there is no benefit from foreign aid, as some critics have argued.[19] It does suggest, however, that planning models should allow for some effect on consumption.[20] Moreover, there is considerable variation in the experience of individual countries. Of the twenty-eight less developed countries in the reduced sample analyzed in Table S13 of the Statistical Appendix for the

[16]Papanek (1972) gives a number of illustrations of this relation.

[17]Papanek (1972) and Mikesell and Zinser (1973) summarize the relevant data from a number of sources. Papanek provides several arguments against the use of cross-section regressions for this purpose.

[18]Chenery and Carter (1973) reached similar conclusions in a wider comparison of time-series results.

[19]Arguments to this effect are given by Griffin and Enos (1970) and Weisskopf (1972). The opposite view is presented by Papanek (1972) and Chenery and Carter (1973).

[20]A two-gap projection model incorporating the type of saving function suggested here is utilized by Chenery and Eckstein (1970).

126

Figure 35: Saving and Capital Inflow

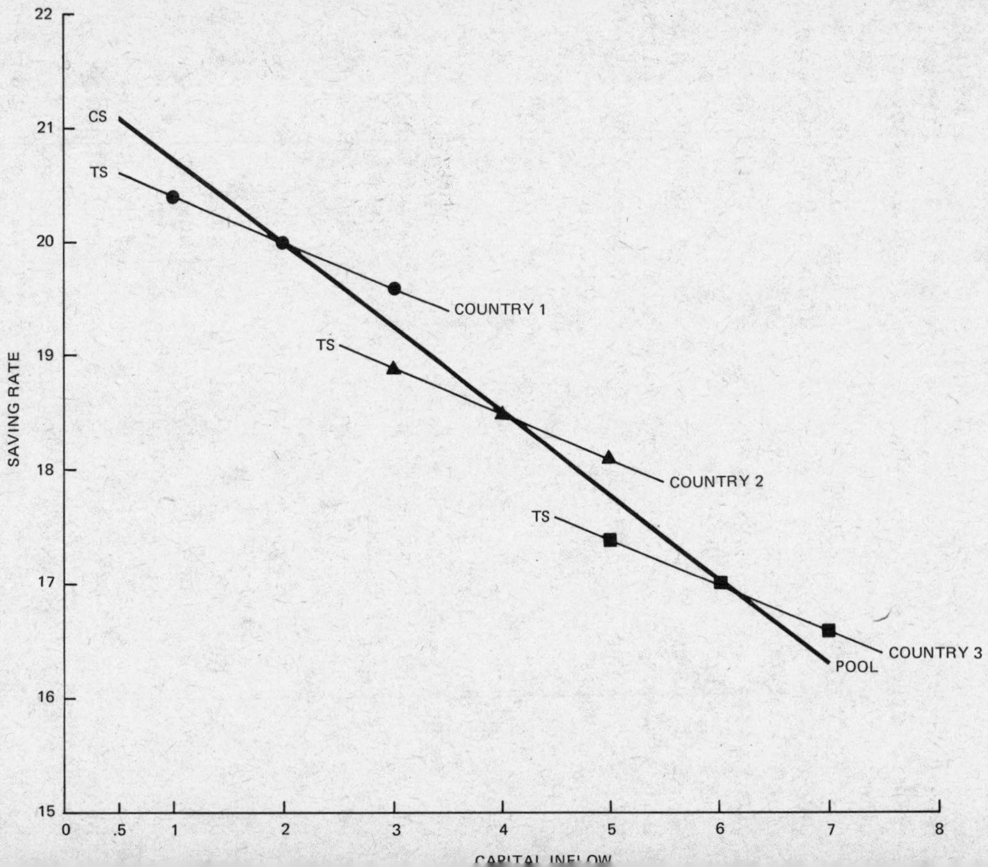

1950–70 period, eighteen showed a significant negative association between the inflow of capital and the rate of saving but ten did not.

The difference between the long-run and the short-run estimates is further illustrated in Figure 35, which shows the net relation between saving and foreign resources after netting out the effect of income. The flat TS lines represent the time-series regressions for individual countries and show the change in the saving rate that accompanied changes in the foreign inflow in the post-1950 period.

The estimate for the intercountry sample (CS) produces a steeper line, since average saving is negatively correlated with the average capital inflow. This negative correlation results from the existence of two different types of countries: the low savers which had large capital inflows; and countries with high export surpluses and capital outflows.[21]

Government Revenue

The short-run income-related changes in levels of government revenue shown in Table 22 are not much different from the changes implied by the long-run patterns. In both cases there is a significant positive association between the share of gross domestic product appropriated by the government and the level of income. Income elasticities are between .2 and .3 for almost all the estimates in Table 22.

In addition to the income effect measured there is also an exogenous upward shift in the share of government revenue of about one percent per decade. This shift appears in both cross-section and time-series estimates and can probably be explained by the fact that governments of developing countries are increasingly aware of their potential role in promoting development.

Several earlier studies reported similar cross-country results for the limited samples then available and found a positive income elasticity for the share of government revenue.[22] This finding has since been questioned by some writers, who suggested that it does not "reflect a continuous tendency but rather a comparison between the averages for low and high income groups" (Musgrave, 1969, p. 118).[23] In the more recent tax literature this claim appears to have been accepted (Bahl, 1971).

---

[21] When all the countries with a capital outflow are excluded from the cross-country regression for the maximal sample, there is a somewhat lower coefficient of the capital inflow in the saving regression (−.77).

[22] See, for example, Oshima (1957), Deutsch (1961), and Williamson (1961) for similar results and various interpretations.

[23] Hinrichs (1966) and Musgrave (1969). The higher ratios in rich countries are then explained through ratchet effects (as in Peacock and Wiseman, 1961, who suggest that sudden increases in revenue during wartime have a lasting effect on expenditure levels) or by referring to differences between the accepted roles of government in poor and rich countries. Both Hinrichs and Musgrave find significant income effects for the whole group of less developed countries and one of them also reports a highly significant relationship for the medium-income group in his study.

In the light of our findings, these earlier results can better be interpreted as suggesting that the association of government revenue with income follows a logistic-type curve: small increases at low and high income levels and an acceleration in the rate of increase over medium income levels. Results in Chapter 4 where separate patterns are estimated for low- and high-income countries also support this interpretation.[24]

The time-series estimates of the effect of capital inflow differ notably from the cross-section estimates. In the short run an increased inflow of foreign capital is likely to be associated with an increase in the proportion of the GDP appropriated by the-government. As in the case of saving, the negative association in the cross section reflects the fact that, on the average, countries with a low tax base had larger inflows of foreign capital. But over time the average experience of these and other countries has been an increase in government revenue, which appears to have been facilitated by the availability of external resources.[25]

ALLOCATION PATTERNS

The patterns of resource allocation are the empirical representation of basic processes such as Engel's law and the accumulation of skills and material capital. On the one hand, the observed universality of such processes is an important factor behind the uniformity of the cross-country patterns, which leads to the expectation of broad similarities in the allocation patterns across countries and over time. On the other hand, the rate of technological change, the development of new products, and variations in trade policies are factors leading to differences between the long-run cross-country associations and the short-run time-series experience.

To compare the two sets of measures, Table 24 (page 124) shows the regression coefficients and total change predicted for a country whose per capita income rises from $300 to $500 over a twenty-year period.

Production

The short-run estimates of the changes in the structure of production are quite similar to the long-run patterns. The only real difference is in the

---

[24]If the association with income were just a reflection of omitted variables leading to differences between countries grouped by income, this would show up in the short-run patterns in the form of significant differences in country levels (through the country-dummy variables) and insignificant income coefficients. But the coefficients of income are quite significant here.

[25]The negative cross-country coefficients of F shown in Table 22 for both saving and government revenue also reflect in part the substitutive relation between primary exports and external resources. After the export variables were introduced in Chapter 2 (Table 6) the impact of the foreign capital variable on saving and government revenue was reduced and is no longer significant for government revenue.

allocation of the total change between income effects and time trends. The lower income effects from the time series are compensated by larger exogenous shifts.

Both sets of time trends show an exogenous shift away from primary production and into services. Behind such a shift there appear to be real phenomena such as the increase in agricultural productivity and the acceleration of the process of urbanization. Such processes would induce a continuation of the decline in the primary share even during short periods of time when income fails to grow, as actually happened in a few stagnant countries in the present sample.

The uniformity of the several time series within countries make the short-run time trends appear to be representative averages of the time-series shifts in the production structure. Since many of the factors responsible for the time shifts have been associated over long periods of time with a rising level of income, part of their effect appears to have been captured by the long-run cross-country income effect.

The comparative analysis of cross-country data in the search for uniformities in development patterns has been most extensively applied to the structure of production. Several authors have compared the few available long-term series of the transformation in the production structure to the cross-section estimates. In general the cross-section projections into the past underestimated the actual changes observed. In Chenery and Taylor (1968) the proportion of the historical decline in the primary share in GDP in nine developed countries explained by the cross section (based on fifty-four countries over the 1950–63 period) ranged from a low of 66 percent for the United Kingdom to a high of 86 percent in Italy, Japan, and Sweden. Kuznets (1971) in a similar long-term comparison for nine countries also found that the backward extrapolation of the cross-section relations (based on over fifty countries for a single year, 1958) in general fell short of the actual changes in the sectoral composition of production. In a short-term comparison of thirty-two countries over a twelve-year period, Kuznets also found the underestimation present mainly in the low-income countries, which were also slower growing.

The available long-term series and Kuznets's 1958 cross section are dominated by the experience of the developed countries, which were the first to industrialize. Future changes in developing countries will be influenced not only by the expected continuation of technological and social innovations but also by the fact that their industrialization is taking place in a world where industrial countries have existed for a long time. It is therefore hard to predict whether the underestimation of past changes will also characterize forward projections based on current cross-section patterns.

Temin (1967) carried out a regression analysis of production shares to test the similarities of the time series in nine developed countries[26] to Chenery's original cross-section results (1960). While Temin's estimates for the share of industry explain only a small portion of the period-by-period variation (each twenty-year interval was taken as an observation), it does support the hypothesis that the aggregate effects of industrialization over the past century have been comparable to the present-day cross-country variation. He found no indication of significant period effects (time trends) in the case of industry, although for agriculture the period effects were dominant.[27]

As Kuznets emphasized, even without the problems of reliability and comparability of the data for the nineteenth century, nine countries are not an adequate sample for a conclusive evaluation of the temporal stability of cross-section relations. Nevertheless the results of these comparisons strengthen the interpretation that cross-section results represent the total effects of rising levels of income in the long run. The cross-section patterns reflect the effects of omitted variables systematically associated with income, but because they do not incorporate the truly independent temporal shifts uncorrelated with income the actual long-term changes are underestimated. In revealing the existence of such shifts the cross-section estimates play a central role—not to substitute for but rather to complement long-term records as they become available.

The Share of Exports

The intercountry patterns and the average time series since 1950 strongly suggest that the overall tendency has been for the share of exports to increase with the level of development. This increase was achieved in spite of the deliberate attempts by many countries to reduce their import and export ratios.

The relatively large time shift shown in the time-series regression is the result of averaging quite different tendencies and is therefore less useful as an indicator of a general trend. In about 50 percent of the countries with observations for the complete twenty-year period, the relation of the export ratio to income per capita was found to be not significantly

---

[26]The Chenery and Taylor (1968) comparison was based on Temin's data for the same nine countries.

[27]The results for agriculture could have been improved in a nonlinear formulation. This is more serious here than for industry; since the actual shares of agriculture were already quite low, the rapid initial fall cannot continue indefinitely as the linear equation would require. In addition, the significant positive income effect of the industry share must be matched by an offsetting negative income effect elsewhere. Services were not analyzed by Temin, but it is hard to imagine the service share compensating for the rise of industry in the countries and periods in the sample.

different from zero or even negative. Although the time-series average shows a net increase in the export ratio since 1950, it is almost impossible to allocate this increase between an income effect and a time trend. When the regression is run without a time trend, the total income effect is not much different from the combined income and time effects shown in Table 24.

During the postwar period spanned by the time series both the attitudes of many countries toward foreign trade and the objective conditions in world markets underwent a considerable change. At the beginning of the 1950s the Korean War and the reconstruction in Europe brought the prices of primary products to an all-time high, and export ratios in value terms reached a relatively high level. This level was not maintained in many countries during the following decade. In some countries the reduction in the share of exports was almost a policy objective (Argentina, Brazil, Mexico, Turkey) and, according to the data for 1960, one that was successfully achieved.

During the 1960s most of the countries that had been following an inward-looking strategy supplemented or replaced it by a more balanced strategy which emphasized the promotion of exports and resulted in a substantial rise in the share of exports in GDP. This tendency also appeared quite strongly within the developed countries, where it was largely related to the rapid increase in the exchange of manufactures against manufacture[28] and the creation of the European Economic Community.

To capture the more homogeneous behavior of the 1960s, which will probably better approximate the future than the mixed experience of the previous decade, an average time-series regression limited to the 1960s was estimated for the compatible sample with the following results:

$$E = \alpha_i + \underset{(3.5)}{.281} \ln Y - \underset{(2.5)}{.0152} (\ln Y)^2 - \underset{(9.1)}{.491} F + \underset{(3.1)}{.0096} T_3$$

$$R^2 = .261 \qquad SEE = .021 \qquad n = 410$$

In a typical country of $300 per capita income in 1960, growing for ten years (to match the estimation period) at the assumed 2.5 percent a year, an overall increase in the export ratio of .016 percentage points is expected. This increase is equivalent to 7 percent of the initial value at $300[29] and is larger than the total change for the complete twenty-year period given in Table 24. (An even stronger rise has taken place since 1970 due to rising prices of primary exports.)

---

[28]For the importance of this interindustry specialization in the developed countries, see Balassa (1966).

[29]This total change is composed of a positive income effect of .026 and a negative time trend of −.010 percentage points.

These average patterns and particularly the recent experience of developed countries are the exact opposite of the decline in the importance of trade first predicted by Sombart early in the present century.[30] This proposition, if proven correct, could have a profound impact on the pattern of economic and political interdependence among nations. In 1961 Deutsch and Eckstein claimed that the long-run trend in several (mostly developed) countries was in agreement with Sombart's generalization.[31] At that time their evidence was dominated by the impact on trade of two world wars, a long and severe depression, and the commercial policies after the Second World War. The experience of the recent past, however, does not support the hypothesis of a general decline in the share of trade, but on the contrary strongly suggests the overall tendency has been for the share of exports to increase with the level of development.

Adjustments to Changes in External Capital

One of the advantages of a uniform approach that has emerged from the present study is that it yields a consistent description of the much-debated effects of changing levels of capital inflow on saving, investment, and the balance of payments. For reasons given above, the time-series results are more appropriate for policy analysis of these relations, since they eliminate the effects of factors related to the level of income that are specific to individual countries. The reduced sample in Table S16, for which there are comparable time series, yields the following consistent description of the overall adjustment to a unit increase or decrease in external capital:

Saving-Investment Adjustment

| Saving | − .56 |
| Investment | + .45 |

Trade Adjustment

| Exports | − .57 |
| Imports | + .43 |

---

[30]Sombart's generalization (1913) was based on the belief that the main source of trade, namely the division of labor between agricultural and industrial countries, would gradually disappear as the former countries industrialized. In 1945 Hirschman criticized this assumption of the law of the declining share of trade and presented convincing evidence to dispel the belief that most of the flows of trade were in the form of exchange of manufactures against primary products.

[31]Based on their evidence Kindleberger concluded in 1962 that the law of declining foreign trade had been established for developed countries (p. 183). For critical comments on the long-run series and on the declining-share thesis, see Lipsey (1963) and Kuznets (1967).

Production Adjustment[32]

Primary	− .24
Industry	+ .12
Services	+ .11

The relations of capital inflow with both saving and exports are remarkably similar. The average trade adjustment indicates that external capital inflows offset export reductions and supply additional imports in similar proportions. As with the saving effect discussed above, however, there is considerable intercountry variation, and in some cases external resources serve to augment rather than replace exports.

CONCLUSIONS

The objective of this chapter has been to compare in a systematic way the cross-section patterns and the time-series experience. For this purpose it was first necessary to average the individual time-series relations so as to derive a single time-series equation for the whole sample. These equations proved to be more representative of general tendencies in some cases than in others. The cases where the average values appear to be less useful have been pointed out in the text.

The time-series results and the comparison with the cross-section patterns may help to clarify the claims of conflicting hypotheses in several fields. In the case of saving, predictions from both the absolute-income and the permanent-income hypotheses of saving behavior received partial support. The marginal saving rate came out significantly above the average rate, implying a rising saving ratio with income, but the short-run propensity to save was found to exceed substantially the long-run propensity. To study the nature of the lag structure linking the two would require a dynamic framework and probably time-series data over a longer period than that of the present study.

In the case of external capital, the short-run and long-run comparison was particularly helpful in measuring and evaluating the two-gap problem, i.e., the adjustments in accumulation and trade in response to a unit change in the available supply of foreign resources. Here the short-run estimates are to be preferred for policy analysis because of the bias due to omission of significant variables in the cross-section relations.

Finally, in spite of some recent evidence to the contrary, a rising level of income was shown to be significantly associated with a rising share of

---

[32]For the production adjustment, the results are shown for the full sample from Table S16 because the reduced sample is inadequately representative of low-income countries; the country-specific factors seem less likely to affect this aspect of the adjustment process. The corresponding estimates from the reduced sample are primary (−.10), industry (.14), and services (−.03).

revenue raised by the government and a rising proportion of the final product exported.

In evaluating these results we have generally adopted the customary interpretation that cross-section results reflect a long-term adjustment and time-series estimates a short or partial adjustment to the change in the exogenous variables. This interpretation requires several significant qualifications. The first qualification stems from the fact that the present analysis covers virtually the whole world.[33] When international phenomena such as trade and capital movements are analyzed, a country's relative income level would appear to be a better proxy for the international influences, although internal supply effects are related to absolute income levels. This qualification is not important for medium-term analysis, but it becomes significant in the longer run.

The interpretation of the cross-section results as representing the normal long-term adaptation to rising income must deal in some way with social and technological change over long periods of time. Many of the time trends of the past twenty years— such as the reduction in the share of primary production—represent the effects of technological change that cannot be expected to continue at the same rate. Others, such as the upward trend in government revenue, result from changing views of the functions of government. Since it would be hazardous to extrapolate these trends for any distance into the future, all trends have been eliminated in analyzing the effects of rising income in the cross-country patterns.

The most difficult qualification to deal with in interpreting the cross-country results as long-term reactions to rising income and size is the effect of omitted variables that are systematically related to income or size. This is especially true of the first group of developed countries. One may hazard a guess that the development patterns of the middle income ranges are likely to prove more valid guides to future change than do present estimates for the upper-income levels.[34]

[33]While most of the communist countries are excluded because of lack of comparable data, the countries in the present sample account for about 85 percent of world trade and capital movements.

[34]This has particular relevance for the next group of countries to reach the developed range of over $1200, since they will have much more diverse political and cultural backgrounds than did the developed countries of 1960.

Chapter 6

CONCLUSIONS

THE MAIN PURPOSE of this study has been to provide a comprehensive statistical analysis of the major features of development that can serve as a basis for economic theory and policy. Our results apply to a particular historical period, 1950–70, during which many countries became independent and development became a major economic and political objective throughout most of the world. By studying the experience of a hundred countries over this period, we have tried to identify universal patterns of change as well as alternative ways in which development can be accomplished.

The principal contribution of this study has been to provide a set of measures of development processes that is based on a uniform set of concepts and makes use of more comprehensive data than were previously available. This broad empirical base has permitted us to compare and partially reconcile time-series and cross-section analyses of the same phenomena to provide an integrated treatment of the basic processes of accumulation, allocation, and distribution.

THE NATURE OF THE TRANSITION

In describing the processes of development we have tried to replace the notion of a dichotomy beweeen less developed and developed countries with the concept of a transition from one state to the other. This transition is defined by a set of structural changes that have almost always accompanied the growth of per capita income in recent decades. Most of these features have already been identified in the history of industrial countries, which Kuznets describes as "modern economic growth."

The present study compares the recent experience of developing countries with the earlier development and present structure of the advanced countries. In this comparison the hypothesis that continuous structural change is related to the growth of income is better supported by our statistical analysis than is the alternative hypothesis that different structural relations characterize developed and developing countries, however defined. We have therefore focused our attention on the nature of the processes that are fundamental to the transition.

Most of the ten processes analyzed here can be described by a logistic or other form of **s**-shaped curve having asymptotes at low and high levels of income. The upper asymptote has an obvious interpretation for such structural characteristics as the rate of saving or investment, the share of industry, the proportion of the population receiving higher education, or the birth rate. These asymptotes provide a set of measures of the direction in which most economies are moving in any historical period. Although these limits may be expected to shift as technology, social objectives, and international conditions change over time, in any given period the logistic curve provides a better basis for analyzing a country's development than the notion of indefinite growth in any single dimension. The estimates for developing countries also suggest that change accelerates in certain periods of a country's development.[1]

This formulation of the structural transition has proved particularly useful in rationalizing the available intercountry evidence on saving rates, industrialization, and trade patterns. A rapid rise in the share of saving or industry during the middle phase of the transition is quite consistent with a leveling off of these shares at higher income levels. The differences between the cross-section measures of these structural relations and the average time series for groups of countries, although significant, are not of a magnitude to cast doubt on the general nature of the transition.

DEVELOPMENT THEORY AND POLICY

These statistical results can be used in several ways to formulate development theory and policy. By establishing a set of "stylized facts" they provide an agenda for theoretical analysis of the interrelated phenomena of development. Although theories cannot be validated by this type of analysis, in a number of cases our statistical results are more consistent with one theoretical formulation than with another, most notably in the fields of saving, taxation, and trade. Our main contribution to the testing of hypotheses has been to describe related phenomena for the same sample of countries and time period so that the results can be taken as manifestations of the same set of underlying processes.

The main focus of this study has been on the general nature of development processes rather than on detailed explanation of individual phenomena. The notable uniformity found among the larger developing countries at similar income levels lends considerable support to theories of balanced growth, which provide a convenient point of departure for interpreting the interrelations between demand, production, and trade patterns. In these countries imports are typically not more than 10 percent of GNP and do not allow for substantial differences between supply and demand in each sector. Smaller countries have a wider range of choice in the

---

[1]Although this formulation has some elements in common with Rostow's (1956) "take-off," we have shown that the periods of more rapid change occur at different levels of income for different processes and vary with the strategy being followed.

nature and extent of their participation in the international economy, suggesting the need for a typology of development patterns.

To apply these results to the formulation of policy, we attempted to classify countries according to the structural similarities of their development strategies. Four principal patterns of resource allocation were thus identified: primary specialization, balanced allocation, import substitution, and industrial specialization. The countries in each classification followed somewhat different sequences of development, stemming partly from initial differences in size, resource endowments, and access to external capital and partly from differences in social philosophy and organization. As a working hypothesis this typology provides a basis for comparing the policies of countries having similar structural characteristics. It may also provide a basis for the refinement of existing theories of resource allocation.

While future policymakers may benefit from such improvement of theory, for the present, development planners must interpret this comparative experience as best they can. Although we have stressed that average parameters such as saving rates or industrial shares have little normative significance, by summarizing the experience of comparable countries the statistical results help test development policies. If a development plan calls for achieving a tax rate of 25 percent of GNP at an income level of $300, it is useful to know that only a small proportion of countries have managed to accomplish this objective. Similarly for long-term projections of fifteen or twenty years, the average structure of those countries which are already at the expected level of income and population may provide a useful reference point. Probably the most that should be claimed for statistical comparisons of this sort is that they are helpful in diagnosing the structural problems of a given country and in suggesting feasible growth patterns. They are of relatively little value in the more detailed definition of policy options.

INTERNATIONAL DEVELOPMENT POLICY

Development policy cannot always wait for the formulation of adequate theories and the preparation of comprehensive country plans. In some instances comparative analysis of development processes has identified both the problems and the successful strategies for meeting them, which might have been disregarded as local peculiarities if studied in the context of only a single country. This is particularly true of international trade and capital movements, where individual countries respond to common forces in the international economy.

One recent example of a successful innovation in international policy is the shift toward industrial exports in a growing number of countries. The

1965 intercountry pattern of industrial exports (which allows for differences in income and size) provides a basis for measuring the conse-quences of this policy shift in the past few years in Taiwan, Korea, Spain, Yugoslavia, Mexico, Brazil, and other countries. An integrated analysis of industrial production and trade can be carried out on a similar basis in order to determine the detailed effects of the changes from previous allocation patterns in these countries.[2]

A second worldwide phenomenon that can be clarified by international comparisons is the observed worsening of income distribution, which was discussed in Chapter 2. International attention focused on this problem when a number of cases were identified through time-series and cross-country comparisons. As a result attempts were made to reformulate development theory for a better understanding of the problem, and programs of international assistance were reconsidered to see whether they could help offset this tendency. International comparisons also show that worsening of the income distribution in the course of growth is by no means inevitable, and they indicate countries in which this tendency has been offset by government action.[3]

FUTURE RESEARCH

In the course of our analysis we have noted a number of questions that could not be adequately treated with present data as well as several prom-ising topics for further research. Among the qualifications to the approach taken here, perhaps the most serious is the lack of an explicit treatment of relative prices and the consequent use of rather crude conversion factors in establishing income levels in constant dollar terms. As argued in the Technical Appendix, we do not feel that our overall results are seriously affected by this procedure, but the completion of research currently under way on international price comparisons[4] should make it possible to treat this problem in a much more satisfactory way and open up new possibilities for intercountry research.

Most of the intercountry patterns described here can be more readily interpreted when they are based on less aggregated data. Although disag-gregation involves some loss of generality because of the smaller number of countries having the required data, this limitation will become less restrictive over time. For example, the production patterns have recently been disaggregated into fourteen sectors (Chenery and Taylor, 1968), and

---

[2]This procedure is followed in Chenery and Hughes (1972).

[3]See Ahluwalia and Chenery (1974).

[4]The first results of a joint UN-World Bank project are being published in Kravis et al. (1974).

the consumption patterns into eight sectors (Lluch and Powell, 1973). In each case more detailed hypotheses can be tested and the results are more useful in policy applications. Other processes such as government revenue and expenditures, employment, and urbanization could probably be analyzed on a less aggregated basis with similar benefits as more comparable data become available.

Finally, with the passage of time it will be possible to make better use of time-series and cross-section analyses in the development of dynamic models. Although we have commented on the varying lags in different development processes, these can be empirically tested only as longer time series become available.

TECHNICAL APPENDIX

EVERY INTERNATIONAL cross-section study has to face a large number of problems; some are common to any econometric study and others arise only in a cross-country framework. The purpose of this Appendix is to analyze a few of the more technical points underlying the econometric formulation in the text and to outline the rationale behind the specific choices we have made among the various competing procedures.

Although many of the problems are discussed in the econometric literature and in specific studies where they are relevant, there is no systematic treatment nor compilation in relation to a comprehensive cross-country study. This Appendix contains brief discussions of the main issues and includes references to the econometric literature for more extended and rigorous treatment of most of these topics.

In selecting among alternative approaches a basic consideration was simplicity in the interpretation of results and feasibility in their application — particularly for country analysis — without undue sacrifice of rigor and accuracy. One can sympathize with Kuznets in his attempts to analyze large bodies of data and still be able "to keep the individual units and the specific groups in continuous view" (1971, p. 103), but even as skilled an analyst as Kuznets has perhaps reached the limit of what can be done without recourse to more powerful statistical methods.

The topics to be discussed are grouped in three broad sections, namely: problems of specification, problems of estimation, and the composition of the sample and its stability over time.

SPECIFICATION

After the processes to be studied and the type of exogenous effects to be measured have been decided, then the functional form of the equations to be estimated and the precise proxies to be used as independent variables must be specified. Some of these specifications are considered below, as well as the related question as to the extent to which the basic underlying "structures" (in the econometric sense) can be determined.

The Functional Form

The following semilog formulation was adopted uniformly for all the development patterns estimated:

$$X = \alpha + \beta_1 \, lnY + \beta_2 \, (lnY)^2 + \gamma_1 \, lnN + \gamma_2 \, (lnN)^2 + \epsilon F + \delta T$$

X, the dependent variable, is measured as a value share in GDP in every case where it is appropriate. The independent variables were defined on page 16 in the text. For any one country there are many other possible candidates for additional variables to include in the reduced form equations, but these candidates vary from country to country. Moreover, in many cases these additional variables represent indirect effects of income and population. Accordingly, it is recognized that the direct effects of the included variables are overstated in cross sections and therefore the residual impact of the additional variables is treated as random. In the time series an attempt has been made to isolate the direct effects of the independent variables from the indirect effects of some omitted factors. (See "Pooling of Cross-section and Time-series Data" below.)

Expressing the dependent variables as shares provides estimates of structural change as this term is commonly understood. When production increases, for example, value added in all sectors usually expands too, but it is the relative rates of expansion which determine the changes in the structure of production. The share formulation allows direct testing of the significance of these changes and not just the significance of the expansion itself. Thus in Chenery's 1960 work the relevant tests were to determine to what extent the various growth elasticities were different from one, whereas in the present case we test directly for significant differences from zero. Also when two monetary magnitudes are divided the share measures are often free of the various problems created by exchange rate conversions.[1]

When converting the absolute values to shares of GDP, the variance is substantially reduced. The coefficients of determination (R^2) are therefore also reduced considerably but are more meaningful.[2] The extreme case would be one where a variable (in absolute value) moved in a fashion similar to that of GDP, leaving its share in the latter almost constant. It might then be possible to obtain coefficients of determination close to one for the variable in absolute value and close to zero in the share form. When the variance to be explained is relatively small, therefore, a low R_2 does not necessarily indicate a poor fit. The standard error of estimate of the regression, which is always provided in the tables and figures, and the t ratios of the coefficients may then be better statistics from which to judge the equation. This point has to be borne in mind when assessing the accuracy of the estimates.

The semilog formulation was chosen over the double-log form to retain the adding-up properties of the shares of a given aggregate. The fitted

---

[1] But not always. See below, the discussion of exchange rate conversions.

[2] In a double-log formulation, both equations have identical implications, in spite of the different R^2s. In fact one can be deduced from the other by adding or substracting $ln Y$ from both sides of the equation and rearranging terms.

equations and derived predicted values of a common semilog formulation for the components of an aggregate add up identically to the fitted equation and predicted value for the aggregate—variable by variable—provided all estimates refer to exactly the same sample.[3] Double-log equations do not share in this property. When the components add up to one, the compensating variation that must have taken place in one or more of the complementary shares can always be found for any change in a particular share induced by income, size, or foreign capital. In studies where changes in structures are an important element, this is a very useful and important property of the function form.

In a semilog equation, income and size elasticities are no longer constant for all values of income and size (as they are in double-log equations). When the quadratic log terms are included, the growth and size elasticities of any variable X are given by:

$$E_{X \cdot Y} = \frac{\beta_1 + 2\beta_2 \ln Y}{\hat{X}}$$

$$E_{X \cdot N} = \frac{\gamma_1 + 2\gamma_2 \ln N}{\hat{X}}$$

where β_1, β_2, γ_1, and γ_2 are the estimated coefficients of the regression given above, and $\hat{X}$ is the predicted value corresponding to the level of income or size at which the elasticity is being computed.

Nonlinearities and Multicollinearity

In the study of patterns of development, theoretical considerations and empirical results have suggested the existence of nonlinearities in the relationships analyzed, even after the usual first step of transforming all or part of the data into logarithms. On the theoretical level, for example, growth elasticities for the shares of any aggregate cannot continue indefinitely to exceed or fall short of one, since the share has an upper level of 100 percent and is bounded from below by zero. Empirically, in the UN study (1963), in Chenery and Taylor (1968), and in our own preliminary tests, significant differences were found when estimating separate *linear* relations (after logging part or all of the data) within income groups or for individual countries grouped by per capita income, suggesting the existence of nonlinearities in the relation encompassing the complete income range.

---

[3]Semilog is not the only form with the adding-up property. Leser (1963) discusses other such forms in a study of total consumption and Engel curves. For a simple statement of the adding-up criterion see Nicholson (1957).

These nonlinearities can be taken into account either by retaining a linear formulation for subsets of data ranked by increasing values of per capita income and population or by fitting nonlinear functional forms. The first procedure has the disadvantage of introducing discontinuities into the relation and of reducing the size of the sample. For analyzing the uniformity of development patterns it is preferable to estimate a single relation for the whole sample[4] and introduce the nonlinearities directly into the functional form. The simplest nonlinear formulation to fit and interpret in this context is to add a quadratic term to the semilog relation. Accordingly, a log quadratic term in income was introduced. For the same reasons nonlinear size effects were postulated as well. Given the large size variation in the sample (from Liberia's 1.1 million to India's 480.9 million in 1965), the assumption of a linear size effect throughout this range becomes untenable.

The log quadratic formulation is one way to take nonlinearities into account, and it has proven particularly useful in this case to represent the transitional range. However, extrapolations of the parabolic equations to either extreme of the income or size scales are subject to large margins of error. For this reason, in the figures of predicted values in Chapter 2 the estimated equations were not used to predict below an income level of $100 and above a $1000 level but were replaced by the actual observed averages of countries in these ranges. These mean values can be interpreted as asymptotic levels of a logistic-type equation.[5] Equations of this type can sometimes be estimated directly and should be explored in the future, especially as the data base expands over time.

Whenever the income or size variation in the sample is small the square terms can be expected to be highly collinear with the lnY or lnN terms. In such a case the coefficients may not be very stable and their t ratios are expected to be small. Dropping the square term, however, may result in a misspecified equation. The greatest danger of multicollinearity is not in the low t ratios it sometimes produces but in the misspecification it leads to when important variables with high standard errors are excluded.[6]

Small t ratios of the lnY and $(lnY)^2$ terms do not necessarily imply unstable or insignificant predicted values and elasticities. It is only the combined result of both estimates (in the form of levels and elasticities) which

---

[4]This does not imply that patterns are unique. Stratification was tried for characteristics like size and availability of resources, but even in these subsamples the reasons for treating the income and remaining size effects as nonlinear still apply.

[5]A simple logistic curve is symmetrical around its point of inflection. For development patterns this may be too restrictive. If the functional form requires nonlinear estimation (nonlinear logarithmic or semilog formulations do not), this has to be weighed against the potential benefits.

[6]This point has recently been nicely illustrated in Shourie (1972). For an earlier reference, see Liu (1960).

is important and not the separate estimated value of either coefficient. The presence of multicollinearity is not a serious problem for prediction in cases where the collinearity can be expected to continue into the future. This certainly applies to the collinearity between $\ln Y$ and $(\ln Y)^2$.

An additional statistical problem arises in the nonlinear framework when estimating the share components of an aggregate: the quadratic term may be found statistically significant in all but one of the shares. In such a case the nonlinear term should be retained in this share, if only to assure the adding-up of the components. The appropriate statistical test is whether there are significant nonlinearities in the changes in the composition of the aggregate and not whether each of its components presents significant nonlinearities.

Real Income, Relative Prices, and Exchange Rate Conversions

Every comparative study based on international cross-section data has to face the problem of how to make commensurable the value figures expressed in the various local currencies. The usual practice is to convert all domestic values into a common currency (U.S. dollars as a rule) through official exchange rates. The resulting international spread in per capita incomes undoubtedly exaggerates the true differences in real income. In our sample, for example, income per capita in the group of countries with lowest income (less than \$100) represented in 1965 no more than 3 to 4 percent of per capita income in the richest nations (over \$2000). The lowest level of income is well below the generally accepted minimum income levels for subsistence. There are two types of difficulties in the income comparisons: the relatively poor statistical coverage in low-income countries and a relative price effect. Only in the latter, however, do the problems of exchange rate conversions appear.

In addition to the problems of collecting the basic data needed to estimate national product and income, the researcher has to confront the existence of a substantial nonmonetized sector in the economies of less developed countries (LDCs). A comparatively large share of economic activity in the poorer countries does not cross the market and has to be estimated to construct the national accounts. This estimation is not only subject to a wide margin for error but also often underestimates the extent of the nonmarket activities.[7] This systematic bias in the income figures can be expected to become less of a problem in the future as statistical techniques improve and the coverage of data expands. Insofar as this type of measurement error does not change much over time but differs greatly

---

[7]For the problems encountered in estimating capital formation in developing countries, see Hooley (1967).

across countries, it resembles an omitted factor. Its effect is partly reflected in the cross-country income effects but not in the time-series or short-run patterns discussed in Chapter 5 and in the section on pooling below.

The second problem related to exchange rate conversions has two distinct aspects. First, official exchange rates are not equivalent to equilibrium exchange rates. The heavy reliance of LDCs—particularly since the Second World War—on high tariffs, import quotas, export subsidies, and other trade interferences as substitutes for open devaluations, and the selective application of these instruments among different industries, gave rise to a price structure with little or no resemblance to relative international prices.[8] In addition, and more important in this context, even under complete free trade the equilibrium set of exchange rates would reflect the equalization of prices of only internationally traded goods.[9] There is evidence to suggest that productivity differentials among countries are larger for traded than for nontraded commodities (primarily services and construction), that the production of the latter is relatively more labor-intensive, and that labor is relatively more abundant and relatively less expensive in low-income countries. Under such conditions the relative prices of the nontraded goods can be expected to increase systematically with real income per capita. This relative-price-of-services effect[10] lies behind the systematic underestimation of the purchasing power of local currencies converted at official exchange rates (even under a free-trade regime), and it contributes to the enormous income differentials mentioned above.

Effect of the Bias on Cross-section Estimates. Reducing the range of the per capita income figures in the sample affects the estimates of the various development patterns. To the extent that there is a negative correlation between income levels and both effective protection and the relative underestimation of the exchange-rate-converted incomes, income or growth elasticities will be underestimated. This point was recognized in Chenery's original 1960 cross-section paper and is graphically illustrated in Figure T1 (from Balassa, 1961).

---

[8]See the evidence on effective protection summarized in Balassa (1971). In Schydlowsky and Syrquin (1972) the effective rates of protection were used as price deflators in estimating CES (constant elasticity of substitution) production functions from intercountry data. Deflating nominal value added had an impact on the coefficients only when additional factors were also taken into account in a covariance framework.

[9]After taking into account transport costs.

[10]Balassa (1964) and Samuelson (1964) derived this effect from simple trade models where at least one of the goods is not traded internationally. Its implications for cross-section studies were the subject of a recent exchange between David (1972, 1973) and Balassa (1973).

Reducing Transition Range by One-Half

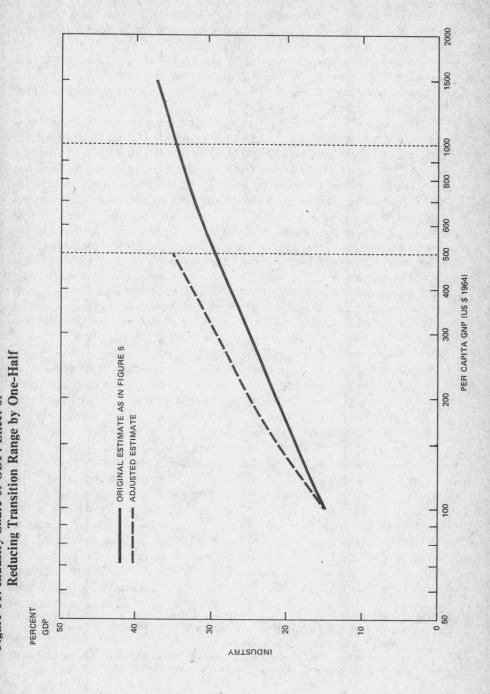

PERCENT
GDP

ORIGINAL ESTIMATE AS IN FIGURE 5
ADJUSTED ESTIMATE

PER CAPITA GNP (US $ 1964)

INDUSTRY

The important conclusion is that as long as the bias affects all components of GDP (on the demand, production, and trade side) equally, our estimates of structural changes during the transition range in all cases underestimate the actual transformations.[11] Thus the large changes in the production structure or the significant increase in accumulation rates cannot be ascribed even in part to this source of bias; on the contrary, we may even have erred on the low side.

The differences in relative prices among countries require different correction factors for different groups of commodities rather than a uniform one for total product, which would leave intact all value figures appearing in the form of shares of GDP. The scant available evidence on international differences in the relative price of real value added for various industries (Balassa, 1971) and in the relative prices of the demand components of final output (Kravis et al., 1974) indicates that the share of industry is relatively overestimated and the share of services underestimated at low levels of income.[12] Compared to consumption goods, government services are also relatively underpriced and capital goods relatively overpriced at low levels of income. The latter situation results from the fact that producers' durables have the most uniform prices across countries,[13] thereby reflecting the large incidence of trade in this category. The price index for construction, on the contrary, like that for government services, rises sharply with the level of income and confirms the relative-price-of-services hypothesis. Both sectors are highly labor-intensive and their output is not traded internationally but consumed domestically.

In sectors or groups of commodities where prices at low-income levels are relatively high (manufacturing, investment goods), there is, in addition to the contraction of the range of variation of real income, a larger change in the real quantities as their relative prices go down with income. Both corrections imply higher growth elasticities than estimated from data converted at exchange rates. In the sectors producing nontraded goods which, as shown above, are relatively more underestimated than total GDP at low-income levels, the relative price effect, when corrected, reduces the sectors' total change during the transition. The original growth elasticities are overstated on this account, but in any specific case it is difficult to determine the combined effect of this upward bias and the downward bias which is due to the exchange rate conversion of per capita income. The principal variables where the two effects offset each other are the share of services in total GDP and the share of government consumption in final

---

[11]Since the dependent variables in this study were defined as shares of GDP, a uniform proportional bias of all GDP components leaves the shares unaltered.

[12]This suggestion was also made by Balassa in 1961.

[13]A uniform price index for producers' durables and an overall rising index for total GDP entail the relative overpricing of the former at low-income levels.

demand. In both cases the growth elasticities estimated were quite low and were therefore not emphasized, since we tried throughout this study to rely on results that appear to be relatively robust.[14]

Alternative Approaches. Among the attempts that have been made to circumvent or overcome the problems of measuring income and converting the various estimates into a common unit of account, the following three have received wide attention in the literature:

1. In the first approach no method is proposed for measuring or converting income but instead it is suggested that per capita income be abandoned as an index of development and replaced by a broader index encompassing various dimensions of the development process. The best example of this approach is the factor-analysis study of Adelman and Morris (1967). But this and other multivariate techniques cannot substitute for a statistical attempt to assess quantitatively the basic development processes. The factor-analysis method is ill suited to the type of questions to which the present study is addressed. As a complementary approach, however, it is to be welcomed, and its many insights should be further explored.

2. The second approach, associated with W. Beckerman[15] (1966), attempts to regress the few available estimates of real income and its components[16] on a few nonmonetary indicators (such as cement production, stock of telephones per head, etc.) which are widely available for most countries. The equation with the highest coefficient of determination corrected for degrees of freedom (R^2) is then used to predict real income for countries where such independent estimates are as yet not available.

   Since most of the real income data in Beckerman and Bacon are for developed countries, the extrapolations for LDCs have at most an ordinal interpretation. For country analysis, using the one single equation on a few indicators[17] will result in large and not easily predictable errors. The estimated coefficients of the nonmonetary indicators look very much like prerequisites needed to attain a certain level of income

---

[14]The growth elasticities of services in the time-series patterns would be affected to a much smaller extent, or not at all, by the corrections based on purchasing power. This point will be discussed again in the conclusions to this section.

[15]For a brief account of this method, see Beckerman and Bacon (1966).

[16]These real income estimates are taken from studies of the purchasing power of various currencies in terms of the currency of one base country (usually the United States). These studies are the third and most ambitious approach to be discussed below.

[17]In predicting real consumption for eighty countries Beckerman and Bacon actually use six to eight different equations for different countries.

and cannot allow for the idiosyncracies of particular countries. For some purposes this regression method might be useful,[18] but not for a quantitative analysis of the processes of structural change.

3. The third and potentially most useful approach to "deflate" nominal income across countries tries to estimate real income and its composition in a group of countries by using a uniform set of prices to aggregate the real quantitites of a large number of goods and services. To date, comparisons of this type have been completed for only a few Western European countries and the United States, for commodities in capital cities in Latin America, and for ten countries differing greatly in their level of development (from India to the United States) and in their organization of economic activity (from Kenya to Hungary).[19] The results broadly confirm the negative correlation between real income and the degree of underestimation of the income figures converted by exchange rates, although the relation is not perfect and not even monotonic. (The main results for specific sectors in the Kravis et al. study were discussed above.)

These as yet partial results have been recently promoted to a rule by David (1972). After analyzing the purchasing power of eleven countries relative to the United States, he postulates the Rule of Four-ninths: ". . . *the 'real' percentage gap between the per capita income of a given country and the United States is only (0.441) four-ninths of the percentage gap indicated by a straight exchange rate conversion expressing all incomes in dollars"* (p. 985, italics in original). Since David's study is a serious one and his proposal to apply the four-ninths rule a seemingly viable alternative to straight exchange rate conversions, the following comments are in order:[20]

a. The purchasing-power parities are obtained from binary comparisons between the United States and the various countries, using a fixed set of price weights. For any country there is a choice between its own weights and the U.S. weights. Because of the expected negative association of prices and quantities, using the U.S. weights yields a higher quantity index than using own weights. In Kravis et al., this gap between the own-weighted and U.S.-weighted quantity

[18]In an unpublished memorandum, for example, Josefina Vial of the IBRD (1972) uses this method to predict real income in 120 countries and then calculates the degree of under-or overestimation of the income figures converted at exchange rates. On the average, she confirms the inverse relation between income and the degree of underestimation, although the individual dispersion over the transition range is considerable.

[19]These countries were chosen to link regional studies to the world project. See Kravis et al. (1974).

[20]The following discussion owes a great deal to Chapter 13 in Kravis et al. (1974) and to Balassa's comment (1973) on David's paper. See, however, David's rejoinder (1973).

indices was found, as expected, to have a systematic negative correlation with income per capita. The impact of this is that, depending on the weights used, different measures of real income will be obtained, and furthermore these differences will be related to income and will carry over to the estimates of cross-section relations such as those presented here.

b. The usual empirical compromise, which has little or no theoretical justification, is to average geometrically both indices and work with the "ideal" or Fisher index. David's solution is to adopt for all binary comparisons the uniform set of price weights of one country. He chooses the United States because it is at one extreme of the real per capita income range. This procedure guarantees "the uniformity of the *direction* of the expected bias present in Laspeyres's quantity comparisons between all possible pairs of countries" (David, 1973, p. 1269). The main point here is that when the bias implicit in the quantity comparisons is recognized there is no longer a clear advantage over the exchange rate conversion. The choice is now reduced to two biased indices.

c. In a mixed cross-section and time-series study, annual estimates of real income are needed. Devaluations and differential rates of inflation are two of the factors that may be expected to alter the degree of underestimation of the exchange-rate-converted income. If there were sectoral price indices for all countries it would be possible to correct the purchasing power of the different currencies by sectors. But differential inflation is not the only factor at work, and in addition the only basis on which a uniform rule such as the four-ninths one could be recommended is its simplicity, which is now lost.

d. The relative spread between real income and per capita income from a straight exchange rate conversion depends on many factors besides the level of income. For a given level of real per capita income a smaller deviation of the exchange-rate-derived measure is expected in countries where inflows of foreign capital and protection levels are high. In such cases the exchange rate is expected to be lower than where such factors are absent. An abundance of natural resources and a greater participation in international trade will also act to reduce the gap between income derived from official exchange rates and from purchasing-power parities.

The typology of development patterns in Chapter 4 resulted in more homogeneous groups with respect to trade. The main factor leading to different behavior in the small and large countries was seen to be the heavier reliance on trade in the former. The bias from converting at exchange rates in the more homogeneous alternative patterns can be expected to be less important than in the uniform equations for the whole sample. Balassa (1973) quotes the results of Clague and Tanzi (1972) for nineteen Latin American countries where little or no relation was found between the ratio of purchasing-power parities to exchange rates and per capita income.

A similar pricing problem, not yet explicitly discussed, arises in within-country time series. The income per capita series within any country were corrected for general changes in the price level. The dependent variables, however, were computed as shares in current prices. The share formulation eliminates the general change in the price level, but, as in the cross-section comparisons, it does not correct for changes in *relative* prices. As previously discussed, it is not at all clear whether an attempt should be made to eliminate any systematic trend in the relative evaluation of the different GDP components. All behavioral decisions on the part of consumers, firms, and the government are based on the concurrent information about income, relative prices, and other pertinent data and not on the relative prices of an arbitrary earlier period. This is not to deny that for some purposes it may be desirable to eliminate the effect of relative prices from both cross-section and time-series comparisons (such as the productivity of investment) but only to question the view that all intercountry and intertemporal comparisons must be of this type. The saving-consumption decisions of individuals and firms—and the resources devoted to and value added derived from a specific production sector (say, manufacturing)—are more meaningfully analyzed at current prices, regardless of their comparative productivity per unit of input which might require a constant price framework for evaluation.

Finally, as in the case of errors of measurement of national income, specific distortions may result from inadequately deflating the values expressed in domestic currencies. But if the distortion has little or no variation within a country over time it will not affect the average time-series patterns but will become part of the country's intercept.[21] We conclude that while the systematic bias in national income converted at official exchange rates is a well-established phenomenon, there is not at present any preferred alternative. The basic question relates to the nature of the systematic distortions introduced by the exchange rates. Insofar as they reflect the commercial policies pursued in the last decades by a large number of developing nations, they will not necessarily continue into the future. However, to the extent that the distortions reflect the relative price effect of differences between traded and nontraded goods, the continuation of their inverse association with real income can be safely predicted. In this case it can be argued that the *uncorrected* estimates are the more relevant, even though they combine both quantity (real) and price effects.

---

[21] Provided also that it enters the estimated equation additively.

A comparison of these estimates with others derived from real income series may yield much interesting information about price elasticities and real income effects of the various developmental processes. To determine levels of feasibility and describe the processes themselves for any given international price structure, however, it is the total not the partial effect which is sought.

The Treatment of Time

When, as in the present case, a cross-country study covers a twenty-year period, questions about the temporal stability of the relations arise. Time itself becomes one of the variables affecting the patterns of development. This section deals first with the nature of potential time shifts, then with alternative ways of incorporating these shifts into the regression, and finally with the interpretation of the estimated coefficients.

In principle the time variables should capture temporal changes in the dependent variables not associated with variations in the explanatory variables. These changes are assumed to be universal and to affect all countries alike. Ideally one should be able to relate the time shift to some identifiable process of change in, for example, the socioeconomic environment, the institutional setting, the level of technology, or the general strategies of development.

In practice, however, it is difficult to identify the estimated time effects with the overall processes of change, largely because of the high correlation between income and time within countries. This is a familiar problem in many areas of empirical analysis, and the large literature on the estimation of production functions and technological change has been concerned mainly with it. In the cross-country patterns there is the additional problem of a changing sample over time. Most of the countries entering the sample during the period are at the low end of the income scale and the results are often sensitive to these new data.

In the average time-series or short-run patterns the multicollinearity between income and time is more severe, but when country-specific effects are eliminated through the country dummy variables, the time coefficients better approximate the effects of exogenous shifts which lead to developmental changes independently of income. The averaging of time series in the short-run patterns also creates some problems of interpretation. The first has to do with the uniformity assumption. Time shifts may differ among countries for several reasons: in some cases they may indicate a delayed adjustment to some previous change or a rectification of a disequilibrium, while in others the time variable may act as a proxy for the effects of omitted variables in some countries. The estimated time trend would then be a combination of all these time adjustments rather than a uniform shift in some universal factors.

Even when the time shifts are uniform for all countries, it is still necessary to consider the extent to which the individual time series being averaged in the short-run patterns differ among themselves. With a high degree of similarity in the time-series experience, an accurate separation of the uniform time shift from the effects of a rising level of income is precluded by the high collinearity between the two. Multicollinearity is less of a problem when there is a wide variation among the individual time series, but then the weighted averages are less representative of the experience within any one country, and the estimated time effect may then just be compensating for systematic deviations from the average income pattern. For example, if for a given variable the time series reveal negative income elasticities within some — primarily low-income — countries, the average may still turn out to be significantly positive, but a negative time shift might then arise to capture the fall in the variable in certain countries over the period. This effect seems to be present to a certain extent in the short-run estimates of saving and export patterns as discussed in Chapter 5. For a proper evaluation of the average short-run income and time effects the range of variation of the individual time-series experience has to be considered too.

The next question is how one measures exogenous shifts over time. In cross-section regressions there are two simple ways of introducing time shifts. The first assumes temporal homogeneous shifts of a given magnitude between any two contiguous periods. An example of this practice is the variable T in Chenery, Elkington, and Sims (1970), which assumes the values 1, 2, 3, and 4 for observations dated 1950, 1955, 1960, and 1965, respectively. This variable stands for an exogenous uniform shift like technological change but is unable to discriminate among periods.

An alternative formulation, which still assumes homogeneity of the shifts across countries but not over time, tests the significance of a time shift between any two subperiods. This formulation, followed in the text, allows every subperiod to have its own level by introducing time dummy variables. Since one-year periods are probably too short to identify any exogenous shifts, five-year intervals were arbitrarily chosen as time units and three dummy variables were attached to the regressions as follows:

$T_1 = 1$ for all observations between 1950 and 1954 (otherwise zero);
$T_2 = 1$ for all observations between 1955 and 1959 (otherwise zero);
$T_3 = 1$ for all observations between 1960 and 1964 (otherwise zero).

The post-1964 observations form the reference period to which the regressions in the tables refer. The appropriate relations for any other subperiods are higher or lower by a constant given by the coefficient of the corresponding T_j variable. Thus, for example, to find the predicted value of any variable in the 1950-54 period, the coefficient of the T_1 variable has to be added to the regression, and similarly for other subperiods.

A negative coefficient for T_1 would imply that by 1964 the relation had shifted *upwards*.

Although significant time shifts may help explain past performance and reconcile the difference between cross-section and long-run time-series studies, they create a problem for projections, particularly when the magnitude of the shift is found to differ over time. In most practical applications projections are made on the assumption that no shift will occur. If there is reason to expect an exogenous time shift and information about its expected nature is at hand, it should, of course, be incorporated explicitly.

The Trade Orientation Index

The availability of natural resources is an important element that is missing from the basic equation, and one that can be expected to have significant influence on the patterns. The various direct measures of the resource base (such as population density or arable land per capita) may indicate the extent of actual exploitation, but they are at best poor indicators of the availability of resources.

In Chapter 2 the impact of the resource base and the development strategies being pursued were measured indirectly through the resulting level and composition of exports. Though significant results were obtained, several considerations suggested that the combined effect of resources and strategies might vary with the level of income. For proper treatment of this variation, either interaction terms between the resource measures and income in the uniform regression should be used, or the sample should be split into more homogeneous groups. In Chapter 4 the second alternative was followed for reasons given below. The question then was how the resource and strategy effects reflected in the level and structure of exports could be .combined into a ranking measure for stratifying the sample.

Given the income level and population size of any country, its expected *absolute export bias,* defined as $\hat{E}_p - \hat{E}_m$, can be calculated. These are the predicted values of the commodity (primary and manufacturing) components of exports from the corresponding equations in Table 6. In Chenery and Taylor (1968) countries were classified by a trade orientation index based on deviations from the normal values of the absolute export bias. A country with normal export levels will have a negative deviation if it emphasizes, because of lack of resources or a deliberate policy not to exploit them, E_m relative to E_p, and a positive one in the opposite case.

When total exports differ significantly from predicted exports the deviation of the absolute export bias includes a scale effect. This effect was found to be particularly important in two extreme cases: the small, high-income countries and the poorest, least developed countries (most of them African). In the former their significant orientation toward industry is obscured by the fact that their level of exports is generally high. At the other extreme the very poor economies are expected to have very low levels of manufactured exports but high levels of primary exports. If exports fall below their expected level it would then appear to be almost exclusively the result of a curtailment of primary exports, since industrial exports are clearly bounded by zero.

To avoid these pitfalls a relative trade orientation index *(TO)* was defined by deviations from the expected *relative export bias* for given income and population levels:

$$TO = \frac{E_p - E_m}{E} - \frac{\hat{E}_p - \hat{E}_m}{\hat{E}}$$

The *TO* index classifies countries according to the relative bias in their exports of *commodities*. Since this bias is expressed relative to actual and predicted *total* exports it indirectly takes into account the level of exports of services, which are very important for a number of countries.[22] The values of the index for all countries and the resulting classification were reported in Tables 10-13.

The various elements that are combined to form the index can be better appreciated with the help of Figure T2, where the normal relation between the per capita values of primary and manufactured exports for a country of 10 million population is plotted for various income levels as in Figures 13 and 14. Isovalue lines can also be plotted for any given value of the *TO* index $\overline{(TO)}$ in the $E_p - E_m$ plane by rewriting the formula given above and making use of the identity $E \equiv E_p + E_m + E_s$

$$\frac{E_p - E_m}{E} = \overline{TO} + \frac{\hat{E}_p - \hat{E}_m}{\hat{E}} \equiv b$$

$$E_p = \frac{b}{1-b} E_s + \frac{1+b}{1-b} E_m, \quad b < 1$$

For a given income level and a preassigned $\overline{TO}$ value, the parameter b can be computed. If service exports per capita are fixed at their predicted value for the given income and size levels, they can be reflected in the

---

[22]Preliminary tests experimented with several alternative indices that lumped service exports with primary or manufactured exports or treated them as a separate factor. The classification of countries was not much affected, but it was necessary to abandon the interpretation of the index as a deviation from a normal export bias that could be compared with a commodity production bias (see Chapter 4).

Figure T2: Normal Export Structure and the Trade-Orientation Index

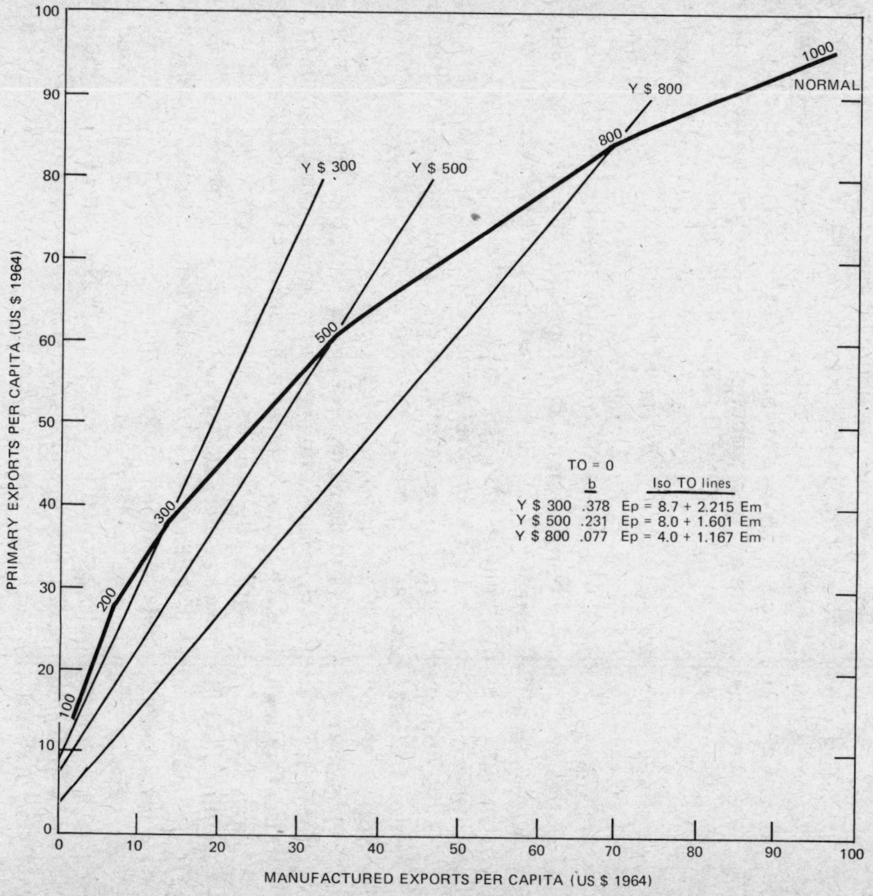

NORMAL

1000

Y $ 800

800

Y $ 500

500

Y $ 300

300

200

100

TO = 0   Iso TO lines

          b
Y $ 300   .378   Ep = 8.7 + 2.215 Em
Y $ 500   .231   Ep = 8.0 + 1.601 Em
Y $ 800   .077   Ep = 4.0 + 1.167 Em

PRIMARY EXPORTS PER CAPITA (US $ 1964)

MANUFACTURED EXPORTS PER CAPITA (US $ 1964)

straight lines in Figure T2 (for TO = zero). These lines show, for any level of income and E_s, all the $E_p - E_m$ combinations that produce a constant trade orientation index. (Varying this value will of course result in a new line.) When TO = zero the line intersects the normal $E_p - E_m$ relation at the corresponding level of income, since TO = zero means there is no deviation from the normal export bias.

A higher level of E_s with an unchanged E_m requires a simultaneous increase in primary exports if the value of the TO index is to remain unchanged. This similarity between industry and service exports was one of the results reported in the last section of Chapter 2.

Finally, the coefficient of E_m in the last equation $[(1 + b)/(1 - b)]$ will exceed unity (for TO = zero) whenever $\hat{E}_p > \hat{E}_m$. [23] In this case a country with a low total export ratio will show a normal export bias only if the low level of exports results from a larger reduction in E_p than in E_m. These relative reductions must be in the ratio of $(1 + b)/(1 - b)$.

Reduced Forms and Structural Relations

Underlying comparative econometric studies is the belief that the observable relations among various development indicators are similar across countries. Initially this was justified by the observation that the structure of production and trade seemed similar in developing countries. Unfortunately, however, the only relations between data which are observable are not structural but reduced form equations, and more than one structure may generate any given reduced form. Thus similar reduced forms may not imply similar structures.

Aside from serious problems of data availability, the major motivation for reduced form estimation is our ignorance of the correct form of the structural equation. The simple quadratic form provides sufficient nonlinearity, at least within the present range of observation, and an examination of the residuals does not reveal any obvious patterns of remaining nonlinearity. The equations presented here should therefore be viewed as reasonable approximations of the true reduced form equations.

Because of the ignorance of the structural equations it was decided not to use simultaneous estimation techniques.[24] (See, however, some tests with instrumental variables in the section below on weighting.) The situation has not changed much since Houthakker wrote in 1965: "Unfor-

---

[23]For a typical country with a population of 10 million this is the case up to a $1000 per capita income level.

[24]In a few studies with some dynamic elements (which made the potential simultaneity problems more serious), two-stage least squares were employed (Modigliani, 1965; Landau in CIAP, 1968; Adelman and Chenery, 1966). In every case the results were about the same as those derived from ordinary least squares.

tunately there is as yet no quantifiable theory of the determination of income levels in different countries, so the single-equation methods used here are probably the best that are available at present" (p. 218).

ESTIMATION

In formulating an econometric study and its precise specification several decisions must be made as to which estimation procedures to follow. In a cross-country study a list of recurrent problems is encountered, to which ad hoc answers are often supplied but not always explicitly discussed. In this section some of the main issues are explored and specific solutions explained, with the stress, as before, on the rationale behind the choices and not on the techniques themselves. These are rigorously treated in the econometric literature which is referred to thoughout this section.

When the classical assumptions of regression analysis regarding the error term hold,[25] ordinary least squares (OLS) yield best (i.e., minimum variance) linear unbiased estimates (BLUE) of the parameters of the equation. When one or more of the assumptions are violated, however, estimators other than OLS may have more desirable properties in some respects.[26] Among the more serious potential violations in the present context is the problem of simultaneity discussed earlier.

The sections below analyze the problems faced in the presence of errors in the variables, heteroscedasticity, and omitted variables (a specification problem). Different problems of estimation arise from the specification of the domain being investigated. These are discussed under "Stratifying the Sample" and "Pooling of Cross-section and Time-series Data."

Errors in the Variables

In most economic contexts errors in the exogenous variables come from two sources: errors in measurement and differences between proxies

---

[25] If μ stands for the vector of error terms and σ^2 for its variance, these are given by: $E(\mu) = 0$ and $\Sigma = \sigma I$, where Σ stands for the variance covariance matrix of the residuals and I is an identity matrix. If the exogenous variables are not fixed the independence of these and the vector μ is also required. The statement in the text is known as the Gauss-Markov theorem. For a more formal statement, see, for example, Goldberger (1964) or any other econometric text.

[26] Competing estimates often improve the results in one respect, but at the cost of worsening some other property. For example, when OLS estimates are biased or inconsistent, as in the case of errors in the variables discussed below, alternative techniques may yield consistent estimates but increase the variance. The resulting trade-off has to be weighed in each particular case.

and unobservable theoretical concepts (e.g., permanent income). When such errors are present in the data ordinary least squares estimates are no longer unbiased or even consistent (see Johnston, 1972). In the classical model of errors in the variables (all errors in the variables are random with no systematic component) one can obtain consistent estimates by using instrumental variable techniques (INVR) or other grouping methods which are variants of INVR. The nonlinear functional form adopted in the text compounds the problem since, as Griliches and Ringstad (1970) have shown, if a variable and the square of this variable appear as "independent" terms in a regression and if the variable in question is measured with error, then not only are both coefficients biased toward zero but also the coefficient of the nonlinear term is biased as the square of the bias factor of the linear term. In the present context the coefficient of the nonlinear income term is expected to be relatively small, and if in addition there are also random errors in the measurement of this variable, its coefficient will be even smaller.[27]

INVR transformations for income per capita, the main independent variable in this study, have been tested. The rank of per capita GNP in 1965 and its square value were selected as instrumental variables on the plausible assumption that they are highly correlated with the original income variables and uncorrelated with all the *random* errors in the equation.[28] The OLS and INVR regressions for the 1965 cross section for the primary share in GDP gave the following results ($n = 85$):

Coefficient of:	Constant	lnY	$(lnY)^2$	lnN	$(lnN)^2$	F	R^2
OLS	2.144	−.4735	.0286	−.0611	.0082	−.6618	.7904
INVR	2.106	−.4601	.0274	−.0609	.0082	−.6601	.7902

In general, the INVR estimates were quite similar to the OLS ones, although such strong similarities were not encountered in every case. Since the INVR is also a remedy for the problem of simultaneity (it is in fact the only method that does not require previous knowledge of the whole structure), these results may also indicate the absence of simultaneity, at least for the income variables.

Another approach would use the grouping solution for the case of one independent variable proposed by Wald and modified by Bartlett (see

---

[27]This provides one more reason for retaining the nonlinear term even when it fails to pass conventional tests of significance.

[28]The case of systematic (i.e., nonrandom) errors of measurement were discussed earlier in the section on exchange rate conversions and are further analyzed below as omitted variables.

Johnston, 1972). This would divide the sample into three groups of approximately the same size according to increasing values of the independent variable and pass the regression line through the means of the two
end groups. A far from simple generalization of this approach to the two
independent variables case has been derived.[29] It was not pursued further
in this study since the added cost (in terms of complexity) was not considered justified by the limited expected benefit in the light of the INVR
results and our belief that most of the "measurement errors" are not random but systematically related to the level of income. The nature of the
resulting bias in this case and the extent to which one may want to correct
for it were discussed in the section on exchange rate conversions above.
(See also the section on omitted variables, below.)

A variation of the grouping method uses all the observations and tries
to minimize the error variance by dividing the sample into more
homogeneous groups and deriving OLS estimates from the group means.
Kuznets's approach to the study of patterns of development can be so interpreted.

Weighted Regression (Heteroscedasticity)

One of the assumptions of the classical regression model under which
OLS estimates are BLUE is that successive disturbances have the same
variance, that is, they are homoscedastic. In many economic contexts it is
reasonable to assume that the variances of the regression errors are related to size, usually to the size of the dependent variable. In the presence
of heteroscedasticity OLS estimates, while still unbiased, are no longer
best (minimum variance), not even asymptotically. In addition, the estimated variances of the coefficients calculated from the least squares
regressions are now biased, and nothing can be said a priori about the
direction of the bias. This has important consequences for hypothesis
testing. (See Theil, 1971.) This source of heteroscedasticity may be
reduced by the use of log transforms or, as in the present case, by the use
of share data rather than absolute values.

Another potential source of heteroscedasticity mentioned in cross-section studies is the averaging-out effect. If the basic units of observation in
the model are specified to be individual and the error term is assumed to
be homoscedastic at the individual level, then aggregating into national
averages causes the variance of the error term to become inversely proportional to the group size. Minimum variance estimates are now given by
Aitken's generalized least squares. Houthakker's studies on saving (1965)

---

[29]The analysis of hierarchical interactions used in Adelman and Morris (1971) can also be
interpreted as a generalization of Wald's method.

and Adelman's study on population (1963) employed weighted regressions to take into account this difference in population sizes. In practice many influences on economic statistics act at country level rather than at the individual level. Government economic policy and the error-control procedures of statistical agencies are just two examples. In this study the national aggregates are regarded as the units of observation and therefore unweighted OLS techniques continue to be employed. This decision implies that the results bear only indirectly on economic theories of individual behavior.

Stratifying the Sample

The rationale behind uniform patterns is based on the existence of "universal factors" important enough to produce some regularity in the behavior of socioeconomic processes. Theory suggests that the level of income and the size of the economy are two of the variables which represent universal factors.

The presence of strong "group factors" (as distinguished from universal and particular) may indicate the existence of group patterns which significantly differ from each other and are inadequately represented in the overall average pattern. In such a case, splitting the sample and estimating separate patterns for the subgroups may contribute to a better analysis of the underlying forces.

Once the decision to split has been made, the actual stratification should rely as much as possible on theoretical arguments. Random splitting, particularly when the samples are large, may result in "significant" (see the discussion below) F tests rejecting the homogeneity assumption, without improving the explanation of the processes at work.[30]

An alternative way to incorporate group factors without splitting would be to include in the estimation the variables which are related to these factors. This is not always a feasible approach since: *(a)* the impact of these additional variables may be quite nonlinear; *(b)* interaction terms between the universal and group variables may be hard to incorporate; and *(c)* the group factors are not always easy to identify.

In any of these cases splitting would be indicated, although the extent of the splitting (i.e., into two, three, or *n* groups) would still remain an open question.[31] Simple statistical tests are of little help here. The classical procedure postulates a general hypothesis (i.e., that each country has separate

---

[30]Clustering techniques may be useful in suggesting ways to quantify theory-based group factors, and its applicability to this problem should be further studied.

[31]Even in large samples, too fine a stratification runs against the problem of subsamples too small for meaningful analysis.

intercepts and regression slopes) and then successively tests the nested hypotheses of homogeneity of subgroups. The level of significance is set a priori for the whole nested procedure.[32]

Splitting the sample is sometimes a useful intermediate step rather than an end in itself, as in the example of splitting by income groups. Even if it is hypothesized that poor countries do not have a different nonlinear pattern from rich countries, splitting by income levels and estimating simple linear regressions within groups can reveal the presence of nonlinearities in the aggregate pattern.

In some cases theory may suggest a causal variable, but difficulties of definition or quantification may preclude its inclusion in the estimation. Splitting by an ordinal estimate of the variable may then be appropriate as an intermediate step.

Tests of Homogeneity. In the analysis of alternative patterns in Chapter 4, three subdivisions were considered. The first and most useful divided the sample by population size into two groups according to whether the 1960 population level was smaller or larger than 15 million. The group of small countries was then subdivided according to the trade orientation index analyzed above. The third step subdivided the sample by the level of development, usually taking a per capita income of $500 in 1960 as the dividing level. In every case it was hypothesized that there was homogeneity in the patterns of the two groups. The hypothesis that the two vectors of regression coefficients are equal (or not significantly different from each other) was tested by computing the F ratio:[33]

$$F = \frac{Q_2 / k}{Q_1 / (m + n - 2k)}$$

with degrees of freedom $(k, m + n - 2k)$,

where: Q_1 equals the total of the two sums of squared residuals from the alternative patterns within the subsamples;

Q_2 equals the difference between the sum of squared residuals from the pooled regression for the whole sample and Q_1; and

m, n, and k stand respectively for the number of observations in the two subgroups and for the number of coefficients estimated in each regression.

The assumption of homogeneity can be rejected if F exceeds the preassigned critical level of F. The critical F for a 5 percent confidence level with $(9, \infty)$ degrees of freedom (which are close to those of the

[32]In some cases, even though the assumption of homogeneity is rejected, pooling may still be desirable in order to obtain an average estimate for the various groups. See below, "Pooling of Cross-section and Time-series Data."

[33]See Johnston (1972); his notation is followed here.

TABLE T1. Tests of Homogeneity (F Tests) of Alternative Patterns Classified by Size, Trade Orientation, and Level of Development

Process	No. of Observations							F Ratios when Split by:		
	Full Sample	Large	Small	SP	SM	Y <$500	Y >$500	Size	Trade Orientation	Level of Development
Saving	1,432	458	974	558	416	979	453	14.3	10.9	5.8
Investment	1,432	458	974	558	416	979	453	14.0	9.9	5.8
Government revenue	1,111	342	769	411	358	775	336	8.7	3.7	9.7
Tax revenue	1,111	342	769	411	358	775	336	9.2	4.5	13.7
School enrollment	433	122	311					4.1		
Private consumption	1,508	451	1,057	633	424	1,056	452	12.5	3.5	3.5
Government consumption	1,508	451	1,057	633	424	1,056	452	25.0	6.0	24.0
Primary production	1,325	439	886	516	370	938	387	5.5	22.8	4.2
Industry production								6.6	18.6	4.0
Utilities production								11.5	8.2	12.6
Services production								15.7	28.9	18.9
Total exports	1,432	458	974	558	416	979	453	8.6	26.9	7.9
Primary exports	413	129	284	173	111			6.1	13.7	
Manufactured exports								4.2	26.7	
Services exports								2.9	29.0	
Imports	1,432	458	974	558	416	979	453	8.7	27.0	7.8
Birth rate	146					101*	45*			3.5

*For birth rates the sample was divided at an income level in 1960 of $800.

TABLE T2. A Summary of Regression Results

| | Standard Error of Estimate | | | | | | | Coefficient of Determination | | | | | | |
| | Full Sample | | | | | | | Full Sample | | | | | | |
Process	Basic Regression	Augmented Regression	L	S	SP	SM	Over $500	Basic Regression	Augmented Regression	L	S	SP	SM	Over $500
Saving	.050	.047	.050	.047	.048	.040*	.050	.71	.78	.54	.78	.73	.86	.59
Investment	.050	.047	.050	.047	.048	.040*	.050	.40	.43	.43	.46	.41	.57	.07
Govt. revenue	.050	.051	.053	.047	.047	.046	.045	.64	.69	.68	.65	.51	.73	.27
School enrollment	.136		.125*	.136				.72		.73	.73			
Private consumption	.068	.052	.070	.065	.071	.052*	.050*	.54	.73	.48	.61	.56	.72	.56
Govt. consumption	.042	.036	.045	.038	.040	.032*	.025*	.15	.26	.18	.22	.20	.32	.33
Primary production	.079	.069*	.057*	.087	.086	.067*	.045*	.75	.82	.89	.69	.66	.59	.61
Industrial production	.057	.043*	.056	.057	.043*	.063	.055	.71	.84	.73	.70	.67	.69	.39
Exports	.115		.052*	.131	.081*	.154	.090*	.28		.38	.15	.42	.23	.39
Primary exports	.060		.028*	.067	.074	.039*		.67		.63	.64	.63	.47	
Manufactured exports	.064		.033*	.072	.014	.093		.31		.45	.33	.23	.38	

SOURCES: For basic regressions, Tables 4 and 5.
For large (L) and small countries (S), Tables S5, S6, S9, and S10.
For small, primary-oriented (SP) and small, industry-oriented countries (SM), Tables S7, S8, S11, and S12.
For over $500, Tables 17 and 20.
For augmented regressions, Table S14.

*Significant improvement from pool results.

basic equation) equals 1.96. Table T1 presents the number of observations and F ratios for the various relevant tests.

Statistical Accuracy. Table T2 presents the two measures that have been computed for all the regressions, the standard error of estimate (SEE), and the coefficient of determination (R^2).[34] Subdivision of the sample may improve the results in one of two ways: by reducing the variance within each group, or by grouping together countries that more nearly satisfy the assumptions underlying the regression equation. In both cases there will be a reduction in the SEE, but only in the second case will R^2 also be increased.[35]

For increased accuracy of estimation, it is most useful to subdivide the sample into large and small countries. There are significant reductions in the standard errors of the large countries for five of the eleven sets of regressions listed in Table T2, most notably in the three export variables and in primary production. The small country regressions show less improvement in production and exports, however, which suggests the need for further subdivision of this group.

When the small countries are subdivided according to their trade orientation, the improvement in accuracy is comparable to that of the large countries in relation to the pooled regression. Within each group accumulation and consumption processes are shown to be more uniform than among the large countries, although production and trade still have somewhat larger unexplained variation.

The augmented regressions employed in the last section of Chapter 2 offer an alternative to splitting the sample, but they require additional information on the levels of each of the three export components. When this condition is met they are able with a single equation to improve estimates of accumulation, consumption, and production as much as the results of the three-way typology. The main advantages of subdividing the sample are therefore that it reveals more accurately the differences in timing concealed in the averages for all countries and results in more accurate estimates of the effects of other variables.

The third approach, which divided the sample by level of development, makes virtually no improvement in the accuracy of the statistical explanations for less developed countries (not shown here). It does demonstrate, however, that the more developed countries have a more uniform structure of production and consumption. The main value of this grouping is to

---

[34]The samples are the same by country and year except for the augmented regression, which is based only on data for the 1960s. However, the pooled regressions for this reduced sample do not differ much from the complete sample.

[35]When the variance to be explained is reduced, R^2 may go down even though the fit is considerably better, as shown by the lower SEE.

describe more accurately the asymptotic characteristics of the underlying relationships. The results also disprove the contention that the only significant variation in several structural characteristics occurs between the developed and underdeveloped countries.

Pooling of Cross-section and Time-series Data

Average Cross Section. It has been only a few years since data have become available for a large number of countries (especially LDCs) over a relatively long period of time (fifteen to twenty years). When these data are used to study development patterns pooling of the temporal cross sections is often considered. It not only adds substantially to the degrees of freedom but also introduces the time dimension to comparative cross-country analysis. The usual practice is to test for the stability of cross-section results over time. If the null hypothesis of homogeneity of the cross-section regressions is not rejected, then pooling follows quite naturally. If the stability assumption is rejected, however, pooling might still be desired to obtain average patterns. In addition to making use of all the information, average patterns are more suitable to use than any one cross section.

The average cross-section estimates can be obtained by adding a set of time dummy variables to the pooled OLS regression, one for each time period. By this procedure all variation *between* time periods is eliminated, and a regression estimate results which is a weighted average of the various cross-section regressions (or within-time-period estimates) with weights related to the within-time-period variances of the explanatory variables.

The estimates of the time dummy variables can be interpreted as indicating the magnitude and significance of exogenous shifts in the patterns from any one time period to another (see "The Treatment of Time" above). These two time effects may reflect the independent effect of universal processes such as changes in technology, but in addition they capture time-related problems of specification. A first order autoregressive pattern of the residuals, for example, if similarly applicable to all countries, would have been absorbed by the time variables without impairing the BLUE properties of the estimators.

Average Time Series. Time can also be incorporated in a more essential way by considering the average time-series experiences of the various countries, which were identified as short-run patterns in the text. These short-run patterns can be estimated by letting each country have its own intercept (using a separate dummy variable for each country) but assuming that *changes* in the characteristics studied are associated with *changes* in income and other pattern variables in the same way for all countries at given values of these variables. This amounts to considering only the *within-country* component of the total variation being studied and is equivalent to estimating a regression equation where deviations are computed from country means.

Although the socioeconomic (dependent) variables have changed considerably within countries over the past two decades, it is still true that most of the variation in the sample is among countries. This is sometimes made explicit by considering only country means and thus eliminating all the within-country variations over time. In fact, the results in Chapters 2—4, which include all the observations, give results similar to those obtained by first averaging over time, but with the added improvement of providing estimates and tests of time shifts for which temporal observations are required. The relatively small variance that exists in short-run patterns (with country dummies) leads to relatively low coefficients of determination (R^2). In this case the SEE of the regression is a more relevant statistic for evaluating and comparing goodness of fit.

As with added time dummies, the estimated pattern with country dummies is interpreted as a weighted average of within-country time series, with weights related to the variances of the explanatory variables in the different countries. The within-country variance of income, and therefore its relative weight in the average estimate, will be larger the higher the level of per capita income, the faster income is growing, and the larger the number of annual observations in the maximal (full) samples. To find out how serious the dominance of the richer countries might be, the SEEs from individual time-series regressions for the primary and industrial shares in GDP were averaged out by income groups, with the following inconclusive results:

Average Standard Errors

Income Group	V_p	V_m
Less than $300	.0683	.0900
$300 to $800	.0661	.0514
More than $800	.0662	.0439

In the case of the industrial share average, standard errors in rich countries were considerably lower than in poor countries, while no such difference was found for the primary share.

Omitted Variables. In comparative analysis of cross-country data we try to isolate and quantify a few important aspects which form part of a complex interdependent process. A host of structural country characteristics are left out of the analysis because of their nonquantifiable nature or lack of data. When these omitted variables are related to income and other explanatory variables, the estimates in the cross-country regressions are biased. In addition to their direct effect, the explanatory variables exert an indirect effect through their association with the omitted variables. For some processes the cross-section association with the included variables (especially income) is also found in the historical data of the developed countries and can be expected to continue into the future. In this case the cross-section income effect can be interpreted as a total or long-run effect as opposed to the direct or short-run effect which eliminates the indirect impact of the omitted variables. (See the section on exchange rate conversions.) In cases where the association with income and other variables is due to some historical accident and is not expected to continue, the bias is more serious, and its elimination may help to prevent unwarranted conclusions as in the case of the cross-section association of saving and external capital.

Nonrandom errors of measurement,[36] when they are systematically associated with income, can be regarded as a particular case of misspecification due to omitted variables. The following discussion therefore applies to them as well.

Many of the omitted variables and systematic errors of measurement associated with income and other pattern variables vary primarily among countries and are relatively invariant within a country over time. When such variables enter the correctly specified equation in an additive form (or multiplicative form in logarithmic and semilogarithmic regressions), the OLS formulation with country dummy variables corrects for the specification bias by lumping together the combined effect of such omitted variables in the country intercept. In the cross-country long-run patterns, however, the specification bias appeared as part of the effect of income and other pattern variables.

THE COMPOSITION OF THE SAMPLE

Since 1950 an increasing number of countries have been collecting and publishing statistical data. Although the quality of the data varies and some questions remain as to its comparability, more representative cross-country studies have been made possible by the larger size of the sample and its broader composition. This changing sample, however, may introduce spurious temporal shifts if the new countries' development patterns do not coincide with those of the original countries. It is therefore of interest to compare the results obtained when using maximal (full) samples with those obtained using a reduced compatible sample whose com-

---

[36]The case of random measurement errors was discussed above in the section on errors in the variables.

position does not vary over time. The detailed analysis of such a comparison for the structure of production is reported elsewhere (Syrquin 1974); a general discussion is presented here.

The Samples

The compatible (reduced) sample includes the forty-two countries with annual observations on all the relevant variables for the 1950—67 period. Full samples range from forty-four countries in 1951 to a maximum of eighty-six countries in 1964. The reduced sample is composed mainly of medium- and high-income countries. LDCs appear in the full samples during the 1950s with the very poor countries entering later. For countries in the full but not in the reduced sample, the average income per capita in 1955 is about one-half of the average per capita income in the reduced sample ($334 and $608 respectively). After that it declines through 1962 in spite of the general increase in income in most of the countries, as new and even poorer countries are added to the sample. Average income for the complete sample also falls during that period but goes up by almost 25 percent within the forty-two countries in the reduced sample.

Annual Cross Sections

Annual cross-section regressions are estimated for both sets of samples: twenty for the full samples (1950—69)[37] and eighteen for the reduced (1950—67).

The coefficients of the income variables are quite significant in almost all the regressions. The curvature of the patterns is more pronounced in the full than in the reduced samples, where the limited representation of countries at the lower end of the income scale makes it harder to detect significant nonlinear effects.

In both sets of cross sections, statistical tests reject the assumption of homogeneity of the annual regressions.[38] When time dummy variables are introduced into the pooled regression as in Chapter 2, uniform production patterns are obtained which are weighted averages of the various

---

[37]No cross-section equation was estimated for 1970 since only twenty-one observations were available. These were included in the regressions for the whole period.

[38]The results of the corresponding F tests are:

| Primary (full) | = | 19.3 | Industry (full) | = | 21.2 |
| Primary (reduced) | = | 9.5 | Industry (reduced) | = | 2.07 |

with (6,1313) degrees of freedom for the full samples and (6,744) degrees of freedom for the reduced samples. For the interpretation of such figures see the section on stratifying the sample.

nonhomogeneous cross-section regressions. (See "Pooling of Cross-section and Time-series Data" above.) To bring out the size and importance of the temporal variation in the annual cross sections for both sets of samples and the differences between the two sets, predicted values from each cross-section regression were calculated at four benchmark levels of income for a typical country of 10 million population and foreign capital inflow of 2 percent. The mean predicted values for the 1950s and 1960s are given in Table T3.

TABLE T3. Average Predicted Values of Production Shares from Yearly Cross Sections

Period	Production	Full Sample Per Capita Income (US$ 1964)				Reduced Sample Per Capita Income (US$ 1964)			
		$50	$300	$800	$1,500	$50	$300	$800	$1,500
1950s:	Primary	64	27	17	17-13	57	28	18	15
	Industry	6	27	35	38	9	28	34	38
	Utilities	3	7	9	10	5	7	10	10
	Services	27	39	39	33-37	29	37	38	37
		100	100	100	100	100	100	100	100
1960s:	Primary	60	26	14	9	59	27	15	11
	Industry	10	25	33	38	4	27	35	39
	Utilities	3	8	10	10	3	7	10	10
	Services	27	41	43	43	34	39	40	40
		100	100	100	100	100	100	100	100

SOURCE: Syrquin (1974), and Table S17.

The predicted primary share at low-income levels is larger when using the full samples but only within the decade of the fifties; in the following years it is almost the same or even lower than the predicted shares from the reduced sample. The reasons have to do with variations in the composition of the sample. There are almost no countries with a very high primary share in the reduced sample. The predictions for the lower-income end of this sample are merely extrapolations of the type of curvature encountered at medium- and high-income levels, but the higher figure for the 1950s in the full samples does represent the structure of economies at such a level of income. Although the countries that were being added to the full samples during the fifties had relatively high primary production shares, they experienced a large drop in the value of the share, only part of which was related to income.

This downward shift over time is even more evident at the upper end of the income scale. This time effect for the higher-income countries was also noted in the regressions within income groups in Chapter 4 (see Tables 20 and 21). There it was noted that the time coefficients in the higher-income groups imply that after 1965 a typical country in this group would have an expected primary share in output almost five percentage points lower than its predicted average value for the 1950—54 period. This is roughly what the figures in Table T3 suggest.

The normal variation with income from the annual regressions for the industrial share indicates that the income pattern tends to rotate in opposite directions for the two sets of samples: "clockwise" for the full sample and "counterclockwise" for the reduced sample. These facts can be reconciled by comparing the industrial structure of the poorer countries not in the reduced sample with that of the remaining countries and by assuming the "true" within-country pattern to have a logistic-type shape. The results of a three-way income split for the industry share in Table T4 support this interpretation, primarily the acceleration of the income-related changes during the medium-income transition.

During the fifties the reduced sample had few observations in the middle region where the process accelerates. Most of the countries were at either end of the income scale. By the sixties, however, many countries moved into the accelerating stage, and at the same time an exogenous upward shift was observed in all but the low-income countries (Table T4). In order to incorporate these changes the annual semilog cross-section regressions for the reduced sample had to shift counterclockwise. This rotation adequately captured the position of countries in the transition range, but it yielded unreasonably low predicted values for the low-income range, with no serious consequences since the reduced samples are unpopulated at that range.

In the full samples, however, there are forty-four countries which are included in the observations at one point or another after 1950, thirty-eight of which had in 1965 a per capita income below $250, and in twenty-one of these it was even lower than $125 per capita. In these twenty-one countries with lowest income per capita, the observed 1965 average industrial share was equal to a relatively high .134. In order to incorporate these observations (relatively high industrial share at low-income levels) into a uniform semilog regression, a typical cross-section curve for the full samples in the 1960s had to shift in a clockwise direction relative to a typical cross section during the 1950s. This rotation, as seen from the predicted values in Table T3, took place in spite of the accelerating industrialization of the countries in the transition range.

In the uniform regressions reported in Chapter 2 the time effects of a small downward shift for the primary share can now be seen as the result of averaging the different trends in low- and high-income countries, and the nonmonotonic shift for the industry share is a result of the varying

TABLE T4. Industrial Patterns by Income Groups

Industry Share of GDP	Constant	$\ln Y$	$(\ln Y)^2$	$\ln N$	$(\ln N)^2$	F	T_1	T_2	T_3	R^2	SEE	Y Mean/Range	No. of Obs.
Y less than $300	−.686 (5.564)	.250 (4.961)	−.018 (3.508)	.038 (7.853)	−.004 (4.595)	.219 (9.870)	.001 (.119)	−.008 (1.710)	−.014 (3.355)	.437	.046	166 46/1089	713
Y $300 to $800	4.536 (6.921)	−1.383 (6.508)	.110 (6.395)	.069 (8.051)	−.009 (4.435)	.149 (3.853)	−.065 (5.997)	−.033 (3.473)	−.016 (1.760)	.456	.057	493 166/1218	340
Y greater than $800	2.028 (2.626)	−.374 (1.722)	.018 (1.211)	.078 (7.052)	−.009 (4.767)	−.204 (3.103)	−.059 (7.597)	−.040 (5.609)	−.015 (2.187)	.552	.037	1431 517/3551	272

t ratios in parentheses.

composition of the sample and the specification of the semilog functional form.

The time effects come out clearer in the average time series discussed in Chapter 5. When the variation between countries is removed the composition of the sample is less important, and time trends become quite significant: downward for the primary share and upward for industry in both samples, but more so in the full.

The composition of the sample seems to be an important factor in analyzing cross sections of country data over time in the post-1950 period. Since the number of yearly observations will increase for all countries and a large number of new countries is not expected to enter the sample, this effect will clearly diminish in importance in the future.

The Share of Services

Although the composition of a sample and its varying coverage over time can affect the uniform regressions, much of the impact of the changing composition of the sample is adequately reflected in the uniform patterns through the time-shift variables. The case of the services sector is treated separately here as a unique example of a situation where the specific characteristics of a few countries dominate the results for any given year. This is not a result of the fact that the sample changes over time for the problem is present throughout the period, although there are signs that over time the exceptional countries are becoming less differentiated in their industrial structure.

In this section we review the empirical evidence on the behavior of the services sector and then interpret it by describing the composition of the sample.

From the uniform regression in Chapter 2 (see Table 5) the normal pattern for a typical country was graphed in Figure 5. This showed an expected services share of about 30 percent for a typical country with a per capita income of less than $100, which then rose, reached a maximum, and even declined within the range of the transition. The time-series experience of high-income countries since 1950, however, indicates no decline in the share of services but on the contrary a rising trend.[39] As will be shown presently, this "hump" in the relation is due to the very high share of services in some medium-income countries. When in addition the very low-income countries not in the reduced sample are considered, the relation becomes even more erratic.

---

[39]The even faster increase in the share of services in the labor force, as relative labor productivity falls in that sector, is adequately represented in the sample. See for example Figure 9.

TABLE T5. Countries with High Services Share of Production around 1965: Main Characteristics

Country	Services % of GDP	Income (US$1964)	Population (mil.)	Capital Inflow % of GDP
Algeria	47	202	11.9	5.0
Angola	69	178	5.2	−3.9
Brazil	47	216	81.3	−2.6
Costa Rica	45	361	1.5	10.4
Dominican Republic	48	215	3.5	2.3
Guatemala	49	278	4.4	2.8
Hong Kong	49	512	3.6	10.2
Israel	48	1,126	2.6	13.0
Jordan	52	217	2.0	20.9
Lebanon	59	446	2.4	20.8
Malagasy	46	84	6.3	7.3
Mexico	51	434	42.7	.1
Morocco	46	179	13.3	−1.5
Panama	46	474	1.2	2.0
Peru	47	289	11.7	1.4
Puerto Rico	52	936	2.6	21.2
Singapore	76	522	1.9	3.9
United States	53	3,201	194.2	−.4
Uruguay	45	498	2.7	−6.0
Vietnam (South)	50	118	16.1	11.7

SOURCE: Tables S2 and S3.

In Table T5 the twenty countries with a 1965 services share exceeding 45 percent are listed together with their main characteristics. Most of the countries in the table are small (the main exceptions are Brazil, Mexico, and the United States); in eleven of them the population around 1965 was below five million. The countries in this group tend to depend heavily on foreign capital; in seven of them the ratio of foreign capital to GDP exceeds 10 percent. In three of the countries (Jordan, Lebanon, and Panama) exports of services account for over 10 percent of GDP.[40]

Annual Cross Sections. The hump in the income pattern of services is present in the cross-section relations for both the full and the reduced samples (Table T3). There is, however, a smaller degree of curvature in the reduced samples, and at a low-income level there appears to be a prevalent and significant upward shift which is absent from the full samples. Both differences are due to the fact that low-income countries are excluded from the reduced sample because of insufficient observations. The preceding section pointed out the relatively high share of industrial and primary production in the countries with lowest per capita income in 1965. The counterpart of those high shares is, of course, a low figure for the share of services, and the fact that these countries enter the full samples

---

[40]This group can also include Jamaica, where the services share equals 44 percent and exports of services 14 percent.

gradually over time tends to increase the curvature and obscures any exogenous increase in services for the low-income countries included.

Services in Large Countries. Since many of the countries with an extremely high share of services are small, a separate regression (for the whole period) for the large countries was run with the following results:

$$V_s = -.443 + .164 \; lnY - .0103 \; (lnY)^2 + .097 \; lnN - .0099 \; (lnN)^2 + .0383 \; F + .004 \; T_1$$
$$\quad (4.0) \quad (5.1) \qquad (3.8) \qquad \qquad (3.3) \qquad (2.8) \qquad \qquad (0.4) \qquad (0.4)$$

$$+ .002 \; T_2 - .004 \; T_3 \qquad \qquad R^2 = .401 \qquad \qquad SEE = .0615$$
$$\quad (0.2) \qquad (0.5)$$

The hump has now disappeared and the expected increase at high levels of income is confirmed.[41]

The Time Series. The income elasticity within countries since 1950 (not shown) is positive for most countries. Among those few with negative elasticities are several of the extreme countries listed in Table T5 (e.g., Guatemala, Jordan, Morocco, and Singapore), while among those with highest positive elasticities are several countries with a very low share of services (e.g., Malawi, Papua, Tanzania, and Zambia). It appears that countries with abnormally low or high shares of services have been approaching the average normal values, while the rest have experienced a relative expansion in their output of services. These trends have brought about a compression of the intercountry variation in the share of services. The standard deviation of the share of services for the forty-two countries in the reduced sample has decreased monotonically over time in spite of the general increase in the value of the share (the coefficient of variation therefore fell even more). In the full samples the standard deviation increases for a while as the low-income, low-services countries are added, but then declines.

To obtain an average of the time-series variation with income across countries, uniform regressions with country dummy variables were estimated for the small and large countries in the reduced sample. (The short-run patterns for the full and reduced pooled samples were presented in Chapter 5.) The results (in Syrquin, 1974) indicate a rising share of services at high-income levels. In the average time series for some of the small, medium-income countries mentioned above there is first a decline toward a more normal value. For large countries there is no such decline.

---

[41] A similar monotonic increase resulted when the eight countries with extreme observations are excluded from the reduced sample: Dominican Republic, Guatemala, Hong Kong, Lebanon, Mexico, Panama, Peru, and the United States.

At a given point in time part of the intercountry variation in the share of services may be due to a price effect (as suggested by Balassa in 1961) because services are relatively underpriced in poor countries or overpriced in rich countries, but the evidence from the time series is relatively free of this distortion.[42] It is therefore not possible to conclude with Balassa that "the Clark hypothesis [of a rising tertiary sector] ... does not stand up in the light of information on cross section data" (1961, p. 397). (See also the section on exchange rate conversions above.)

---

[42]Balassa (1964) and Samuelson (1964) argue convincingly that the relative-price-of-services effect can also be found within a country over time. Over a twenty-year period, however, it is most unlikely that it could by itself account for the significant increase in the share of services.

STATISTICAL APPENDIX

THE DATA

The basic statistics used for this study cover 101 countries for the 1950–70 period to the extent that data were available. The countries and number of observations in each sample are listed in Table 2 in the text. The data were compiled in June 1972 by the Economic and Social Data Division of the World Bank and represent for the most part a revision and expansion of the series circulated by the Bank in 1971 under the title *World Tables*. The original sources of the data include the United Nations Statistical Office, UN specialized agencies, World Bank country economic reports, and national statistical publications. Sources of data not available in the IBRD data bank are noted below under "Definitions of Variables."

In order to achieve maximum coverage, data were in some cases estimated by IBRD staff. Additional adjustments were made in a number of other cases to remove discrepancies and inconsistencies evident in the original series. In general the study includes all countries with a midyear population of one million or more in 1960. Countries with centrally planned economies were excluded from the study because their basic data for income, product, and resources are not comparable with those of countries whose national accounts are compiled according to the standard United Nations system.

The World Bank has a continuing program for expanding and strengthening the quality of these and other series of economic and social statistics used in the Bank's operations and research activities. Some of the series used here appear routinely in World Bank publications such as the *Atlas,* the *World Tables,* the *Annual Report,* and *Trends in Developing Countries.* Other series maintained by the Bank and used almost exclusively by Bank staff are published only infrequently. A number of these series which are of special interest are available from the Bank at cost, on request, including the data base for the present study. Inquiries may be directed to the Economic and Social Data Division, World Bank, Washington, D.C., 20433.

EXCHANGE RATES

For most countries conversion into U.S. dollars was made on the basis of par or official exchange rates, but in a number of cases where these rates appeared to have become unrealistic as the result of inflation or other causes appropriate adjustments were made. For countries with multiple exchange-rate systems, the rates used were those which appeared to be closest to an equilibrium rate.

A list of the exchange rates used to convert domestic currencies to U.S. dollars is given in Table S1. For three countries (Brazil, Indonesia, and Pakistan), where exchange rate fluctuations had been large or where multiple rates were in use, principal trading rates were used when it was felt they were more realistic.

DEFINITIONS OF VARIABLES

Definitions of the economic and social variables used in the study are based on the standard international classification systems of the United Nations and specialized agencies, as follows:

Gross national product. GNP at constant factor cost (in millions of 1964 U.S. dollars) is the value of the gross national product, excluding indirect taxes net of subsidies. The estimates for 1964 were computed directly from the domestic currency estimates of GNP at current prices.

The estimates of GNP in 1964 U.S. dollars for years other than 1964 were extrapolated on the basis of real growth rates computed from the domestic currency estimates at constant prices. Indirect taxes net of subsidies are excluded to minimize the possible distorting effect of differing tax policies on relative country ranking.

Population. The data are midyear estimates. Where the series in the original sources appeared to be inconsistent over time, the figures have been appropriately adjusted.

Percent of gross domestic product. All computations under this head are based on domestic currency values at current market prices.

Accumulation Processes

1a. *Gross domestic saving as percent of GDP.* Gross domestic investment at current prices *plus* exports of goods and nonfactor services *less* imports of goods and nonfactor services constitutes gross domestic saving. Transfers of all categories are excluded from the computation.

1b. *Gross domestic investment as percent of GDP.* Gross domestic investment, valued at current market prices, consists of gross domestic fixed investment (GDFI) plus the increase in stocks in both the private and public sectors.

GDFI comprises purchases and own-account construction of fixed assets, including expenses directly related to the acquisition, improvement, or transfer of capital goods. Not included are: improvements in dwellings or purchases of consumer durables other than new dwellings; expenses only indirectly related to the acquisition of capital goods (e.g., commissions and financing costs); normal repair and maintenance of

TABLE S1. Annual Average Exchange Rate

	Country	1964 Atlas*		Country	1964 Atlas*
1.	Afghanistan	45.00	51.	Lebanon	3.08
2.	Algeria	4.937	52.	Liberia	1.00
3.	Angola	28.63	53.	Libya	0.357
4.	Argentina	140.39	54.	Malagasy	246.85
5.	Australia	0.447	55.	Malawi	0.357
6.	Austria	25.83	56.	Malaysia	3.07
7.	Belgium	49.74	57.	Mali	246.85
8.	Bolivia	11.88	58.	Mexico	12.49
9.	Brazil	991.9	59.	Morocco	5.06
10.	Burma	4.798	60.	Mozambique	28.75
11.	Cambodia (Khmer)	98.50	61.	Netherlands	3.607
12.	Cameroon	246.85	62.	New Zealand	0.358
13.	Canada	1.078	63.	Nicaragua	7.00
14.	Central African Republic	246.85	64.	Niger	246.85
15.	Ceylon (Sri Lanka)	4.756	65.	Nigeria	0.357
16.	Chad	246.85	66.	Norway	7.16
17.	Chile	3.57	67.	Pakistan	4.774
18.	China (Taiwan)	40.10	68.	Panama	1.00
19.	Colombia	10.62	69.	Papua	0.893
20.	Congo (Zaire)	165.0	70.	Paraguay	126.00
21.	Costa Rica	6.62	71.	Peru	26.82
22.	Dahomey	246.85	72.	Philippines	3.91
23.	Denmark	6.92	73.	Portugal	28.94
24.	Dominican Republic	1.00	74.	Puerto Rico	1.0
25.	Ecuador	18.58	75.	Rhodesia	0.357
26.	El Salvador	2.50	76.	Saudi Arabia	4.50
27.	Ethiopia	2.500	77.	Senegal	246.85
28.	Finland	3.22	78.	Sierra Leone	0.714
29.	France	4.90	79.	Singapore	3.06
30.	Germany (West)	3.975	80.	Somalia	7.143
31.	Ghana[†]	0.357	81.	South Africa	0.720
32.	Greece	29.875	82.	Spain	59.96
33.	Guatemala	1.00	83.	Sudan	0.348
34.	Guinea	246.85	84.	Sweden	5.156
35.	Haiti	5.0	85.	Switzerland	4.319
36.	Honduras	2.0	86.	Syria	4.04
37.	Hong Kong	5.74	87.	Tanzania	7.143
38.	India	4.794	88.	Thailand	20.84
39.	Indonesia[‡]	250.00	89.	Togo	246.85
40.	Iran	75.75	90.	Tunisia	0.446
41.	Iraq	0.357	91.	Turkey	9.00
42.	Ireland	0.358	92.	Uganda	7.143
43.	Israel	3.00	93.	U.A.R. (Egypt)	0.435
44.	Italy	624.45	94.	United Kingdom	0.358
45.	Ivory Coast	246.85	95.	U.S.A.	1.00
46.	Jamaica[§]	0.357	96.	Upper Volta	246.85
47.	Japan	360.9	97.	Uruguay	21.06
48.	Jordan	0.357	98.	Venezuela	4.50
49.	Kenya	7.143	99.	Vietnam (South)	60.0
50.	Korea (South)	255.0	100.	Yugoslavia	750.0
			101.	Zambia	0.357

* Units of domestic currency per US$1.

† Ghana pound.

‡ Old rupiah.

§ Jamaica pound.

capital goods, which are regarded as current expenditures; and government defense expenditures, which are included under general government consumption.

The increase in stocks comprises the current value of physical change in privately owned raw materials and finished goods, work in progress (except work on dwellings and nonresidential buildings which is included in fixed capital investment), and changes in stocks of strategic materials or emergency supplies held by the government.

1c. *Capital inflow (net imports of goods and services) as percent of GDP.* Capital inflow is defined as the total imports of goods and services *less* the total exports of goods and services. Factor payments and transfers to and from abroad are excluded from the calculation. (As indicated above, capital inflow is also equal to gross domestic investment minus gross domestic saving.)

2a. *Government revenue as percent of GDP.* Included in this measure are direct taxes on households and corporations, indirect taxes, and nontax revenue of all agencies of central, state, and local government other than government enterprises or public corporations, *plus* interest on the public debt, *less* current transfers to general government from abroad. Revenues of the social security system are included. All computations are based on values at current prices. Where data from all branches of government were not available, data from central government alone were used.

2b. *Tax revenue as percent of GDP.* Direct taxes on households and corporations as well as indirect taxes make up tax revenue.

Direct taxes on households: All taxes and surtaxes levied as a charge on the income of households, nonprofit institutions, and unincorporated enterprises, including social security contributions of both employers and employees.

Direct taxes on corporations: All taxes and surtaxes levied as a charge on the income of corporations, including corporate income and excess profits taxes, and taxes which are levied at regular intervals on undistributed profits or capital stock. Taxes levied at irregular intervals on capital or wealth are excluded. Where it is not possible to isolate and exclude one-time taxes on property, these taxes are included.

Indirect taxes: Taxes other than those levied on income and wealth and in the assessment of which no account is taken of the personal circumstances of the taxpayer. Also included are all taxes chargeable to business expenses of enterprises. The bulk of indirect taxes consists of sales taxes and customs duties; other main categories are entertainment duties, betting taxes, business licenses, stamp duties, and motor vehicle duties. Profits of state monopolies are also included. Real estate and land taxes are treated as indirect taxes unless they are considered merely as administrative devices for the collection of income taxes.

3a. *Education expenditure by government as percent of GDP.* Included here are both current and capital expenditures for education by central, state, and local government.

Current expenditure refers to financial charges incurred on behalf of schools for services and goods such as textbooks, teachers' salaries, scholarships, welfare services, maintenance and operation of buildings, and other consumable materials and supplies.

Capital expenditure refers to the purchase and development of land, buildings, and durable instructional equipment. Data on expenditure refer to public education only and do not include grants to privately operated schools.

Where only partial information was available, it has been given as an approximation. For some countries information is published on current expenditure only, i.e., excluding the value of investment in school buildings and equipment. In such cases the understatement of total expenditure may be considerable.

3b. *Primary and secondary school enrollment (adjusted).* This ratio expresses total enrollment at the primary and secondary level as a percent of the total 5- to 19-year-old population and corresponds more closely than a crude rate to the actual duration of schooling in each country. It does not allow for national differences in the age range of pupils and the length of schooling.

Resource Allocation Processes

4b. *Private consumption as percent of GDP.* Private consumption is measured as the value at current market prices of final expenditure by households and private nonprofit institutions on current goods and services (not including household purchases of land and buildings), *less* sales of similar goods (mainly secondhand) and services, *plus* the value of gifts in kind (net) received from the rest of the world.

Income in kind such as food, shelter, and clothing furnished to employees is included at cost, and a similar imputation is made for rent in respect to owner-occupied dwellings and for the value of home-grown food consumed by farm families and others.

4c. *Government consumption as percent of GDP.* The consolidated net expenditure incurred by all agencies of central, state, and local government constitutes government consumption. It includes compensation of employees and purchases from enterprises and from the rest of the world by general government (all central, state, or local government agencies, including social security systems but excluding agencies defined as public enterprises), *less* sales of goods and services to enterprises and households other than sales of stores which are treated as decreases in government stocks.

Among the items included in general government consumption are: *(a)* expenditure jointly financed by households and government in which government actually makes the purchase or in which households pay only a nominal amount (household contributions to such expenditures are treated as a transfer to general government); *(b)* expenditure of a capital nature for national defense (excluding civil defense); *(c)* transfers in kind received by general government from abroad, except transfers of military equipment; *(d)* transfer of military equipment by general government to the rest of the world.

Among the items *not* included in general government consumption are expenditure on capital formation for civil purposes (considered part of gross domestic investment) and transfer in kind other than transfer of military equipment made by general government to the rest of the world (treated as exports).

4d. *Food consumption as percent of GDP.* Food consumption (excluding beverages and tobacco) is measured at current purchaser's values as a percent of total consumption expenditure of households and private non-profit institutions (according to the UN *Yearbook of National Accounts Statistics,* 1970, and various years). This share is applied against private consumption as a percent of GDP.

5. *Value added by sector:* In principle, distributions have been calculated on the basis of values at current factor cost.

5a. *Primary output as percent of GDP.* Primary production is the share of GDP contributed by agriculture (including forestry, hunting, and fishing) and mining (including quarrying). (ISIC Divisions 0 + 1)

5b. *Industrial output as percent of GDP.* Industrial production is that contributed by manufacturing and construction. (ISIC Divisions 2 − 4)

5c. *Utilities output as percent of GDP.* Contributing to the share of utilities are electricity, gas, and water, as well as transportation and communication, including storage. (ISIC Divisions 5 + 7)

5d. *Services output as percent of GDP.* Services are contributed by the wholesale and retail trade; banking, insurance, and real estate; ownership of dwellings; service industries such as education, medicine, and recreation; public administration and defense; and other branches not elsewhere classified. (ISIC Divisions 6 + 8 − 81)

Source: *Classification of Commodities by Industrial Origin,* Department of Economic and Social Affairs of the United Nations Secretariat, Statistical Papers Series M, No. 43, 1966.

6a. *Exports as percent of GDP.* Exports of goods and nonfactor services is the value at current market prices of merchandise (f.o.b.), transportation, insurance, and other services sold to the rest of the world, not including factor payments from abroad (i.e., payment accruing to domestically owned factors of production operating abroad, which represent the claim of domesticm residents on the GDP's of other countries). The value of gifts *in kind* and other exports financed by means of international transfers is included, but the value of military equipment transferred between governments is excluded. Where factor receipts from abroad cannot be identified and where labor income earned abroad is relatively small, investment income from abroad may be deducted from the total value of exports of goods and all services as an approximation of exports of goods and nonfactor services.

6b. *Primary exports as percent of GDP.* Calculated as

$$E_p = (100 - ME) \cdot MR \cdot XPR.$$

6c. *Industry exports as percent of GDP.* Calculated as

$$E_m = XPR \cdot ME \cdot MR.$$

6d. *Service Exports as Percent of GDP.* Calculated as

$$E_s = (100 - MR) \cdot XPR,$$

where XPR = total exports as percent of GDP defined above.

MR = merchandise export ratio, i.e., merchandise share of exports of goods and services (IBRD, *World Tables,* 1971, Table VII, col. 10).

ME = manufactures as percent of exports of all merchandise derived from "Total A" of United Nations Committee on Trade and Development (UNCTAD) as defined in UN, *Trade in Manufactures of Developing Countries, 1970 Review,* at current f.o.b. prices. This includes the first stage of processing for most minerals in primary exports. Standard International Trade Classification (SITC) Groups 5-8 form the basis of the UNCTAD series.

6e. *Imports as percent of GDP.* Imports of goods and nonfactor services is the value at current market prices of purchases of merchandise (f.o.b.), transportation, insurance, and other services from the rest of the world, not including factor payments abroad. The value of gifts *in kind* and other imports financed by means of international transfers is included, but the value of military equipment transferred between governments is excluded. Where factor payments abroad cannot be identified and where labor income accruing to nonresidents is relatively small, investment income accruing abroad may be deducted from total imports of goods and services as an approximation of imports of goods and nonfactor services.

Demographic and Distributional Processes

7. *The labor force by branch total* represents the total number of economically active persons at midyear (July 1) as a sum of those in the various branches of economic activity, as defined by the International Standard Industrial Classification (ISIC). In countries where the unemployed are not classified according to the branch of economic activity in which they are usually or were most recently engaged, the unemployed are frequently included under "other" ("activities not adequately described").

The percentages have been calculated mostly on the basis of the total labor force, i.e., including employed and unemployed. Where this information was not available the employed population has been used.

7a. *Share of primary labor.* This includes all persons economically active in agriculture, forestry, logging, fishing, hunting, mining, and quarrying.

7b. *Share of industry labor.* Included here are all persons economically active in manufacturing and construction.

7c. *Share of services labor.* All persons economically active in all other sectors are included in this category.

8. *Urbanization (urban percent of total population).* The definition of urban population varies from country to country. At least one of the following five major concepts or criteria is utilized in the definition of each country providing data: administrative status; population size; form of local government; urban characteristics; characteristics of economic activity. The criteria of administrative area and urban character seem to be used more frequently in Latin America; type of administration plus population size is predominant in Europe, and the type of local government predominates in the British Commonwealth countries.

Source: *Urban and Rural Population: Individual Countries 1950–1985 and Regions and Major Areas 1950–2000,* prepared by the Population Division, Department of Economic and Social Affairs of the United Nations Secretariat, September 1970 (ESA/P/WP.33/Rev. 1).

For a discussion of the problems of statistical definition, see *Growth of the World's Urban and Rural Population, 1920–2000,* Population Division, Department of Economic and Social Affairs of the United Nations Secretariat, 1969 (ST/SOA/A/44), pp. 7–10.

9a. *Birth Rate.* This is the crude live birth rate per 1,000 population.

9b. *Death rate.* This is the crude death rate per 1,000 population. Source: UN *Demographic Yearbook,* 1970, and various years.

10. *Income distribution, highest 20 percent and lowest 40 percent.* Source: Shail Jain and Arthur E. Tiemann: "The Size Distribution of Income: A Compilation of Data." IBRD Development Research Center, Discussion Paper no. 4, August 1973. Data selected refer to national coverage of households and/or individuals, ignoring occupational and sectoral classifications.

TABLE S2. Accumulation Processes: Data for 1965 or Closest Available Year

Country	Y	N	Investment			Government Revenue		Education	
			S	I	F	GR	TR	EDEXP	SCHEN
1. Afghanistan	64.4	15.1	—	—	.0445	.0630	.0437	.0833	.1100
2. Algeria	202.4	11.9	.0496[5]	.2553[5]	.0496	.2010	.1872	.0414	.3900
3. Angola	178.0	5.2	.1162[9]	.0772[9]	-.0390	.1538[9]	.0908[9]	.0074[9]	.1000[6]
4. Argentina	786.6	21.7	.2115	.1975	-.0140	—	.2257	.0324	.6400
5. Australia	1680.4	11.4	.2690	.2944	.0254	.2577	.3516	.0321	.9200
6. Austria	1052.3	7.3	.2624	.2728	.0104	.3586	—	.0365	.8100
7. Belgium	1538.0	9.5	.2268	.2253	-.0015	.3065	.3002	.0560[10]	.9300[10]
8. Bolivia	124.0	4.3	.1097	.1699	.0601	.1459	.1299	.0379	.4340
9. Brazil	216.3	81.3	.2093	.1837	-.0256	.2013	.1504	.0114	.4700
10. Burma	59.1	24.7	.1410	.1837	.0427	.2618	.2372	.0274[6]	.3100[6]
11. Cambodia (Khmer)	101.8	6.5	.1374	.1469	.0095	.2481	.2102	.0379	.4300
12. Cameroon	108.0	5.3	—	—	.0147	—	—	.0308[10]	.6900
13. Canada	2056.7	19.6	.2562	.2596	.0038	.2895	.2572	.0592	.7600
14. Central African Republic	96.7	1.4	.1206	.1868	.0662	.1821	.1564	.0309	.3500
15. Ceylon (Sri-Lanka)	141.8	11.2	.1291	.1250	-.0041	.2187	.1780	.0456	.7400
16. Chad	58.5	3.3	.0136	.0915	.0780	.1385	.1074	.0271	.2000
17. Chile	418.7	8.7	.1894	.1812	-.0081	.2780	.2672	.0347	.7700
18. China (Taiwan)	201.0	12.4	.1979	.2306	.0327	.2005	.1440	.0277	.7400
19. Colombia	227.9	18.0	.1869	.1767	-.0102	.1207	.1117	.0210	.5200
20. Congo (Zaire)	71.0	16.4	.1529[11]	.1365[11]	-.0164[11]	—	—	.0396[10]	.3400[2]
21. Costa Rica	360.7	1.5	.1811	.2850	.1038	.1632	.1488	.0382	.8100
22. Dahomey	72.3	2.4	.0237	.1355	.1118	.1234	.1082	.0405	.2000
23. Denmark	1727.1	4.8	.2230	.2362	.0132	.3138	.2934	.0573	.9000
24. Dominican Republic	215.4	3.5	.0728	.0955	.0227	.1255	.1092	.0271[11]	.6400[11]
25. Ecuador	195.3	5.2	.1363	.1342	-.0021	.2254	.1504	.0294	.6700
26. El Salvador	240.5	2.9	.1300	.1541	.0241	—	—	.0275	.5100
27. Ethiopia	51.6	22.7	.1018	.1210	.0191	.0871	.0782	.0123	.0800
28. Finland	1485.9	4.6	.2743	.2934	.0191	.3349	.2972	.0595	.7100
29. France	1705.7	48.8	.2654	.2569	-.0086	.3755	.3691	.0337	.9100
30. Germany (West)	1613.7	59.0	.2874	.2861	-.0011	.3552	.3348	.0331	.9000

	[1]1953	[2]1955	[3]1957	[4]1958	[5]1959	[6]1960	[7]1961	[8]1962	[9]1963	[10]1964	[11]1966	[12]1967	[13]1968	[14]1969
31. Ghana					155.6	7.6		.0920	.1692	.0771	.1603	.1546	—	.7200
32. Greece					585.0	8.5		.1437	.2706	.1269	.2331	.2147	.0237	.8300
33. Guatemala					277.9	4.4		.1071	.1354	.0282	.1123	.0973	.0200	.3500
34. Guinea					52.4	3.5		.1337	.2532	.1195	—	—	.0758	.1900
35. Haiti					80.4	4.4		.0055	.0480	.0425	—	—	.0118	.2700
36. Honduras					207.4	2.2		.1600	.1571	-.0029	.1118	.1072	.0284	.4600
37. Hong Kong					511.8	3.6		.1335	.2351	.1017	.1314	.0922	.0241	.7500
38. India					83.9	480.9		.1573	.1781	.0208	.1436	.1262	.0229[10]	.4100
39. Indonesia					83.8	104.9		.0623	.0669	.0046	.0389	.0368	.0068[6]	.4200
40. Iran					217.8	24.8		.2232	.1643	-.0589	.1631	.0597	.0240	.3700
41. Iraq					249.2	8.1		—	—	-.1588	.2544	.2197	.0475	.5000
42. Ireland					815.1	2.9		.1419	.2311	.0892	.2776	.2554	.0429	.9800
43. Israel					1126.2	2.6		.1505	.2808	.1303	.2911	.2611	.0659	.8200
44. Italy					980.1	51.6		.2232	.1971	-.0261	.3151	.2888	.0504	.7000
45. Ivory Coast					178.7	4.3		.2238	.1896	-.0342	.2158	.2104	.0486	.3200
46. Jamaica					419.7	1.8		.1768	.1966	.0198	.1664	.1631	.0125	.7500
47. Japan					780.4	98.0		.3452	.3307	-.0146	.2080	.1897	.0443	.9300
48. Jordan					216.7	2.0		-.0436	.1659	.2094	.1683	.1181	.0322	.6800
49. Kenya					95.5	9.6		.1545	.1446	-.0099	.1181	.1138	.0452	.4500
50. Korea (South)					123.4	28.4		.0729	.1483	.0755	.1186	.0868	.0183	.7200
51. Lebanon					446.4	2.4		.0166	.2249	.2084	.1377	.1107	.0226	.6100
52. Liberia					179.3	1.1		—	—	-.0807	.1426	.1265	.0212	.3000
53. Libya					695.0	1.6		.4943	.2755	-.2189	.3075	.0698	.0504	.4800
54. Malagasy					84.4	6.3		—	—	.0727	.2103	.1582	.0085	.4100
55. Malawi					57.5	3.9		.0207	.1404	.1197	—	—	.0299[12]	.3100[11]
56. Malaysia					258.1	9.4		.2050	.1593	-.0457	.1875	.1520	.0406	.5700
57. Mali					57.0	4.5		.0996	.2080	.1084	.1383	.1316	.0442	.1400
58. Mexico					434.2	42.7		.1747	.1755	.0008	.0864	.0775	.0181	.6600
59. Morocco					179.1	13.3		.1212	.1061	-.0152	.1431	.1123	.0378	.3300
60. Mozambique					157.0	7.0		.0682[9]	.0824[9]	.0142[9]	—	—	.0081[9]	.2600[9]

Country	Y	N	Investment			Government Revenue		Education	
			S	I	F	GR	TR	EDEXP	SCHEN
61. Netherlands	1335.4	12.3	.2617	.2673	.0056	.3679	.3406	.0647	.9100
62. New Zealand	1806.4	2.6	.2484	.2750	.0263	.2940	.2557	.0372	.9200
63. Nicaragua	330.3	1.7	.1774	.2014	.0240	.1427	.1164	.0156	.4800
64. Niger	72.9	3.5	.1053	.1107	.0054	.1048	.0836	.0143	.0600
65. Nigeria	87.8	48.7	.1177	.1390	.0214	.1114	.0824	.0214[8]	.2500
66. Norway	1608.9	3.7	.2961	.2977	.0016	.3767	.3460	.0523	.9100
67. Pakistan	84.3	113.9	.1307	.1880	.0573	.1167	.0815	.0159	.2900
68. Panama	474.4	1.2	.1555	.1755	.0200	.1673	.1391	.0356	.7500
69. Papua	168.0	2.1	.1450	.3059	.1609	—	—	.0208	.4300
70. Paraguay	200.1	2.0	.1431	.1510	.0080	.0924	.0808	.0162[10]	.6200
71. Peru	288.7	11.7	.1723	.1862	.0139	.1782	.1750	.0333[9]	.7100[10]
72. Philippines	149.3	31.8	.1933	.2025	.0092	.1007	.0929	.0286	.8400
73. Portugal	361.1	9.2	.1371	.1875	.0504	.2071	.1912	.0149	.6700
74. Puerto Rico	935.8	2.6	.0846	.2961	.2115	—	—	.0532	.9700
75. Rhodesia	199.8	4.5	—	—	-.0747	.1011	.0756	.0369[11]	.5700
76. Saudi Arabia	270.8	6.8	.5467	.1218	-.4249	.2859	.2502	.0494	.1500
77. Senegal	192.7	3.5	—	—	.0177	.1964	.1813	.0245[10]	.2400
78. Sierra Leone	134.9	2.4	.1139	.1534	.0395	.1396	.1154	.0268	.1600
79. Singapore	522.2	1.9	—	—	.0392	.2053	.1211	.0418	.8300
80. Somalia	45.9	2.5	-.0300	.1100	.1400	.1484	.1375	.0141	.0600
81. South Africa	552.2	17.9	.2770	.2790	.0004	.1966	.1666	.0332[7]	.7100[6]
82. Spain	572.2	31.6	.2242	.2627	.0385	.1753	.1616	.0140	.7500
83. Sudan	87.8	13.7	.1049	.1487	.0438	.1546	.1082	.0275	.1400
84. Sweden	2242.7	7.7	.2465	.2587	.0122	.4204	.3726	.0623	.8500
85. Switzerland	2112.8	6.0	.2374	.2884	.0010	.2533	.2159	.0388[10]	.6400[10]
86. Syria	173.6	5.2	.1091	.1126	.0035	.1408	.1052	.0323	.5700
87. Tanzania	67.1	11.7	.1535	.1445	-.0381	.1351	.0926	.0262	.2300
88. Thailand	110.4	31.0	.1886	.2017	.0130	.1364	.1293	.0297	.5600
89. Togo	86.8	1.6	.1747	.2368	.0621	.1093	.1041	.0173	.3300
90. Tunisia	198.0	4.4	.1361	.2791	.1430	.2466	.2281	.0585	.6200

	[1]1953	[2]1955	[3]1957	[4]1958	[5]1959	[6]1960	[7]1961	[8]1962	[9]1963	[10]1964	[11]1966	[12]1967	[13]1968	[14]1969
91. Turkey						244.3	31.1	.1369	.1510	.0141	.1492	.1324	.0281	.5400
92. Uganda						82.9	8.7	.1468	.1357	−.0111	.1044	.1007	.0193	.3200
93. United Arab Republic (Egypt)						137.7	29.4	.1415	.1724	.0253	—	.3000	.0498	.5200
94. United Kingdom						1534.4	54.4	.1810	.1898	.0088	.3248	—	.0515	1.0200
95. United States of America						3200.7	194.2	.1896	.1857	−.0039	—		.0530	.9300
96. Upper Volta						35.1	4.9	.0585	.1525	.0940	.1387	.1285	.0275[8]	.0800
97. Uruguay						497.5	2.7	.1582	.0977	−.0604	.2350	.2332	.0372	.6730
98. Venezuela						829.6	8.7	.3047	.2084	−.0963	.2126	.1545	.0361	.7400
99. Vietnam (South)						117.7	16.1	.0035	.1203	.1168	.1105	.1084	.0197	.5400
100. Yugoslavia						414.8	19.5	.3070	.3004	.0066	.3032	.3021	.0431	.7800
101. Zambia						178.8	3.7	.4101	.2399	−.1702	.2862	.2625	.0555	.4200

TABLE S3. Resource Allocation and Trade Processes: Data for 1965 or Closest Available Year

Country	Domestic Demand			Structure of Production					Exports			Imports
	C	G	C_f	V_p	V_m	V_u	V_s	E	E_p	E_m	E_s	M
1. Afghanistan	.6454	.1986	—	.3191	.1560	.0567	.4681	.1986[5]	—	—	—	.4043[5]
2. Algeria	.7534[9]	.1304[9]	—	.2273[9]	.0464[9]	.0358[9]	.6905[9]	.2107[9]	—	—	—	.1717[9]
3. Angola	.6831	.1053	—	.1871	.3772	.0989	.3368	.0844	.0688	.0072	.0084	.0703
4. Argentina	.6193	.1015	.1380	.1381	.3646	.1105	.3867	.1523	.1036	.0243	.0244	.1777
5. Australia	.6028	.1347	.1828	.0896	.4919	.0967	.3218	.2575	.0212	.1539	.0824	.2678
6. Austria	.6423	.1309	.1641	.0783	.3942	.0943	.4332	.3634	.0587	.2393	.0654	.3618
7. Belgium	.7733	.1170	—	.3750	.1792	.0850	.3608	.2077	.1823	.0026	.0228	.2678
8. Bolivia	.6759	.1148	—	.2255	.2202	.0873	.4671	.0882	.0683	.0119	.0079	.0626
9. Brazil	—	—	—	—	—	—	—	—	—	—	—	—
10. Burma	—	—	—	—	—	—	—	.1373	.1217	.0088	.0069	.1800
11. Cambodia (Khmer)	.6849	.1777	.3882	.4011	.1507	.0337	.4145	.1211	.1069	.0046	.0097	.1306
12. Cameroon	.6734	.1748	—	.4269	.1061	.0802	.3868	—	—	—	—	—
13. Canada	.5778	.1323	.0951	.1038	.3347	.1175	.4440	.1962	.0743	.0925	.0294	.2000
14. Central African Republic	.6690	.2104	—	.3822	.1113	.1132	.3933	.1986	.1866	.0059	.0060	.2648
15. Ceylon (Sri Lanka)	.7271	.1438	.3536	.3411	.1607	.1052	.3930	.2581	.2330	.0018	.0232	.2539
16. Chad	.8441	.1424	—	.5295	.0867	.0092	.3745	.1576	.1512	.0033	.0032	.2356
17. Chile	.6997	.1110	—	.2091	.3218	.0678	.4013	.1401	.1042	.0177	.0182	.1319
18. China (Taiwan)	.6334	.1678	.3048	.2784	.2503	.0784	.3930	.1837	.0733	.0865	.0239	.2164
19. Colombia	.7481	.0650	—	.3380	.2191	.0762	.3667	.1142	.0869	.0067	.0206	.1040
20. Congo (Zaire)	.6386[11]	.2085[11]	—	.2819[11]	.2090[11]	.0675[11]	.4416[11]	.2427[11]	.2314[11]	.0016[11]	.0097[11]	.2262[11]
21. Costa Rica	.6852	.1336	—	.2784	.2097	.0601	.4517	.2255	.1568	.0280	.0406	.3293
22. Dahomey	.8108	.1656	—	.4269	.1061	.0802	.3868	.1312	.0721	.0052	.0538	.2430
23. Denmark	.6227	.1542	.1334	.1113	.3822	.1132	.3933	.2979	.0898	.1366	.0715	.3110
24. Dominican Republic	.7457	.1813	.3151[10]	.2726	.1792	.0643	.4839	.1519	.1272	.0064	.0182	.1746
25. Ecuador	.7272	.1365	.3216[10]	.3600	.2141	.0521	.3738	.1741	.1579	.0022	.0139	.1719
26. El Salvador	.7661	.0868	.2873	.2995	.1969	.0620	.4416	.2656	.1927	.0437	.0292	.2897
27. Ethiopia	.8023	.0960	—	.6207	.1212	.0391	.2189	.1152	.0853	.0011	.0288	.1343
28. Finland	.5801	.1455	.1869	.1859	.3510	.0998	.3632	.2128	.0165	.1580	.0383	.2319
29. France	.6084	.1262	.1775	.0867	.4516	.0667	.3950	.1374	.0238	.0806	.0330	.1288
30. Germany (West)	.5535	.1509	.1568	.0635	.4958	.0756	.3652	.1918	.0174	.1399	.0345	.1907

	[1] 1953	[2] 1955	[3] 1957	[4] 1958	[5] 1959	[6] 1960	[7] 1961	[8] 1962	[9] 1963	[10] 1964	[11] 1966	[12] 1967	[13] 1968	[14] 1969
31. Ghana				.4733	.7805	.1275	.2645	.2322	—	—	.1567	.1119	.0266	.2338
32. Greece					.7380	.1183	.2885	.1589	.0084	.4149	.0929	.0307	.0465	.2198
33. Guatemala					.8193	.0735	.5065	—	.0648	.4878	.1679	.1212	.0252	.1962
34. Guinea					.7354	.1309	—	.1344	—	—	.1849	.0740[11]	—	.3044
35. Haiti					—	—	.4241	.1782	.0372	.3219	.1103	.0148[11]	.0212	.1528
36. Honduras				.3260[10]	.7484	.0916	.0224	.4197	.0684	.3293	.2649	.0941	—	.2620
37. Hong Kong					—	—	.4892	.1924	.0650	.4929	.6586	.0173	.0037	.7603
38. India					.7480	.0955	.6120	.0942	.0515	.2670	.0394	.0482	.0071	.0602
39. Indonesia					.8816	.0561	.4452	.1611	.0221	.2716	.0528	—	—	.0574
40. Iran				.3302[11]	.6414	.1348	—	—	.0662	.3274	.2096	.1851	.0147	.1508
41. Iraq				.2578	.4893	.2021	.5374[11]	.1124[11]	.0790[11]	.2712[11]	.3177	.1357	.0921	.4069
42. Ireland				.2369	.7255	.1326	.0794	.3535	.0837	.4833	.1891	.0380	.0756	.3194
43. Israel				.1748	.6512	.1983	.1398	.3421	.0945	.4236	.1685	.0199	.0539	.1424
44. Italy				.2465	.6354	.1414	.4173	.1417	.1136	.3274	.3247	.2157	.0747	.2905
45. Ivory Coast					.6389	.1368	.2137	.2571	.0875	.4418	.3594	.1889	.1402	.3792
46. Jamaica				.2346	.7144	.1064	.1114	.3235	.1580	.4070	.1083	.0040	.0152	.0937
47. Japan				.1961	.5623	.0925	.2425	.1431	.0948	.5195	.1700	.0407	.1207	.3795
48. Jordan				.4260	.8234	.2196	.3537	.1539	.1055	.3870	.3347	.1857	.1138	.3249
49. Kenya					.7023	.1494	.4326	.2081	.0511	.3082	.0859	.0309	.0077	.1615
50. Korea (South)				.4648	.8383	.0952	—	—	—	—	—	—	—	—
51. Lebanon				.3299[12]	.8829	.1006	.1161	.1881	.1047	.5912	.1896	.0294	.1535	.3979
52. Liberia					—	—	.5849	.0755	.0572	.2824	—	—	—	—
53. Libya					.3887	.1170	.5924	.0954	.0398	.2724	.5642	.5359	.0282	.3453
54. Malagasy					.7418	.2273	.2930[11]	.1444[11]	.1007[11]	.4619[11]	—	.0001	—	—
55. Malawi					.8300	.1499	.5780	.1275	.0483	.2462	.1818	.1383	.0017	.3015
56. Malaysia				.2782	.6298	.1652	.4136	.1441	.0689	.3734	.4587	.3814	.0406	.4130
57. Mali					.7478	.1759	.5017	.1251	.0387	.3345	.1261	.1031	.0028	.2345
58. Mexico					.7347	.0701	.1538	.2888	.0434	.5141	.0972	.0463	.0101	.0980
59. Morocco					.7424	.1364	.3486	.1651	.0275	.4587	.2045	.1284	.0270	.1894
60. Mozambique					.8096[9]	.1222[9]	—	—	—	—	.1423[9]	—	—	.1566[9]

Country	Domestic Demand			Structure of Production				E	Exports			Imports M
	C	G	C_f	V_p	V_m	V_u	V_s		E_p	E_m	E_s	M
61. Netherlands	.5833	.1550	.1615	.0962	.3829	.1072	.4137	.4502	.1333	.2269	.0900	.4558
62. New Zealand	.6080	.1345	—	.1606	.3098	.1090	.4205	.2168	.1904	.0134	.0130	.2432
63. Nicaragua	.7276	.0950	.3263[2]	.3614	.1554	.0695	.4137	.2795	.2164	.0184	.0447	.3035
64. Niger	.7800	.1161	.4962	.6119	.1105	.0310	.2466	.1484	.1450	.0034	—	.1538
65. Nigeria	.8032	.0578	—	.5926	.1221	.0496	.2357	.1687	.1526	.0026	.0135	.1901
66. Norway	.5426	.1614	.1589	.0985	.3411	.2046	.3558	.4001	.0566	.1475	.1960	.4017
67. Pakistan	.8000	.0638	—	.4785	.1539	.0741	.2935	.0605	.0321	.0181	.0103	.1178
68. Panama	.7348	.1097	.3037	.2598	.2071	.0688	.4644	.3640	.1445	.0011	.2184	.3840
69. Papua New Guinea	.7014	.1536	—	.6934	.0656	.0348	.2062	.1624	.1252	.0031	.0341	.3233
70. Paraguay	.7889	.0680	—	.3683	.1796	.0497	.4024	.1498	.1268	.0110	.0120	.1577
71. Peru	.7189	.1088	.2871[1]	.2641	.2077	.0543	.4739	.1793	.1103	.0493	.0197	.1932
72. Philippines	.7209	.0858	.3871	.3329	.2217	.0437	.4017	.1605	.1023	.0132	.0449	.1696
73. Portugal	.7397	.1231	—	.2160	.3834	.0771	.3235	.2584	.0335	.1242	.1008	.3088
74. Puerto Rico	.7778	.1375	.1929	.0783	.3056	.0970	.5191	.4369	—	—	—	.6484
75. Rhodesia	.6608	.1244	.1474	.2562	.2455	.1165	.3819	—	—	—	—	—
76. Saudi Arabia	.3007	.1458	—	.5906	.0634	.0906	.2554	.5776	.5256	—	.0520	.1527
77. Senegal	.7169	.1860	—	.3206	.1540	.0788	.4466	—	—	—	—	—
78. Sierra Leone	.7979	.0759	.3539	.5050	.0990	.0857	.3103	.2857	.2482	.0004	.0371	.3252
79. Singapore	.7851	.1012	.2360	.0460	.1791	.0177	.7571	—	—	—	—	—
80. Somalia	.8487	.1813	—	—	—	—	—	.2301	.1699	.0142	.0460	.3701
81. South Africa	.6364	.1180	.1673	.2173	.2842	.1123	.3862	.2654	.1040	.0367	.1247	.2674
82. Spain	.6887	.0871	.3046	.1934	.3274	.0832	.3960	.1106	.0230	.0246	.0630	.1491
83. Sudan	.7779	.1172	.4953[11]	.5439	.1137	.0053	.3370	.1810	.1572	.0003	.0235	.2248
84. Sweden	.5654	.1872	.1454	.0812	.4284	.1062	.3842	.2314	.0252	.1645	.0417	.2436
85. Switzerland	.5969	.1156	.1464	—	—	—	—	.3062	.0135	.2131	.0796	.3072
86. Syria	.7409	.1500	—	.2915	.1888	.0883	.4315	.2075	.1282	.0150	.0643	.2110
87. Tanzania	.5660	.1257	—	.5665	.0785	.0515	.3035	.2575	.2121	.0145	.0309	.2485
88. Thailand	.6951	.0985	.3256	.4114	.1863	.0871	.3150	.1827	.1171	.0327	.0329	.1957
89. Togo	.7448	.0805	.4948	—	—	—	—	.2092	.1771	.0091	.0230	.2713
90. Tunisia	.7040	.1599	—	.2552	.2318	.1038	.4092	.1990	.0883	.0331	.0776	.3420

	[1]1953	[2]1955	[3]1957	[4]1958	[5]1959	[6]1960	[7]1961	[8]1962	[9]1963	[10]1964	[11]1966	[12]1967	[13]1968	[14]1969
91. Turkey			.7179	.1452	—	.3694	.2221	.0834	.3251	.0617	.0394	.0038	.0185	.0759
92. Uganda			.7437	.0987	—	.5641	.0672	.0460	.3227	.2379	.2173	.0016	.0190	.2268
93. United Arab Republic (Egypt)			.6609	.1976	—	.2966	.2629	.1015	.3390	.1859	.0919	.0252	.0688	.2112
94. United Kingdom			.6464	.1720	.1619	.0569	.4157	.1168	.4106	.1849	.0199	.1169	.0481	.1937
95. United States of America			.6281	.1823	.1230	.0536	.3309	.0869	.5285	.0488	.0121	.0265	.0102	.0449
96. Upper Volta			.8298	.1117	—	—	—	—	—	.1064	.0989	.0053	.0021	.2004
97. Uruguay			.6957	.1461	—	.1467	.3084	.0939	.4510	.1816	.1285	.0096	.0436	.1211
98. Venezuela			.5719	.1235	.1660	.3459	.1940	.0590	.4011	.3071	.2943	.0005	.0123	.2108
99. Vietnam (South)			.7678	.2287	.3804	.3083	.1276	.0597	.5045	.0844	.0167	.0002	.0675	.2013
100. Yugoslavia			.5163	.1768	.2235	.2331	.3920	.1025	.2733	.2243	.0471	.1192	.0584	.2182
101. Zambia			.4619	.1280	.1218	.4806	.1447	.0687	.3060	.5664	.5528	.0023	.0113	.3962

TABLE S4. Demographic and Distributional Processes: Data for 1965 or Closest Available Year

Country	Labor Allocation			Urbani-zation	Demographic Transition		Income Distribution	
	L_p	L_m	L_s	UBR	BR	DR	Low	High
1. Afghanistan	—	—	—	.0698	.4800	—	—	—
2. Algeria	.6258[11]	.0697[11]	.3045[11]	.3770	.1960[9]	.1600[6]	—	—
3. Angola	—	—	—	.1046[6]	—	—	.1590[7]	.5310[7]
4. Argentina	.1837[6]	.3075[6]	.5089[6]	.7717	.2140	.0820	—	—
5. Australia	.1056[11]	.3585[11]	.5358[11]	.8265	.1970	.0880	—	—
6. Austria	.2430[7]	.3843[7]	.3727[7]	.5199	.1790	.1300	—	—
7. Belgium	.0856[10]	.4130[10]	.5013[10]	.6766	.1640	.1210	—	.5770[13]
8. Bolivia	.5315[4]	.0956[4]	.3729[4]	.3202	.4500	.0470	.0920[13]	.6220[14]
9. Brazil	.5417[6]	.1232[6]	.3350[6]	.5134	.4100	.1000	.1000[14]	—
10. Burma	.1114[1]	.2055[1]	.6831[1]	.1710	.4700	—	—	—
11. Cambodia (Khmer)	.8040[8]	.0364[8]	.1596[8]	.1122	—	.1970[6]	—	—
12. Cameroon	—	—	—	.1642	.2140	.0760	.2000	.4020
13. Canada	.0954[11]	.2972[11]	.6074[11]	.7296	—	.0810	—	—
14. Central African Republic	—	—	—	—	—	—	—	—
15. Ceylon (Sri Lanka)	.4915[9]	.1152[9]	.3934[9]	.1843	.3320	.0810	.1370[9]	.5230[9]
16. Chad	—	—	—	—	—	—	.1800[4]	.4300[4]
17. Chile	.3152[6]	.2365[6]	.4483[6]	.6880	.3320	.1040	.1300[13]	.5680[13]
18. China (Taiwan)	.5169[3]	.1296[3]	.3535[3]	.6063	.3270	.0550	.1400[7]	.5220[7]
19. Colombia	.4883[10]	.1708[10]	.3409[10]	.5426	.3670	.0990	.0940[14]	.5950[14]
20. Congo (Zaire)	.8760[2]	.0561[2]	.0680[2]	.0830[2]	.4300[5]	.3500[2]	—	—
21. Costa Rica	.4937[9]	.1722[9]	.3342[9]	.3487	.4230	.0850	.1470[15]	.5060[15]
22. Dahomey	—	—	—	—	.1800	—	.1550[5]	.5000[5]
23. Denmark	.1767[6]	.3567[6]	.4666[6]	.7776	.1800	.1010	.1670[11]	.4180[11]
24. Dominican Republic	.6163[6]	.1072[6]	.2643[6]	.3396	.4600	.0900[6]	—	—
25. Ecuador	.5586[8]	.1788[8]	.2626[8]	.3605	.4900	.1450	—	—
26. El Salvador	.6035[7]	.1685[7]	.2280[7]	.3914	.4690	.1060	.1200[13]	.6140[13]
27. Ethiopia	—	—	—	.0675	—	—	—	—
28. Finland	.3581[6]	.3020[6]	.3399[6]	.5705	.1690	.0960	.1110[8]	.4930[8]
29. France	.2144[8]	.3517[8]	.4339[8]	.6359	.1780	.1070	.0950[8]	.5370[8]
30. Germany (West)	.1294	.4558	.4148	.7886	.1790	.1120	.1540[10]	.5290[10]

	[1]1953	[2]1955	[3]1957	[4]1958	[5]1959	[6]1960	[7]1961	[8]1962	[9]1963	[10]1964	[11]1966	[12]1967	[13]1968	[14]1969	[15]1970
31. Ghana					.5972[6]		.1191[6]	.2837[6]		.2709	.1770		.2400[6]	—	—
32. Greece					.4845[14]		.1981[14]	.3174[14]		.4567	.4530		.0790	.2100[3]	.4950[3]
33. Guatemala					.6553[10]		.1397[10]	.2050[10]		.2927			.1680	—	—
34. Guinea															
35. Haiti										.1590			.2200[6]	—	—
36. Honduras					.6708[7]		.0986[7]	.2306[7]		.2383	.4580		.0860	.0730[13]	.6750[13]
37. Hong Kong					.0529[11]		.4405[11]	.5065[11]		.9014	.2810			—	—
38. India					.7397		.1058[7]	.1603[7]		.1922	.3840		.1290	.1400[6]	.5200[6]
39. Indonesia					.6743		.0689	.2568		.1582			.2140[6]	—	—
40. Iran					.4708[11]		.2407[11]	.2886[11]		.3736	.4230		.0820	.1250[13]	.5450[13]
41. Iraq					.4808[4]		.1398[4]	.3794[4]		.4353	.3500			.0680[3]	.6800[3]
42. Ireland					.3166[11]		.2630[11]	.4204[11]		.4503	.2210		.1150		—
43. Israel					.1250		.3454	.5296		.7794	.2580		.0630	.2020[3]	.3940[3]
44. Italy					.2581		.3893	.3526		.5019	.1920		.1000	—	—
45. Ivory Coast					.8665[10]		.0174[10]	.1161[10]		.1785	.4950			.1750[5]	.5500[5]
46. Jamaica					.3679[6]		.2137[6]	.4183[6]		.3341	.3890		.0860	.0820[4]	.6150[4]
47. Japan					.2499		.3121	.4380		.6791	.1860		.0710	.1530[8]	.4600[8]
48. Jordan					.3769[7]		.1872[7]	.4359[7]		.4407	.4810			—	—
49. Kenya										.0846					
50. Korea (South)					.5365[11]		.1328[11]	.3307[11]		.3294	.4500			.1730[15]	.4620[15]
51. Lebanon										.3547				.1300[6]	.6100[6]
52. Liberia										.2466	.3230			—	—
53. Libya					.3926[1]		.1481[1]	.4593[1]						—	—
54. Malagasy										.1206	.3230			.1350[6]	.6100[6]
55. Malawi											.5800			—	—
56. Malaysia					.5495[12]		.1199[12]	.3306[12]		.3996	.3670		.0790	.1090[13]	.5520[13]
57. Mali										.1084	.5070			—	—
58. Mexico					.4859[13]		.2114[13]	.3027[13]		.5290	.4420		.0950	.1090	.6110
59. Morocco					.5756[6]		.0990[6]	.3254[6]		.3226	.3600		.1870[6]	—	—
60. Mozambique														—	—

Country	Labor Allocation L_p	L_m	L_s	Urbanization UBR	Demographic Transition BR	DR	Income Distribution Low	High
61. Netherlands	.1219[6]	.3958[6]	.4824[6]	.6912	.1990	.0800	.1360[12]	.4850[12]
62. New Zealand	.1374[11]	.3587[11]	.5039[11]	.7686	.2290	.0870	.2200[11]	.3900[11]
63. Nicaragua	.6042[9]	.1516[9]	.2442[9]	.3963	.4580	—	.1020[11]	.5930[11]
64. Niger	.9686[6]	.0059[6]	.0255[6]	.2020	—	.2700[6]	.1800[6]	.4200[6]
65. Nigeria	—	—	—	—	—	.1180[6]	—	—
66. Norway	.2013[6]	.3492[6]	.4495[6]	.5083	.1780	.0910	.1660[9]	.4050[9]
67. Pakistan	.6766	.1178	.2057	.1289	.4900	.1540	.1750[10]	.4500[10]
68. Panama	.4629[6]	.1187[6]	.4184[6]	.4409	.3940	.0730	.1540[13]	.4560[13]
69. Papua New Guinea	—	—	—	—	—	—	—	—
70. Paraguay	.5478[8]	.1843[8]	.2679[8]	.3703	.4500	.1200	—	—
71. Peru	.5190[7]	.1651[7]	.3158[7]	.4803	.3920	.0900	.0650[15]	.6000[15]
72. Philippines	.5289	.1320	.3390	.3196	.4470[11]	.0730	.1160	.5540
73. Portugal	.4305[6]	.2707[6]	.2988[6]	.3513	.2290	.1030	—	—
74. Puerto Rico	.1707[11]	.2805[11]	.5488[11]	.4572	.3020	.0670	.1370[9]	.5060[9]
75. Rhodesia	—	—	—	.1833	.4800	.0780	—	—
76. Saudi Arabia	—	—	—	.1996	—	—	—	—
77. Senegal	—	—	—	.2411	.4250	.1600[6]	.1000[6]	.6400[6]
78. Sierra Leone	.7995[9]	.0612[9]	.1397[9]	.1275	.4360	.1860	.1000[13]	.6700[13]
79. Singapore	—	—	—	1.0000	.3110	.0560	—	—
80. Somalia	—	—	—	.1907	—	—	—	—
81. South Africa	.4027[6]	.1608[6]	.4365[6]	.4856	.4560	.1130	.0620	.5800
82. Spain	.3443	.3357	.3200	.5864	.2130	.0870	.1730	.4540
83. Sudan	.8693[3]	.0569[3]	.0874[3]	.0926	—	—	—	—
84. Sweden	.1241	.4151	.4609	.7710	.1590	.1000	.1400[9]	.4400[9]
85. Switzerland	.1139[6]	.4932[6]	.3929[6]	.5485	.1880	.0930	—	—
86. Syria	.5639	.1713	.2647	.4014	.3310	—	—	—
87. Tanzania	.8213[6]	.0390[6]	.1397[6]	.0580	—	.0780	.1380[12]	.5850[12]
88. Thailand	—	—	—	.1360	.3640	—	—	—
89. Togo	—	—	—	—	.5000	—	—	—
90. Tunisia	—	—	—	.4050	.4400	.1170	—	—

	[1]1953	[2]1955	[3]1957	[4]1958	[5]1959	[6]1960	[7]1961	[8]1962	[9]1963	[10]1964	[11]1966	[12]1967	[13]1968	[14]1969	[15]1970
91. Turkey					.7247		.0951	.1802		.3008	—	—		—	—
92. Uganda					—		—	—		.0638	—	.2000[6]		—	—
93. United Arab Republic (Egypt)					.5687[6]		.1108[6]	.3205[6]		.4048	.4160	.1480		.1880[13]	.3900[13]
94. United Kingdom					.0547[11]		.4249[11]	.5204[11]		.7955	.1830	.1150		.1500[11]	.4400[11]
95. United States of America					.0689		.3201	.6110		.7201	.1940	.0940		—	—
96. Upper Volta					—		—	—		—	—	—		—	—
97. Uruguay					.1811[9]		.2599[9]	.5630[9]		.7531	.3120	.0900		.1430[12]	.4740[12]
98. Venezuela					.3411[7]		.1757[7]	.4832[7]		.6346	.4280	.0710		.1330[8]	.4970[8]
99. Vietnam (South)					—		—	—		.2149	.2770	.0640		—	—
100. Yugoslavia					.5867[7]		.1572[7]	.2561[7]		.3184	.2090	.0870		.1850[13]	.4150[13]
101. Zambia					.2727[7]		.1212[7]	.6061[7]		.1872	.5200	.0800		.1460[5]	.5700[5]

TABLE S5. Accumulation Processes: Large Countries

Process	Constant	lnY	$(lnY)^2$	lnN	$(lnN)^2$	F	T_1	T_2	T_3	R^2	SEE	Y Mean/Range	No. of Obs.
Saving	−.335 (4.293)	.220 (10.020)	−.016 (8.580)	−.083 (3.461)	.009 (3.163)	−.810 (10.300)	−.022 (3.145)	−.013 (1.953)	−.007 (1.063)	.537	.050	602 34/3614	458
Investment	−.342 (4.370)	.219 (9.938)	−.016 (8.476)	−.080 (3.323)	.009 (3.063)	.206 (2.612)	−.023 (3.323)	−.013 (1.997)	−.007 (1.087)	.425	.050	602 34/3614	458
Government revenue	.185 (1.983)	−.130 (4.661)	.017 (6.831)	.092 (3.482)	−.011 (3.314)	−.104 (1.109)	.003 (.278)	.004 (.455)	−.001 (.132)	.676	.053	527 34/2191	342
Primary and secondary school enrollment ratio	−1.356 (3.085)	.342 (2.648)	−.014 (1.271)	.229 (1.895)	−.026 (1.777)	1.749 (4.473)	−.047 (1.280)	−.019 (.561)	−.031 (1.098)	.726	.125	563 47/3207	122

Normal Variation in Economic Structure with Level of Development*

	Per Capita Income (US$ 1964)							Variation with size at $Y = \$300$		
	$100	$200	$300	$500	$800	$1,000	$1,500	$N = 15$	$N = 30$	$N = 60$
Saving	.140	.182	.199	.213	.219	.219	.215	.222	.204	.194
Investment	.157	.199	.216	.230	.236	.236	.233	.238	.221	.212
Government revenue	.133	.156	.178	.212	.252	.273	.316	.153	.173	.182
Primary and secondary school enrollment ratio	.450	.591	.667	.757	.833	.867	.926	.605	.654	.678

t ratios in parentheses.
*N = 40; F = .02

TABLE S6. Accumulation Processes: Small Countries

Process	Constant	lnY	(lnY)²	lnN	(lnN)²	F	T_1	T_2	T_3	R^2	SEE	Y Mean/ Range	No. of Obs.
Saving	.100 (2.063)	-.011 (.645)	.004 (3.104)	-.013 (1.431)	.007 (2.277)	-.841 (45.410)	-.009 (1.898)	-.014 (3.233)	-.010 (2.509)	.776	.047	493 35/2356	974
Investment	.114 (2.370)	-.015 (.926)	.005 (3.374)	-.014 (1.533)	-.007 (2.411)	.150 (8.105)	-.009 (1.939)	-.014 (3.262)	-.011 (2.720)	.461	.047	493 35/2356	974
Government revenue	.123 (2.031)	-.043 (2.101)	.009 (4.900)	.065 (6.743)	-.017 (5.296)	-.137 (7.006)	-.017 (3.020)	-.009 (1.682)	-.010 (2.313)	.649	.047	540 35/2356	769
Primary and secondary school enrollment ratio	-1.845 (7.179)	.636 (7.239)	-.036 (4.743)	-.011 (.234)	.011 (.741)	.506 (6.317)	-.060 (2.224)	-.037 (1.515)	-.022 (1.220)	.734	.136	425 35/2243	311

Normal Variation in Economic Structure with Level of Development*

	Per Capita Income (US$ 1964)							Variation with size at Y = $300		
	$100	$200	$300	$500	$800	$1,000	$1,500	N = 2	N = 3	N = 10
Saving	.125	.148	.163	.184	.206	.217	.238	.160	.160	.173
Investment	.146	.168	.184	.205	.227	.238	.260	.181	.181	.194
Government revenue	.162	.191	.211	.241	.273	.289	.320	.189	.202	.209
Primary and secondary school enrollment ratio	.337	.529	.625	.729	.808	.840	.889	.611	.615	.648

t ratios in parentheses.
*N = 5; F = .02

TABLE S7. Accumulation Processes: Small, Primary-oriented Countries

Process	Constant	lnY	$(lnY)^2$	lnN	$(lnN)^2$	F	T_1	T_2	T_3	R^2	SEE	Y Mean/Range	No. of Obs.
Saving	.293 (3.982)	−.074 (2.883)	.010 (4.462)	−.046 (3.719)	.018 (4.211)	−.808 (30.250)	.007 (1.038)	−.009 (1.528)	−.013 (2.469)	.728	.048	327 49/1857	558
Investment	.302 (4.106)	−.077 (2.987)	.010 (4.557)	−.048 (3.861)	.018 (4.380)	.190 (7.121)	.006 (.971)	−.009 (1.591)	−.013 (2.536)	.414	.048	327 49/1857	558
Government revenue	.145 (1.525)	−.044 (1.348)	.008 (2.859)	.054 (4.017)	−.014 (2.890)	−.195 (7.794)	−.022 (2.752)	.000 (.029)	−.011 (1.928)	.511	.047	376 53/1857	411

Normal Variation in Economic Structure with Level of Development*

	Per Capita Income (US$ 1964)						
	$100	$200	$300	$500	$800	$1,000	$1,500
Saving	.122	.141	.156	.180	.206	.220	.249
Investment	.143	.160	.175	.199	.225	.239	.268
Government revenue	.162	.187	.205	.231	.259	.273	.302

t ratios in parentheses.
*$N = 5$; $F = .02$.

TABLE S8. Accumulation Processes: Small, Industry-oriented Countries

Process	Constant	$\ln Y$	$(\ln Y)^2$	$\ln N$	$(\ln N)^2$	F	T_1	T_2	T_3	R^2	SEE	Y Mean/ Range	No. of Obs.
Saving	−.180 (2.976)	.074 (3.588)	−.003 (1.614)	.056 (4.571)	−.015 (3.544)	−.874 (30.890)	−.031 (5.153)	−.023 (4.113)	−.007 (1.235)	.859	.040	715 35/2356	416
Investment	−.166 (2.784)	.070 (3.444)	−.003 (1.477)	.058 (4.744)	−.015 (3.687)	.104 (3.747)	−.031 (5.266)	−.023 (4.184)	−.008 (1.525)	.568	.040	715 35/2356	416
Government revenue	.131 (1.679)	−.052 (1.930)	.010 (4.273)	.053 (3.792)	−.014 (2.951)	−.008 (.196)	−.008 (.971)	−.011 (1.556)	−.009 (1.405)	.729	.046	729 35/2356	358

Normal Variation in Economic Structure with Level of Development*

	Per Capita Income (US$ 1964)						
	$100	$200	$300	$500	$800	$1,000	$1,500
Saving	.135	.167	.185	.205	.223	.231	.244
Investment	.156	.186	.203	.222	.239	.247	.260
Government revenue	.151	.182	.205	.239	.274	.292	.328

t ratios in parentheses.
*$N = 5$; $F = .02$

TABLE S9. Resource Allocation and Trade Processes: Large Countries

Process	Constant	$\ln Y$	$(\ln Y)^2$	$\ln N$	$(\ln N)^2$	F	T_1	T_2	T_3	R^2	SEE	Y Mean/Range	No. of Obs.
Private consumption	1.368 (10.960)	−.248 (6.850)	.016 (5.412)	.085 (2.565)	−.009 (2.361)	.428 (3.736)	.020 (2.051)	−.018 (1.925)	.008 (.896)	.481	.070	612 47/3615	451
Government consumption	.161 (2.038)	−.015 (.635)	.003 (1.483)	−.026 (1.231)	.003 (.991)	.277 (3.817)	.007 (1.194)	−.004 (.625)	−.005 (.824)	.183	.045	612 47/3615	451
Primary production	2.476 (24.180)	−.512 (17.280)	.032 (12.680)	−.147 (5.399)	.016 (4.838)	−.345 (3.694)	−.008 (.949)	−.004 (.462)	.001 (.099)	.886	.057	608 47/3551	439
Industry production	−.966 (9.509)	.290 (9.865)	−.018 (7.090)	.080 (2.946)	−.009 (2.831)	.357 (3.848)	.010 (1.221)	.003 (.334)	.001 (.123)	.731	.056	608 47/3551	439
Total exports	.477 (5.909)	−.080 (3.502)	.007 (3.675)	−.022 (.892)	−.003 (.826)	−.811 (9.966)	−.014 (1.879)	−.015 (2.120)	−.007 (1.140)	.380	.052	603 34/3615	458
Primary exports	.537 (6.047)	−.075 (2.999)	.004 (2.105)	−.068 (2.638)	.005 (1.534)	−.729 (8.006)				.633	.028	662 51/3551	129
Manufactured exports	−.079 (.751)	−.009 (.316)	.003 (1.167)	.037 (1.208)	−.005 (1.280)	.121 (1.123)				.451	.033	662 51/3551	129
Total imports	.475 (5.941)	−.081 (3.611)	.007 (3.779)	−.019 (.789)	−.003 (.928)	.202 (2.497)	−.013 (1.759)	−.014 (2.016)	−.007 (1.110)	.253	.050	603 34/3615	458

Normal Variation in Economic Structure with Level of Development*

	Per Capita Income (US$ 1964)							Variation with size at $Y = \$300$		
	$100	$200	$300	$500	$800	$1,000	$1,500	$N = 15$	$N = 30$	$N = 60$
Private consumption	.768	.709	.682	.656	.639	.633	.627	.658	.677	.687
Government consumption	.099	.109	.116	.125	.136	.141	.152	.125	.118	.113
Primary production	.458	.320	.254	.185	.136	.117	.092	.297	.263	.245
Industry production	.171	.253	.292	.334	.364	.375	.392	.272	.288	.295
Total exports	.130	.123	.123	.126	.132	.136	.144	.160	.134	.105
Primary exports	.082	.062	.049	.038	.029	.026	.021	.088	.060	.036
Manufactured exports	.016	.029	.038	.051	.064	.071	.084	.031	.037	.039
Imports	.149	.143	.142	.145	.151	.155	.164	.180	.154	.126

TABLE S10. Resource Allocation and Trade Processes: Small Countries

Process	Constant	$\ln Y$	$(\ln Y)^2$	$\ln N$	$(\ln N)^2$	F	T_1	T_2	T_3	R^2	SEE	Y Mean/Range	No. of Obs.
Private consumption	.598 (9.039)	.070 (3.114)	−.009 (4.772)	.006 (.472)	−.009 (2.176)	.734 (31.070)	.033 (5.470)	.029 (5.125)	.015 (2.980)	.607	.065	467 35/2356	1,057
Government consumption	.218 (5.655)	−.034 (2.624)	.003 (2.729)	.003 (.354)	.004 (1.490)	.156 (11.380)	−.028 (7.975)	−.019 (5.956)	−.005 (1.761)	.222	.038	467 35/2356	1,057
Primary production	2.018 (17.190)	−.457 (11.540)	.028 (8.402)	−.057 (3.283)	.012 (2.041)	.611 (18.620)	.016 (1.784)	.016 (1.908)	.014 (1.858)	.693	.087	461 52/2307	886
Industry production	−.257 (3.369)	.053 (2.059)	.003 (1.331)	.079 (7.049)	−.017 (4.503)	.200 (9.381)	.015 (2.508)	.004 (.797)	−.006 (1.252)	.699	.057	461 52/2307	886
Total exports	−.180 (1.329)	.141 (3.051)	−.009 (2.284)	−.044 (1.733)	.008 (.915)	−.422 (8.138)	−.003 (.210)	−.010 (.821)	−.012 (1.097)	.154	.131	493 35/2357	974
Primary exports	.254 (1.877)	.040 (.882)	−.007 (1.718)	−.091 (5.085)	.017 (3.489)	−.997 (20.450)				.642	.067	542 35/2357	284
Manufactured exports	−.020 (.135)	−.039 (.799)	.007 (1.727)	.056 (2.939)	−.012 (2.225)	.070 (1.335)				.332	.072	542 35/2357	284
Total imports	−.174 (1.284)	.139 (3.009)	−.009 (2.245)	−.044 (1.752)	.008 (.942)	.577 (11.130)	−.003 (.225)	−.010 (.837)	−.012 (1.115)	.192	.131	493 35/2357	974

Normal Variation in Economic Structure with Level of Development*

	Per Capita Income (US$ 1964)							Variation with size at $Y = \$300$		
	$100	$200	$300	$500	$800	$1,000	$1,500	$N = 2$	$N = 3$	$N = 10$
Private consumption	.724	.709	.697	.676	.653	.640	.616	.710	.706	.676
Government consumption	.142	.139	.139	.140	.142	.144	.148	.129	.132	.150
Primary production	.441	.319	.261	.200	.157	.141	.119	.287	.273	.253
Industry production	.136	.193	.227	.272	.315	.335	.373	.191	.210	.236
Total exports	.216	.251	.267	.284	.295	.299	.303	.291	.279	.258
Primary exports	.179	.162	.149	.130	.109	.098	.077	.195	.171	.133
Manufactured exports	.014	.035	.051	.075	.100	.113	.138	.025	.039	.058
Total imports	.237	.273	.289	.306	.317	.321	.326	.313	.301	.280

t ratios in parentheses.

*$N = 5$; $F = .02$.

TABLE S11. Resource Allocation and Trade Processes: Small, Primary-oriented Countries

Process	Constant	lnY	$(lnY)^2$	lnN	$(lnN)^2$	F	T_1	T_2	T_3	R^2	SEE	Y Mean/Range	No. of Obs.
Private consumption	.483 (4.701)	.109 (3.044)	−.013 (4.073)	.026 (1.485)	−.016 (2.704)	.758 (22.960)	.022 (2.407)	.021 (2.733)	.015 (2.133)	.563	.071	308 50/1857	633
Government consumption	.107 (1.848)	−.002 (.118)	.001 (.328)	.018 (1.804)	−.000 (.095)	.129 (6.922)	−.029 (5.800)	−.017 (3.948)	−.004 (1.007)	.199	.040	308 50/1857	633
Primary production	2.209 (14.830)	−.516 (9.974)	.034 (7.494)	−.078 (3.470)	.015 (1.988)	−.698 (15.920)	.002 (.186)	.009 (.796)	.017 (1.802)	.656	.086	315 52/1808	516
Industry production	−.213 (2.888)	.064 (2.485)	.001 (.295)	.039 (3.517)	−.010 (2.594)	.268 (12.330)	.011 (1.835)	.004 (.715)	−.008 (1.717)	.672	.043	315 52/1808	516
Total exports	.122 (.983)	.066 (1.536)	−.006 (1.482)	−.115 (5.495)	.039 (5.534)	−.816 (18.090)	−.020 (1.839)	−.011 (1.164)	−.011 (1.256)	.421	.081	327 50/1857	558
Primary exports	.505 (2.501)	−.071 (1.020)	.005 (.808)	−.074 (3.392)	.015 (2.572)	−1.043 (16.480)				.632	.074	356 57/1857	173
Manufactured exports	−.146 (3.665)	.050 (3.667)	−.004 (3.164)	.001 (.246)	.000 (.164)	.049 (3.907)				.225	.014	356 57/1857	173
Total imports	.131 (1.058)	.064 (1.471)	−.005 (1.421)	−.116 (5.573)	.040 (5.627)	.183 (4.052)	−.020 (1.883)	−.012 (1.205)	−.011 (1.304)	.099	.081	327 50/1857	558

Normal Variation in Economic Structure with Level of Development*

	Per Capita Income (US$ 1964)						
	$100	$200	$300	$500	$800	$1,000	$1,500
Private consumption	.728	.715	.701	.679	.652	.637	.607
Government consumption	.139	.141	.143	.145	.147	.149	.151
Primary production	.457	.334	.277	.222	.186	.175	.163
Industry production	.139	.188	.217	.254	.288	.304	.334
Total exports	.209	.217	.219	.219	.216	.214	.209
Primary exports	.181	.165	.158	.152	.148	.147	.146
Manufactured exports	.009	.018	.021	.024	.025	.025	.024
Total imports	.229	.236	.238	.238	.235	.233	.227

TABLE S12. Resource Allocation and Trade Processes: Small, Industry-oriented Countries

Process	Constant	$\ln Y$	$(\ln Y)^2$	$\ln N$	$(\ln N)^2$	F	T_1	T_2	T_3	R^2	SEE	Y Mean/ Range	No. of Obs.
Private consumption	.754 (9.434)	.033 (1.224)	−.006 (2.804)	−.036 (2.269)	.003 (.625)	.608 (16.080)	.049 (6.450)	.039 (5.353)	.014 (2.057)	.717	.052	704 35/2356	424
Government consumption	.411 (8.284)	−.094 (5.670)	.008 (5.654)	−.024 (2.422)	.011 (3.292)	.220 (9.357)	−.023 (4.831)	−.019 (4.245)	−.006 (1.435)	.315	.032	704 35/2356	424
Primary production	1.408 (7.187)	−.319 (4.061)	.019 (3.649)	−.036 (1.718)	.018 (2.586)	−.158 (3.443)	.048 (4.641)	.032 (3.252)	.015 (1.615)	.589	.067	664 69/2307	370
Industry production	−.980 (5.318)	.283 (4.672)	−.016 (3.160)	.125 (6.376)	−.025 (3.719)	.020 (.455)	.004 (.411)	−.004 (.414)	−.006 (.683)	.688	.063	664 69/2307	370
Total exports	−.610 (2.642)	.310 (3.961)	−.022 (3.282)	−.067 (1.417)	−.007 (.418)	−.219 (2.032)	−.007 (.298)	−.014 (.666)	−.025 (1.248)	.232	.154	715 35/2356	416
Primary exports	.139 (1.099)	.041 (1.019)	−.006 (1.754)	−.041 (1.539)	.003 (.366)	−.481 (7.057)				.466	.039	833 35/2356	111
Manufactured exports	−.374 (1.231)	.090 (.919)	−.004 (.534)	.154 (2.391)	−.044 (2.235)	−.376 (2.289)				.379	.093	833 35/2356	111
Total imports	−.607 (2.632)	.309 (3.949)	−.022 (3.272)	−.066 (1.399)	−.007 (.435)	.781 (7.234)	−.007 (.294)	−.014 (.684)	−.025 (1.245)	.319	.154	715 35/2356	416

Normal Variation in Economic Structure with Level of Development*

	Per Capita Income (US$ 1964)						
	$100	$200	$300	$500	$800	$1,000	$1,500
Private consumption	.732	.710	.695	.673	.649	.637	.614
Government consumption	.141	.131	.129	.130	.134	.137	.146
Primary production	.333	.244	.201	.155	.122	.109	.091
Industry production	.127	.216	.260	.309	.347	.363	.387
Total exports	.220	.283	.310	.334	.345	.347	.346
Primary exports	.136	.124	.114	.099	.083	.074	.056
Manufactured exports	.076	.109	.126	.145	.161	.168	.180
Total imports	.241	.304	.331	.355	.367	.369	.367

t ratios in parentheses.
*$N = 5$; $F = .02$.

TABLE S13. Saving Reduced Sample: Time-series Coefficients

Country	lnY	F	R^2	SEE	Y Mean/Range
Argentina	.102 (3.512)	−.342 (2.048)	.555	.012	697 580/809
Australia	.005 (.132)	−.436 (3.502)	.420	.021	1464 1202/1857
Austria	.076 (7.241)	−.070 (.559)	.770	.012	854 517/1248
Brazil	.061 (2.457)	−.300 (1.020)	.320	.017	195 147/238
Burma	−.033 (.553)	.566 (2.249)	.432	.030	49 34/59
Ceylon (Sri Lanka)	.089 (1.965)	−.831 (11.230)	.905	.014	136 118/162
Chile	.059 (1.007)	−.662 (2.680)	.319	.021	384 342/432
China (Taiwan)	.148 (10.640)	−.710 (5.027)	.951	.014	158 95/252
Colombia	.154 (2.980)	−.919 (3.662)	.464	.014	216 185/247
Costa Rica	.036 (.800)	−.437 (2.269)	.287	.018	329 253/429
Israel	−.046 (1.437)	−.568 (2.354)	.246	.031	859 534/1337
Italy	.054 (2.638)	−.176 (.517)	.551	.017	796 462/1190
Jamaica	.226 (7.775)	−.317 (1.735)	.885	.024	338 212/457
Japan	.091 (5.675)	.126 (.176)	.690	.032	573 251/1218
Mexico	.061 (2.839)	−.693 (2.010)	.493	.015	373 290/495
Netherlands	.079 (5.450)	−.369 (3.764)	.711	.012	1115 800/1495
Norway	−.014 (.872)	−.656 (5.247)	.638	.012	1359 1030/1836
Paraguay	−.157 (1.361)	−.055 (.280)	.139	.019	188 177/202
Peru	−.102 (2.402)	−.086 (.456)	.253	.024	251 194/296
Philippines	.089 (2.976)	−.706 (3.075)	.437	.019	136 97/176

Country						
Denmark	.081 (4.540)	−.386 (1.794)	.549	.013	1436	1190/1961
Dominican Republic	−.027 (.252)	−.648 (2.964)	.521	.033	215	172/245
Ecuador	−.054 (1.267)	−.285 (1.758)	.497	.011	177	150/205
Finland	.058 (3.631)	−.496 (2.743)	.456	.013	1194	802/1680
France	.143 (11.860)	−.936 (3.500)	.894	.012	1413	987/2091
Germany (West)	.065 (7.117)	−.411 (1.831)	.772	.011	1274	703/1862
Ghana	−.025 (.318)	−.695 (4.370)	.733	.027	144	114/162
Greece	.129 (10.550)	−.147 (1.011)	.868	.016	449	268/712
Guatemala	.062 (1.035)	−.154 (.526)	.060	.020	258	227/300
Honduras	.195 (2.542)	−1.105 (6.691)	.748	.018	195	170/220
Ireland	.173 (9.554)	−.485 (7.555)	.931	.011	713	579/940
Portugal	.083 (6.907)	−.727 (4.120)	.798	.013	289	194/436
Puerto Rico	.160 (7.419)	−.580 (3.466)	.955	.015	749	453/1195
South Africa	.094 (7.636)	−.414 (6.106)	.861	.009	471	369/634
Switzerland	.243 (14.840)	.115 (.966)	.930	.011	1823	1359/2296
Thailand	.193 (14.720)	−.810 (5.380)	.928	.011	94	67/138
Turkey	.114 (8.429)	−.568 (2.610)	.816	.010	219	156/294
United Kingdom	.154 (10.230)	−.345 (2.024)	.882	.008	1352	1093/1610
U.S.A.	−.026 (1.268)	−1.071 (1.410)	.212	.011	2871	2358/3614
Venezuela	−.090 (3.039)	−.072 (.398)	.352	.026	669	446/852
Yugoslavia	.043 (1.570)	.019 (.030)	.162	.035	306	166/473

t ratios in parentheses.

TABLE S14. Regressions with Exogenous Trade Variables

Process	Constant	$\ln Y$	$(\ln Y)^2$	$\ln N$	$(\ln N)^2$	F	E_p	E_m	E_s	R^2	SEE	Y Mean/Range	No. of Obs.
Production													
Primary	1.546	−.342	.020	−.029	.006		.559	−.244	−.303	.816	.069	567	304
	(11.670)	(7.569)	(5.395)	(2.512)	(3.002)		(12.300)	(4.173)	(2.848)			52/3551	
	1.613	−.353	.021	−.035	.006	−.136	.473	−.255	−.306	.817	.069	567	304
	(11.550)	(7.728)	(5.551)	(2.858)	(3.148)	(1.489)	(6.396)	(4.332)	(2.883)			52/3551	
Industry	−.345	.131	−.006	.039	−.005		−.297	.323	.089	.836	.043	567	304
	(4.210)	(4.681)	(2.537)	(5.394)	(4.429)		(10.560)	(8.928)	(1.351)			52/3551	
	−.330	.128	−.006	.037	−.005	−.030	−.317	.320	.088	.836	.043	567	304
	(3.808)	(4.514)	(2.445)	(4.946)	(4.343)	(.536)	(6.902)	(8.785)	(1.339)			52/3551	
Utilities	−.001	.007	.000	.012	−.002		−.017	−.003	.267	.381	.024	567	304
	(.016)	(.460)	(.284)	(2.950)	(2.640)		(1.070)	(.130)	(7.132)			52/3551	
	.013	.005	.001	.011	−.002	−.027	−.034	−.005	.266	.382	.024	567	304
	(.254)	(.309)	(.388)	(2.536)	(2.536)	(.838)	(1.318)	(.231)	(7.110)			52/3551	
Services	−.200	.204	−.015	−.022	.001		−.245	−.076	−.052	.320	.061	567	304
	(1.735)	(5.175)	(4.502)	(2.135)	(.764)		(6.180)	(1.496)	(.566)			52/3551	
	−.296	.220	−.016	−.013	.001	.193	−.122	−.061	−.048	.333	.060	567	304
	(2.443)	(5.560)	(4.813)	(1.277)	(.509)	(2.442)	(1.903)	(1.199)	(.522)			52/3551	

Resource Use

Private consumption

1.092	−.019	−.003	−.055	.005		−.648	−.405	−.274	.692	.056	592	400
(12.000)	(.607)	(1.024)	(6.840)	(3.692)		(20.010)	(5.811)	(3.617)				
.865	.023	−.006	−.039	.005	.458	−.368	−.305	−.302	.733	.052	35/3551	
(9.628)	(.782)	(2.189)	(5.003)	(3.485)	(7.739)	(7.802)	(4.600)	(4.271)				

Government consumption

.458	−.123	.011	.014	−.004		−.021	−.030	.220	.186	.037	592	400
(7.512)	(5.840)	(6.004)	(2.602)	(3.677)		(.952)	(.638)	(4.340)				
.333	−.100	.009	.023	−.004	.252	.133	.025	.204	.259	.036	35/3551	
(5.400)	(4.869)	(5.337)	(4.280)	(4.217)	(6.200)	(4.122)	(.557)	(4.218)				

Investment

−.053	.050	−.002	.006	−.000		.057	.216	.115	.387	.048	592	400
(.674)	(1.810)	(.838)	(.845)	(.319)		(2.030)	(3.569)	(1.751)				
−.197	.076	−.004	.016	−.001	.290	.235	.280	.097	.430	.047	35/3551	
(2.443)	(2.844)	(1.636)	(2.298)	(.659)	(5.448)	(5.531)	(4.690)	(1.531)				

Accumulation

Saving

−.464	.105	−.005	.050	−.003		.644	.204	.316	.630	.061	584	348
(4.700)	(3.096)	(1.647)	(5.368)	(1.852)		(16.870)	(4.207)	(3.717)				
−.202	.075	−.003	.018	−.001	−.732	.209	.064	.205	.782	.047	35/3551	
(2.599)	(2.839)	(1.421)	(2.441)	(.892)	(15.360)	(5.121)	(1.669)	(3.112)				

Government revenue

.334	−.125	.016	.023	−.004		.148	.148	.051	.688	.051	607	269
(3.421)	(3.682)	(5.438)	(2.387)	(1.995)		(4.032)	(2.384)	(.609)				
.346	−.125	.016	.021	−.004	−.053	.119	.147	.051	.688	.051	35/2356	
(3.482)	(3.685)	(5.401)	(2.154)	(1.962)	(.670)	(2.081)	(2.352)	(.608)				

t ratios in parentheses.

TABLE S15. Saving and Export Patterns: Income Split

Process	Constant	$\ln Y$	$(\ln Y)^2$	$\ln N$	$(\ln V)^2$	F	R^2	SEE	Y Mean/Range	No. of Obs.
Saving										
Per capita GNP less than $200	.399 (.937)	-.157 (.854)	.022 (1.140)	-.001 (.073)	.000 (.218)	-.909 (14.910)	.667	.048	133 35/252	157
Per capita GNP $200 to $800	-1.810 (2.103)	.595 (2.123)	-.043 (1.891)	-.029 (2.110)	.009 (3.032)	-.912 (18.890)	.798	.048	493 215/1218	123
Per capita GNP greater than $800	-.349 (.137)	.185 (.270)	-.014 (.304)	.013 (.655)	-.004 (1.276)	-1.298 (9.623)	.732	.029	1792 1052/3551	68
Exports										
Per capita GNP less than $200	-.203 (.359)	.181 (.741)	-.016 (.618)	-.022 (1.625)	-.003 (1.160)	-.772 (9.527)	.541	.063	133 35/252	157
Per capita GNP $200 to $800	.408 (.228)	-.058 (.099)	.009 (.178)	-.054 (1.862)	-.004 (.583)	-.805 (7.964)	.589	.100	493 215/1218	123
Per capita GNP greater than $800	2.246 (.355)	-.408 (.240)	.020 (.179)	-.009 (.178)	-.007 (.784)	-1.104 (3.304)	.501	.072	1792 1052/3551	68

t ratios in parentheses.

LE S16. Short-run Patterns: Full and Reduced Samples

ss	$\ln Y$	$(\ln Y)^2$	F	T_1	T_2	T_3	R^2	SEE	Y Mean/Range	No. of Obs.
g: Full	.109 (3.755)	−.002 (1.004)	−.649 (29.626)	.002 (.582)	−.003 (1.077)	−.002 (1.081)	.511	.028	528 34/3614	1,432
Reduced	.158 (4.568)	−.004 (1.536)	−.555 (17.313)	.019 (4.327)	.016 (4.457)	.010 (3.722)	.491	.024	653 34/3614	820
ment: Full	.127 (4.370)	−.004 (1.712)	.337 (15.343)	.000 (.008)	−.004 (1.528)	−.004 (1.619)	.314	.028	528 34/3614	1,432
Reduced	.179 (5.120)	−.006 (2.178)	.448 (13.767)	.018 (4.045)	.015 (4.234)	.010 (3.560)	.402	.024	653 34/3614	820
al inflow: Full	.160 (4.500)	−.018 (6.300)		−.037 (8.100)	−.016 (4.500)	−.006 (2.300)	.078	.035	528 34/3614	1,432
Reduced	.093 (2.400)	−.012 (4.000)		−.030 (6.200)	−.017 (4.400)	−.010 (3.400)	.075	.027	653 34/3614	820
ts: Full	.015 (.347)	.000 (.062)	−.580 (18.259)	.007 (1.312)	.002 (.382)	−.001 (.332)	.224	.040	528 34/3614	1,432
Reduced	.089 (2.296)	−.000 (.030)	−.570 (15.849)	.024 (6.346)	.024 (6.197)	.010 (3.213)	.362	.027	653 34/3614	820
ts: Full	.018 (.432)	−.000 (.038)	.420 (13.215)	.007 (1.296)	.002 (.372)	−.001 (.394)	.120	.040	528 34/3614	1,432
Reduced	.089 (2.294)	−.000 (.032)	.433 (12.012)	.032 (6.416)	.025 (6.286)	.010 (3.244)	.218	.027	653 34/3614	820
nment revenue: Full	−.096 (3.855)	.012 (5.878)	.043 (2.337)	−.018 (7.756)	−.018 (6.862)	−.012 (6.905)	.399	.019	536 34/2356	1,111
Reduced	−.034 (.796)	.009 (2.851)	.105 (3.404)	−.018 (3.202)	−.015 (3.752)	−.012 (3.912)	.495	.019	792 34/2306	468
ry production: Full	−.073 (2.313)	.003 (.954)	−.241 (11.491)	.059 (15.751)	.040 (13.674)	.022 (10.099)	.521	.027	510 47/3551	1,325
Reduced	−.036 (.901)	−.003 (.868)	−.100 (4.005)	.040 (8.928)	.020 (5.744)	.008 (3.019)	.589	.022	677 67/3432	756
ry production: Full	.160 (7.190)	−.009 (5.141)	.115 (7.721)	−.018 (6.847)	−.014 (6.993)	−.010 (6.236)	.380	.019	510 47/3551	1,325
Reduced	.158 (4.945)	−.009 (3.349)	.138 (6.804)	−.008 (2.068)	−.007 (2.285)	−.003 (1.097)	.351	.018	677 67/3432	756
es: Full	−.140 (4.658)	.011 (4.381)	.105 (5.224)	−.031 (8.552)	−.021 (7.375)	−.010 (5.020)	.143	.026	510 47/3551	1,325
Reduced	−.248 (6.020)	.020 (5.995)	−.031 (1.170)	−.029 (6.270)	−.014 (3.676)	−.007 (2.330)	.190	.024	677 67/3432	756

s in parentheses.

TABLE S17. Structure of Production: Cross Sections

Shares of Production	Year	Constant	lnY	(lnY)²	lnN	(lnN)²	F	R²	SEE	No. of Obs.
Full Sample										
Primary:	1955	2.295 (5.562)	−.553 (3.985)	.037 (3.153)	−.022 (.837)	.000 (.031)	−.673 (5.483)	.804	.068	54
	1965	2.144 (7.384)	−.474 (4.792)	.029 (3.420)	−.061 (2.526)	.008 (1.855)	−.662 (6.079)	.790	.082	85
Industry:	1955	−.965 (2.646)	.294 (2.399)	−.017 (1.661)	.066 (2.787)	−.009 (1.777)	.154 (1.415)	.717	.060	54
	1965	−.457 (2.340)	.122 (1.840)	−.003 (.574)	.066 (4.067)	−.008 (2.865)	.261 (3.563)	.763	.055	85
Services:	1955	−.470 (.916)	.306 (1.774)	−.025 (1.752)	−.058 (1.732)	.012 (1.672)	.512 (3.352)	.333	.085	54
	1965	−.593 (2.322)	.312 (3.594)	−.023 (3.195)	−.014 (.661)	.002 (.466)	.389 (4.066)	.379	.072	85
Reduced Sample										
Primary:	1955	1.809 (3.261)	−.395 (2.169)	.024 (1.599)	−.015 (.582)	−.001 (.204)	−.623 (3.574)	.730	.064	42
	1965	1.851 (3.567)	−.405 (2.456)	.024 (1.838)	−.010 (.368)	−.002 (.474)	−.619 (3.617)	.796	.054	42
Industry:	1955	−.594 (1.057)	.179 (.967)	−.008 (.540)	.072 (2.702)	−.011 (1.935)	.099 (.561)	.629	.065	42
	1965	−.949 (1.589)	.286 (1.507)	−.016 (1.083)	.073 (2.381)	−.011 (1.949)	.045 (.230)	.643	.062	42
Services:	1955	−.236 (.370)	.225 (1.075)	−.018 (1.067)	−.073 (2.402)	.015 (2.446)	.501 (2.502)	.313	.073	42
	1965	.189 (.347)	.084 (.484)	−.006 (.467)	−.069 (2.460)	.014 (2.760)	.538 (2.992)	.365	.059	42

t ratios in parentheses.

BIBLIOGRAPHY

Adelman, I. 1963. An economic analysis of population growth. *American Economic Review* 53 (June): 314-39.

Adelman, I., and H. B. Chenery. 1966. Foreign aid and economic development: The case of Greece. *Review of Economics and Statistics* 48 (February): 1-19.

Adelman, I., and C. Morris. 1967. *Society, Politics, and Economic Development.* Baltimore: Johns Hopkins University Press.

———. 1971. An anatomy of income distribution patterns in developing nations: A summary of findings. IBRD Staff Working Paper no. 116.

———. 1973. *Economic Growth and Social Equity in Developing Countries.* Stanford: Stanford University Press.

Ahluwalia, M. S., and H. B. Chenery. 1974. The economic framework. In *Redistribution with Growth,* H. B. Chenery and associates. London: Oxford University Press.

Arrow, K., H. B. Chenery, B. Minhas, and R. Solow. 1961. Capital-labor substitution and economic efficiency. *Review of Economics and Statistics* 43 (August): 225-50.

Bahl, R. 1971. A regression approach to tax effort and tax ratio analysis. International Monetary Fund, *Staff Papers* 18 (November): 570-612.

Balassa, B. 1961. Patterns of industrial growth: Comment. *American Economic Review* 51 (June): 394-7.

———. 1964. The purchasing-power parity doctrine: A reappraisal. *Journal of Political Economy* 72 (December): 584-96.

———. 1966. Tariff reductions and trade in manufactures among the industrial countries. *American Economic Review* 56 (June): 466-73.

———. 1971. *The Structure of Protection in Developing Countries.* Baltimore: Johns Hopkins University Press.

———. 1973. Just how misleading are official exchange rate conversions? *Economic Journal* 83 (December): 1258-66.

Becker, G. S. 1960. An economic analysis of fertility. In *Demographic and Economic Change in Developed Countries.* Universities–National Bureau Conference, Series 11. Princeton: Princeton University Press.

Beckerman, W. 1966. International comparisons of real incomes. Paris: Development Centre, Organization for Economic Cooperation and Development.

Beckerman, W., and R. Bacon. 1966. International comparisons of income levels: A suggested new measure. *Economic Journal* 76 (September): 519-36.

Behrman, J. R. 1972. Sectoral investment determination in a developing economy. *American Economic Review* 62 (December): 825-41.

Bhagwati, J. 1964. The pure theory of international trade. *Economic Journal* 74 (March): 1-84.

Bogue, D. J. 1969. *Principles of Demography.* New York: Wiley.

Bruno, M. 1962. *Interdependence, Resource Use, and Structural Change in Israel,* Special Studies no. 2. Jerusalem: Bank of Israel Research Department.

Carter, N. G. and H. Elkington. 1974. A handbook of expected values of structural characteristics. IBRD Staff Working Paper no. 154 (revised).

Chenery, H. B. 1960. Patterns of industrial growth. *American Economic Review* 50 (September): 624-54.

―――. 1961. Comparative advantage and development policy. *American Economic Review* 51 (March): 18-51.

―――. 1964. Land: The effects of resources on economic growth. In *Economic Development with Special Reference to East Asia,* ed. K. Berrill. New York: St. Martin's.

―――. 1965. The process of industrialization. Paper presented to the World Congress of the Econometric Society, Rome.

―――. 1970. Alternative patterns of development. Harvard University Center for International Affairs, Economic Development Report no. 163.

―――. 1971. Targets for development. In *The Widening Gap,* ed. B. Ward, I. D. Runnalls, and L. D'Anjou. New York: Columbia University Press.

―――. 1973. Alternative strategies for development. IBRD Staff Working Paper no. 165.

Chenery, H. B., and associates. 1974. *Redistribution with Growth.* London: Oxford University Press.

Chenery, H. B., and N. G. Carter. 1973. Foreign assistance and development performance. *American Economic Review* 63 (May): 459-68.

Chenery, H. B., and P. Eckstein. 1970. Development alternatives for Latin America. *Journal of Political Economy* 78 (August): 966-1006.

Chenery, H. B., H. Elkington, and C. Sims. 1970. A uniform analysis of development patterns. Harvard University Center for International Affairs, Economic Development Report no. 148.

Chenery, H. B., and H. Hughes. 1972. The international division of labor: The case of industry. In *Towards a New World Economy,* Papers and proceedings of the 5th European Conference of the Society for International Development, The Hague, 1971. Rotterdam: Rotterdam University Press.

Chenery, H. B., S. Shishido, and T. Watanabe. 1962. The patterns of Japanese growth, 1914-54. *Econometrica* 30 (January): 98-139.

Chenery, H. B., and L. Taylor. 1968. Development patterns: Among countries and over time. *Review of Economics and Statistics* 50 (November): 391-416.

CIAP. 1968. La brecha externa de la América Latina, 1968-73. Comité Inter-Americano de la Alianza para el Progreso (Pan American Union), Washington, D.C.

Clague, C., and V. Tanzi. 1972. Human capital, natural resources, and the purchasing-power parity doctrine: Some empirical results. *Economia Internazionale* 25 (February): 3-17.

Clark, C. 1940 (2d ed. 1951, 3d ed. 1957). *The conditions of economic progress.* London: Macmillan.

Cline, W. R. 1973. Income distribution and economic development: A survey, and tests for selected Latin American cities. Paper presented for Estudios Conjuntos Sobre Integración Económica Latino Americana (ECIEL) International Conference on Consumption, Income, and Prices; Hamburg. Washington, D.C.: The Brookings Institution. Mimeographed.

David, P.A. 1972. Just how misleading are official exchange rate conversions? *Economic Journal* 82 (September): 979-90.

————. 1973. A reply to Professor Balassa. *Economic Journal* 83 (December): 1267-76.

Deutsch, K. W. 1961. Social mobilization and political development. *American Political Science Review* 55 (September): 493-514.

Deutsch, K. W., and A. Eckstein. 1961. National industrialization and the declining share of the international economic sector, 1890-1959. *World Politics* 13 (January): 267-99.

Fei, J. C., and G. Ranis. 1964. *Development of the Labor Surplus Economy.* Homewood, Ill.: Irwin.

Fisher, A.G.B. 1939. Production, primary, secondary, and tertiary. *Economic Record* 15 (June): 24-38.

Fishlow, A. 1972. Brazilian size distribution of income. *American Economic Review* 62 (May): 390-402.

Friedlander, S., and M. Silver. 1967. A quantitative study of the determinants of fertility behavior. *Demography* 4 (February): 30-70.

Friedman, M. 1957. *A Theory of the Consumption Function.* Princeton: Princeton University Press.

Fuchs, V., ed. 1969. *Production and Productivity in the Service Industries.* New York: National Bureau of Economic Research, distributed by Columbia University Press.

Goldberger, A. S. 1964. *Econometric Theory.* New York: Wiley.

Gregory, P. 1970. *Socialist and Nonsocialist Industrialization Patterns: A Comparative Appraisal.* New York, Washington, and London: Praeger.

Griffin, K. B., and J. L. Enos. 1970. Foreign assistance: objectives and consequences. *Economic Development and Cultural Change* 18 (April): 313-27.

Griliches, Z., and V. Ringstad. 1970. Error-in-the-variables bias in nonlinear contexts. *Econometrica* 38 (March): 368-70.

Harris, J. R., and M. P. Todaro. 1968. Urban unemployment in East Africa: An economic analysis of policy alternatives. *East African Economic Review,* Nairobi, vol. 4, New Series, no. 2 (December): 17-36.

Heer, D. M. 1966. Economic development and fertility. *Demography* 3 (May): 423-44.

Hinrichs, H. H. 1965. Determinants of government revenue shares among less developed countries. *Economic Journal* 75 (September): 546-56.

————. 1966. *A General Theory of Tax Structure Change during Economic Development.* Cambridge: Law School of Harvard University.

Hirschman, A. O. 1945. *National Power and the Structure of Foreign Trade.* Berkeley: University of California Press.

————. 1958. *The Strategy of Economic Development.* New Haven: Yale University Press.

Hooley, R. W. 1967. The measurement of capital formation in underdeveloped countries. *Review of Economics and Statistics* 49 (May): 199-208.

Houthakker, H. S. 1957. An international comparison of household expenditure patterns: Commemorating the centenary of Engel's Law. *Econometrica* 25 (October): 532-51.

————. 1961. An international comparison of personal saving. Proceedings of the 32d Session of the International Statistical Institute, Tokyo. *Bulletin de l'Institut International de Statistique* 38, pt 2: 56-69.

————. 1965. On some determinants of savings in the developed and underdeveloped countries. In *Problems of Economic Development,* ed. E.A.G. Robinson. London: Macmillan.

Jain, S., and A. Tiemann. 1973. The size distribution of income: A compilation of data. IBRD Development Research Center, Discussion Papers no. 4.

Johansen, L. 1960. *A Multisectoral Study of Economic Growth.* Amsterdam: North Holland.

Johnston, J. 1972. *Econometric Methods.* 2d ed. New York: McGraw-Hill.

Kelley, A. C., and J. G. Williamson. 1973. Modelling economic development and general equilibrium histories. *American Economic Review* 63 (May): 450-8.

Kelley, A. C., J. G. Williamson, and R. J. Cheetham. 1972. *Dualistic Economic Development.* Chicago: University of Chicago Press.

Kindleberger, C. 1962. *Foreign Trade and the National Economy.* New Haven: Yale University Press.

Kravis, I. B., Z. Kenessey, A. Heston, and R. Summers. 1974. A system of international comparison of gross product and purchasing power. UN International Comparison Project. Washington, D.C.: IBRD. Mimeographed draft. Also forthcoming from Johns Hopkins University Press under same or similar title.

Kuznets, S. 1955. Economic growth and income inequality. *American Economic Review* 49 (March): 1-28.

———. 1960*a*. Economic growth of small nations. In *Economic Consequences of the Size of Nations,* ed. E.A.G. Robinson. London: Macmillan.

———. 1960*b*. Quantitative aspects of the economic growth of nations, V: Capital formation proportions: International comparisons for recent years. *Economic Development and Cultural Change,* vol. 8, no. 4, pt. 2 (July): 1-96.

———. 1962. Quantitative aspects of the economic growth of nations, VII: The share and structure of consumption. *Economic Development and Cultural Change,* vol. 10, no. 2, pt. 2 (January): 1-92.

———. 1963. Quantitative aspects of the economic growth of nations, VIII: Distribution of income by size. *Economic Development and Cultural Change,* vol. 11, no. 2, pt. 2 (January): 1-80.

———. 1966. *Modern Economic Growth.* New Haven: Yale University Press.

———. 1967. Quantitative aspects of the economic growth of nations, X: Level and structure of foreign trade: Long-term trends. *Economic Development and Cultural Change,* vol. 15, no. 2, pt. 2 (January): 1-140.

———. 1971. *Economic Growth of Nations: Total Output and Production Structure.* Cambridge: Belknap Press of Harvard University Press.

Landau, L. 1969. Differences in saving ratios among Latin American countries. Unpublished doctoral dissertation at Harvard University.

———. 1971. Saving functions in Latin America. In *Studies in Development Planning,* ed. H. B. Chenery. Cambridge: Harvard University Press.

Leontief, W. et al. 1953. *Studies in the Structure of the American Economy.* New York: Oxford University Press.

Leser, C.E.V. 1963. Forms of Engel functions. *Econometrica* 31 (October): 694-703.

Lewis, W. A. 1954. Economic development with unlimited supplies of labor. *The Manchester School* 22 (May): 139-91.

———. 1955. *The Theory of Economic Growth.* London: Allen and Unwin.

Linder, S. B. 1961. *An Essay on Trade and Transformation.* New York: Wiley.

Lipsey, R. E. 1963. *Price and Quantity Trends in the Foreign Trade of the United States.* New York: National Bureau of Economic Research.

Little, I. M., T. Scitovsky, and M. Scott. 1970. *Industry and Trade in Some Developing Countries: A Comparative Study.* London: Oxford University Press.

Liu, Ta-Chung. 1960. Underidentification, structural estimation, and forecasting. *Econometrica* 28 (October): 855-65.

Lluch, C. 1973. The extended linear expenditure system. *European Economic Review* 4 (April): 21-32.

Lluch, C., and A. Powell. 1973. International comparisons of expenditure and saving patterns. IBRD Development Research Center, Discussion Papers no. 2.

Lluch, C., and R. Williams. 1973. Cross-country demand and savings patterns: An application of the extended linear expenditure system. IBRD Development Research Center (mimeo).

Lotz, J. R., and E. R. Morss. 1967. Measuring "tax effort" in developing countries. International Monetary Fund, *Staff Papers* 14 (November): 478-97.

Meerman, J. 1972. Fiscal incidence in empirical studies of income distribution in poor countries. U.S. Agency for International Development, AID Discussion Paper no. 25.

Mikesell, R. F., and J. E. Zinser. 1973. The nature of the savings function in developing countries: A survey of the theoretical and empirical literature. *Journal of Economic Literature* 11 (March): 1-26.

Modigliani, F. 1965. The life cycle hypothesis of saving. Paper read at the First Congress of the Econometric Society, Rome.

Musgrave, R. A. 1969. *Fiscal Systems.* New Haven and London: Yale University Press.

Myrdal, G. 1957. *Economic Theory and Underdeveloped Regions.* London: Duckworth.

Nicholson, J. L. 1957. The general form of the adding-up criterion. *Journal of the Royal Statistical Society,* Series A (General), vol. 120, pt. 1: 84-5.

Nurkse, R. 1959. *Patterns of Trade and Development.* The Wicksell Lectures. Stockholm: Almquist and Wiksell.

Ofer, G. 1973. *The Service Sector in Soviet Economic Growth: A Comparative Study.* Cambridge: Harvard University Press.

Oshima, H. T. 1957. Share of government in gross national product for various countries. *American Economic Review* 47 (June): 381-90.

Pack, H. 1971. *Structural Change and Economic Policy in Israel.* New Haven and London: Yale University Press.

Papanek, G. F. 1972. The effect of aid and other resource transfers on savings and growth in less developed countries. *Economic Journal* 82 (September): 934-50.

Peacock, A. T., and J. Wiseman. 1961. *The Growth of Public Expenditures in the United Kingdom.* National Bureau of Economic Research. Princeton: Princeton University Press.

Phillips, L., H. Votey, and D. E. Maxwell. 1969. A synthesis of the economic and demographic models of fertility: An econometric test. *Review of Economics and Statistics* 51 (August): 298-308.

Please, S. 1967. Saving through taxation—reality or mirage. IBRD *Finance and Development* 4 (March): 24-32.

Rich, W. 1973. Smaller families through social and economic progress. Monograph Series no. 7. Washington: Overseas Development Council.

Rosenstein-Rodan, P. N. 1943. Problems of industrialization of Eastern and Southeastern Europe. *Economic Journal* 53 (June–September): 202-11.

Rostow, W. W. 1956. The take-off into self-sustained growth. *Economic Journal* 66 (March): 25-48.

Samuelson, P. A. 1964. Theoretical notes on trade problems. *Review of Economics and Statistics* 46 (May): 145-54.

Schydlowsky, D., and M. Syrquin. 1972. The estimation of CES production functions and neutral efficiency levels using effective rates of protection as price deflators. *Review of Economics and Statistics* 54 (February): 79-83.

Scitovsky, T. 1959. Growth—balanced or unbalanced? In *The Allocation of Economic Resources,* ed. M. Abramovitz et al. Stanford: Stanford University Press.

Shourie, A. 1972. The use of macroeconomic regression models of developing countries for forecasts and policy prescription: Some reflections on current practice. *Oxford Economic Papers* 24 (March): 1-35.

Sombart, W. 1913. *Die Deutsche Volkswirtschaft im neunzehnten Jahrhundert.* 3d ed. Berlin: Bond.

Syrquin, M. 1970. Production functions and regional efficiency in the manufacturing sector in Mexico, 1965. Unpublished doctoral dissertation at Harvard University.

———. 1974. The effect of sample composition on the estimation of development patterns. IBRD Working Paper forthcoming.

Taylor, L. 1969. Development patterns: A simulation study. *Quarterly Journal of Economics* 83 (May): 220-41.

Temin, P. 1967. A time-series test of patterns of industrial growth. *Economic Development and Cultural Change* 15 (January): 174-82.

Theil, H. 1971. *Principles of Econometrics.* New York: Wiley.

Todaro, M. P. 1969. A model of labor migration and urban unemployment in less developed countries. *American Economic Review* 59 (March): 138-48.

United Nations, Department of Economic and Social Affairs. 1963. *A Study of Industrial Growth.* New York.

Weintraub, R. 1962. The birth rate and economic development: An empirical study. *Econometrica* 15 (October): 812-17.

Weisskoff, R. 1969. Income distribution and economic growth: An international comparison. Unpublished doctoral dissertation at Harvard University.

———. 1970. Income distribution and economic growth in Puerto Rico, Argentina and Mexico. *Review of Income and Wealth,* vol. 16, no. 4 (December): 303-32.

————. 1971. Demand elasticities for a developing economy: An international comparison of consumption patterns. In *Studies in Development Planning,* ed. H. B. Chenery. Cambridge: Harvard University Press.

Weisskopf, T. E. 1972. The impact of foreign capital inflow on domestic savings in underdeveloped countries. *Journal of International Economics* 2 (February): 25-38.

Williamson, J. G. 1961. Public expenditure and revenue: An international comparison. *The Manchester School* 29 (January): 43-56.

————. 1968. Personal saving in developing nations: An intertemporal cross-section from Asia. *Economic Record* 44 (June): 194-210.

Willis, R. J. 1973. A new approach to the economic theory of fertility behavior. *Journal of Political Economy,* vol. 81 (March–April), no. 2, pt. 2: S14–S64.

SUBJECT INDEX

The letter *f, t,* or *n* indicates the reference will be found in a figure, table, or note, respectively. The tabular material following page 185 of the Statistical Appendix is not indexed.

A

Absolute export bias, 69n, 155
Accumulation estimates, 124t
Accumulation pattern, 122-128
  and income effect, 122
  and time trends, 122
Accumulation process, 8, 23-31, 122
  basic regressions, 26, 30t
  definition, 23
  developed countries, 110t
  and income distribution, 22
  income level effect on, 108
  less developed countries, 111t
  regression analysis, 69
  statistical analysis, 25-26
Aggregation of data and cross-country patterns, 138
Agriculture, 34, 34n, 60
Agriculture share time trends effect, 130n
Allocation; allocation pattern, etc.; *see* resource allocation, etc.; *see also* development pattern
Argentina, 54
  exports pattern, 88
  exports share reduction, 131
  income distribution, 60
Asymptotes,
  of development process, 8, 135-136
Australia, 10
Austria, 10
Average time series, 118, 167

B

Balance of payments
  and capital inflow, 132
Balanced allocation; *see* balanced countries pattern
Balanced countries pattern, 23, 32, 33, 54, 105, 137
  analysis, 103t
  definition, 104

Balanced export strategy in developed countries, 131
Balanced growth theory; *see* balanced countries pattern
Basic allocation pattern; *see* resource allocation pattern
Basic development process; *see* development process
Basic metal industry, 78
Belgium, 10
Best linear unbiased estimates, 159
Birth rate, 7
  augmented regressions, 59t
  effect on labor supply, 47
  and income level, 56, 57f
  Mexico, 58
  Nicaragua, 58
  per capita GNP, 57t
  South Africa, 58
  Venezuela, 58
Brazil, 54
  exports pattern, 89
  exports share reduction, 131

C

Canada, 10
Capital inflow
  adjustment changes in, 132-133
  and allocation of capital and labor, 65
  and balance of payments, 132
  and cross-section analysis, 123
  and development policy, 137
  at excessive levels, 106
  and exports, 133
  and GDP, 128
  and government revenue, 26
  impact on trade pattern, 65
  and investment, 132
  Korea, 101
  long- and short-run comparison, 133
  and low income level, 31
  Pakistan, 101

and primary exports, 67, 101
and saving, 126f, 132, 133
and saving and investment, 123, 125
statistical use defined, 18n
and tax base, 128
and time-series analysis, 123
time-series and cross-section estimates, 128
and trade, 43
Capital movements, 134
Capital outflow, 127n
Ceylon (Sri Lanka)
income distribution, 63
Chemicals industry, 78
Chile, 54
primary export bias, 90
Clustering techniques, 162n
Colombia, 54
exports pattern, 89
Commodities
relative prices, 148
Comparative analysis; see cross-country pattern; cross-section analysis
Consumption
and income variation, 119
Consumption, food; see food consumption
Consumption functions, 117
Consumption, private; see private consumption
Convergence hypothesis, 33, 66
Costa Rica
income distribution, 63
Cross-country pattern, 3-22; see also cross-section analysis
and aggregation of data, 138
and basic processes, 128
and industry exports, 138
long-run, 129
Cross-section analysis, 117-121, 141, 167-169; see also cross-country pattern
basis for, 16
capital inflow relationship, 123
and lags in development pattern, 107-108
and process interaction, 43
sample for, 119
and social/technological change, 134
statistical procedure, 16
and time series compared, 133
and trade orientation index, 68

Cross-section estimates
bias effect, 146, 148
Cross-section patterns; see cross-section analysis
Cross-sections, annual, 170-172, 175
Czechoslovakia, 10

D

Death rate, 7, 58n
effect on labor supply, 47
and income level, 56
and per capita GNP, 57f
Declining trade theory, 132
Demand factor, 5
Demand growth, 32
Demand shift, 45
Demographic process, 47-63
basic regressions, 49t
Demographic transition 7, 56-59
Denmark, 10
Developed countries
accumulation processes, 110t
balanced export strategy, 131
code names, 51t
decline in primary share of production, 129
definition, 10
dichotomy with less developed, 107
growth compared with less developed, 135
leadership role in, 108
list of those in study, 12t
regression technique problems in, 108
and resource allocation, 113t
sampling for statistical study of patterns, 107-108
socioeconomic variables effect, 58
time trends vs. less developed countries, 116
trade patterns, 132
Development level
and exports, 130, 132
normal variability by income, 21t
Development pattern, 11, 64-116; see also resource allocation pattern
defined, 4
demand effect on, 5
and development policy, 137
equations discussed, 141-142

regression analysis, 112
and trade orientation index, 68
typology, 101-107
Development policy, 3
  and capital inflow, 137
  and industry exports, 137
  and trade, 137
Development process, 6, 7, 65, 135
  asymptote setting, 8
  large countries, advantages in, 89
  regression analysis, 66
  timing differences, 22
Development strategy, 10, 65
Development theory, 7, 64, 106, 136, 137
  and income distribution, 138
Disaggregated model, 7
Distributional process, 47-63
  basic regression, 49t
Domestic demand, 9t, 32
  and per capita GNP, 35f
  and trade, 40
  and trade pattern, 65
Domestic production
  and trade pattern, 74
Double-log form, 142
Dual economy theory, 6, 23, 48, 60, 61, 63

E

Econometric procedure, 10
Economic dualism; see dual economy theory
Education, 9t, 25
  and GNP, 29f
  and income distribution, 60, 63
Employment, 32
  factor inequality effect, 48
  factors determining, 48
  and labor force growth, 48
  and primary output, 48
  and urban population, 54
Engel's law, 6, 24, 32, 33, 34, 128
  and time-series, 118, 118n
Equilibrium exchange rates, 146
Estimation, 118n, 141, 159, 164
European economic community, 131
Exchange rate conversion, 145-146
Exogenous shift, 154
Exports
  and capital inflow, 44, 44t

and development policy, 68
government policy effect, 34
and income groups, 115f
index of composition, 69
large vs. small countries per capita
  GNP, scatter, 79f
per capita GNP, 37f
and population, 41f
primary orientation, 90
regression analysis, 44t
and resource allocation, 113f, 114f
in small countries, 89
small countries scatter
  industry-oriented, 91f
  primary-oriented, 91f
and trade pattern, 44
Exports, manufactured; see manufactured exports
Exports, primary; see primary exports
Exports share, 130-132
  and development level, 130, 132
  income and time effect in regression, 131
  and income per capita, 130
  in time-series analysis, 131
  time shift in, 130
External borrowing, 102, 106
External process
  interaction with internal, 42-43
  regression analysis, 43

F

Factor-analysis approach, 149
Fertility
  lag factor in cross-section analysis, 107-108
  and socioeconomic processes, 56
Finland, 10
Fisher index, 151
Food consumption
  and Engel's law, 33, 34
  and per capita GNP, 35f, 40
Food demand elasticity, 34n
Foreign capital inflow; see capital inflow
Foreign exchange, 101
Functional form equations, 141

G

Gauss-Markov theorem, 159n
General equilibrium system, 10, 117

German Federal Republic, 10
General consumption
  and per capita GNP, 35f
  and resource allocation, 113f, 114f
Government policy, 42
  and exports, 34
Government revenue, 9t, 28f, 127
  and development expenditure, 24,
    26
  and income level, 127
  large countries scatter, 85f
  small countries scatter
    industry-oriented, 97f
    primary-oriented, 97f
  small vs. large countries, 88
  time-series and cross-section com-
    parisons of, 127
  time trends in, 134
  and transition, 31
Greece
  export pattern, 100
Gross domestic investment
  and per capita GNP, 35f
Gross domestic product
  and capital inflow, 128
Group factors, 162
Growth elasticity, 17, 142, 149n

                    H

Heckscher-Ohlin theory, 33
Heteroscedasticity; see weighted
    regression
Homogeneity tests, 163-164
Hong Kong
  exports pattern, 100

                    I

Import level
  small countries' needs, 89
Import substitution, 102
Import substitution countries, 54, 88,
    137
  country pattern analysis, 103f
  defined, 104
  and industry exports, 105
Imports, 45, 46
  in trade structure, 37f
Income
  problems of measurement, 149
  public sector share, 7
Income distribution, 9t, 11, 60-63

cross-country pattern, 60
  and development process, 22
  and development theory, 138
  factors determining, 47
  scatter for 55 countries, 62f
Income effect
  in time-series analysis, 120
Income elasticity, 5, 120, 120n, 176
Income groups
  and exports, 115f
Income level, 5, 6, 138
  and accumulation process, 108-109
  and birth/death rates, 56, 58
  and composition of exports, 69
  and export growth, 90
  and labor force, 53
  long-run effect in cross-section
    results, 130
  long-term reactions to change in,
    134
  and natural resources effect, 100
  and primary export bias, 100
  and primary exports in small coun-
    tries, 89
  and primary production, 63
  and production, 53
  and regularity of socioeconomic pro-
    cess, 162
  scale effect, 112
  statistical use defined, 17
Income per capita
  as explanatory variable, 5
Income-related change, 5, 7
Income share
  regression, 61
Industrial exports; see manufactured
    exports
Industrial production
  value added per capita GNP, 36f,
    113f, 114f
Industrial specialization pattern, 4, 137
  country pattern analysis, 103f
  defined, 104
Industrialization, 78, 129
  aggregate effects, 130
  and income distribution, 60
  and investment in small countries,
    100
  of large countries, 88
  and problems caused by delay, 107
  and saving in small countries, 100

and small countries growth, 101
in transition, 42
Industry orientation
and natural resources, 100
Industry-oriented countries, 54
exports, per capita GNP, scatter, 91f
government revenue, per capita
GNP, 97f
industry share of production, per
capita GNP, 99f
investment, per capita GNP, 95f
manufactured exports, per capita
GNP, 100
manufactured exports, per capita
GNP, scatter, 93f
primary exports, per capita GNP,
scatter, 92f
primary share of production, per
capita GNP, 98f
private consumption, per capita
GNP, 96f
saving, per capita GNP, 94f
and trade orientation index, 69
trade pattern, 72t
Industry share of exports
and resource allocation pattern, 101
Industry share of labor, 48, 50f
Industry share of labor productivity,
52f
Industry share of production
large countries scatter, 87f
small countries scatter
industry-oriented, 99f
primary oriented, 99f
Input-output analysis, 33, 45
Instrumental variable techniques, 160
Intercountry analysis, relations, etc.;
see cross-country pattern; cross-
section analysis
Internal process
interaction with external, 42-43
regression analysis, 43
International trade; see trade
Investment, 122-128; see also gross
domestic investment
and accumulation process, 31
and capital inflow, 27f, 125, 132
in cross-section and time-series
analyses, 122
in large countries, 88
large countries scatter, 83
and resource increase, 46

and saving, 27f
small countries scatter
industry-oriented countries, 95f
primary-oriented countries, 95f
Ireland, 10
Israel, 10, 54
exports pattern, 100
Italy, 10
decline in primary share of production, 129

J

Japan, 10
decline in primary share of production, 129

K

Keynesian hypothesis; see propensity
to save
Korea
capital inflow, 74, 100-101
income distribution, 63
Kuznets-Myrdal hypothesis, 60-61

L

Labor
rural-urban supply-demand, 48
Labor allocation, 9t, 50f
and income level, 48
interaction with supply, 47
Labor force
and employment, 48
income level effect, 53
per capita GNP, 50f
regression analysis, 48, 49f
Labor productivity
Argentina, 53
Canada, 53
indices per capita GNP, 52f
New Zealand, 53
in poor countries, 53
and population growth, 63
Labor supply
factors effecting, 47
interaction with demand, 47
Lag
in adjustment process, 48
in consumption, 119
in development process, 139
of fertility, 108

structure of in time series, 119
in transformation, 100
Large countries, 4,67
  advantages in development process,
    89
  exports vs. small countries per capita
    GNP, scatter, 79f
  government revenue, 85f
  industry share of production, 87f
  investment, per capita GNP, scatter,
    83f
  manufactured exports, per capita
    GNP, scatter, 81f
  primary exports scatter, 80f
  primary share of production, 86f
  private consumption, 84f
  resource allocation vs. small coun-
    tries, 78-88
  and scale effect, 74
  trade pattern, 70t
Laspeyres index, 151
Lebanon
  exports pattern, 100
Less developed countries, 10
  accumulation process, 111t
  capital inflow-rate of saving associa-
    tion, 125
  classified by development pattern,
    103t
  classified by stage of development,
    102
  code names, 51t
  dichotomy with developed, 107
  and education, 25
  income distribution, 47
  list of those included in study, 12t
  nonmonetized sector, 145
  and resource allocation, 114f
  socioeconomic variables effect, 58
  structural differences, 65
  time trends vs. developed countries,
    116
Life-cycle theory
  of saving behavior, 122
Linder's theory; see representative demand theory
Log quadratic formulation, 144
Logistic curve, 8n, 17, 135, 144n, 172

M

Manufactured exports

behavior in transition, 40
and cross-country patterns, 138
and development policy, 137
large countries, per capita GNP,
  scatter, 81f
and population, 41f
and primary exports, country scatter,
  77f
and primary exports, per capita, 157f
small countries scatter
  primary-oriented, 93f
  industry-oriented, 93f
in trade structure, 37f
Manufacturing-oriented countries; see
  industry-oriented countries
Market size
  and trade, 40
Mexico
  exports pattern, 89
  exports share reduction, 131
Migration
  rural to urban, 54
Mining, 34, 34n
Multicollinearity, 143-145, 153-154

N

National accounts, 4
National income, 152
Natural resources, 34n
  and development policy, 64
  effect on production, 40
  effect on trade, 40
  and industry orientation, 100
  and trade policy, 67
Net resource inflow, 18
Netherlands, 10
New Zealand, 10
Nigeria
  exports, 74
Nonfood consumption, 33
  and per capita GNP, 35f
Nonlinearities, 16, 143-145, 160
Nonmonetized sector
  in less developed countries, 145
Normal trade bias, 73
Norway, 10

O

Omitted variables, 168
  in time-series equation, 118, 119
Ordinary least squares, 159

P

Pakistan
  capital inflow, 74, 101
Paper industry, 78
Permanent income theory, 24n, 119, 122, 133
Petty's law, 32
Poorer countries; see less developed countries
Population
  statistical use defined, 17
Population growth, 56
  and income distribution, 63
  see also demographic transition
Population, urban
  relation to employment, 54
Portugal
  exports pattern, 100
Primary employment, 48
Primary exports
  and capital inflow, 66, 101
  and economic dualism, 63
  large countries, per capita GNP, scatter, 80
  and manufactured exports, scatter, 77t
  and natural resources, 90
  and per capita GNP, 40
  and population, 41f
  small countries scatter, 92f
  in trade structure, 37f
Primary-oriented countries, 54, 90-99
  exports, per capita GNP, scatter, 91f
  government revenue, per capita GNP, 97f
  industry share of production, per capita GNP, 99f
  investment, per capita GNP, 95f
  manufactured exports, per capita GNP, 93f, 100
  primary exports, per capita GNP, scatter, 92f
  primary share of production, per capita GNP, 98f
  private consumption, per capita GNP, 96f
  saving, per capita GNP, 94f
  and trade orientation index, 69
  trade pattern, 71t
Primary output
  and employment, 48

Primary production
  and income distribution, 61
  and resource allocation, 113t, 114t
  value added per capita GNP, 36f
Primary products, 40
Primary sector
  labor productivity indices, 52f, 53
Primary share of exports
  and capital inflow, 101
Primary share of labor, 48
Primary share of labor productivity, 52f
Primary share of production
  decline in developed countries, 129
  large countries scatter, 86f
  small country scatter
    industry-oriented, 98f
    primary-oriented, 98f
  time trends in, 134
Primary specialization pattern, 4, 106, 137; see also primary-oriented countries
  country pattern analysis, 103t
Primary trade bias
  of Chile, 90
  of Uruguay, 90
Private consumption
  large countries scatter, 84
  and resource allocation, 113f
  and resource increase, 46
  small country scatter
    industry-oriented, 96f
    primary-oriented, 96f
Production, 9t, 33
  and agricultural productivity, 129
  exogenous shifts, 129
  income distribution, 47
  income level effect, 53
  and natural resources, 64
  scale effect, 40
  sectoral composition change, 129
  share regression analysis, 130
  time-series vs. cross-section analysis, 128-130
  time shifts in structure, 129
  and urbanization, 129
  value added per capita GNP, 36f
Production, domestic; see domestic production
Production functions, 117
Production, industry share of; see industry share of production

Production, primary share of; *see* primary share of production
Production shift, 45
Productivity
  and income distribution, 60
Propensity to save, 23, 24, 67
  from capital inflow, 125
  short-run, 122, 133
Puerto Rico, 10
  income distribution, 60
Purchasing-power parity, 150

R

Ratchet effects, 127n
Rate of change, 8
Real income
  and cross-section analysis, 151
  deflation of, 150, 151
  and per capita income, 151
  and time-series study, 151
Real income conversion, 145-146
Real income regression, 149
Reduced form equations, 10, 158-159
Reduced samples, 120
Regression, weighted; *see* weighted regression
Relative prices, 138, 148, 152
Relative prices conversion, 145-146
Representative demand theory, 33
Resource allocation pattern, 10, 128-134; *see also* development pattern
  classification, 103t, 104-105
  estimates, 124t
Resource allocation process, 3, 10, 23, 32-46, 68
  basic regression, 38t, 39t
  definition, 32
  and import substitution countries, 106
  and income distribution, 22
  income level, 112
  in large countries, 88
  regression analysis, 69
  rising income effect, 33
  and side effect, 78, 88-89
  statistical analysis, 34
  and trade processes, 113t
  in transition, 42
Resource effects
  small country patterns, 89-100

Resource endowment; *see* natural resources
Resource mobilization, 3
Richer countries; *see* developed countries
Resource shift, 45
Rubber products industry, 78
Rule of four-ninths, 150

S

Sample, 169-170
  compatible, 169
  in cross-country and time series, 119
  stratification of, 162-164
  and trade orientation, 100
Saving, 122-128
  behavior of groups, 24
  capital inflow, 125, 126f, 132
  in cross-section and time-series analysis, 122
  and income distribution, 47
  and income level, 123
  and industrialization, 100
  Keynesian hypothesis, 23
  large countries, per capita GNP, scatter, 82
  Lewis hypothesis, 24
  marginal rate of, 133
  national income effect on, 24
  rate constancy, 123
  small countries scatter
    industry-oriented, 94f
    primary-oriented, 94f
  time-series regressions for, 123
Scale effect, 43, 74-88
  and accumulation process, 88
  and capital inflow, 26, 43
  for exports, 112t
  large country patterns, 74-88
  on production, 40, 78, 87f
  and resource allocation process, 78-88
  for saving, 112t
  and time trends, 112
  on trade, 40
Scale index, 67
School enrollment, 31
  and income distribution, 61
  as exogenous variable, 56
Semilog formulation, 141, 142, 172

Services
  value added per capita GNP, 36t
Services exports
  and population, 41f
  trade structure, 37f
Services share, 174-175
  in large countries, 176
  and time series, 176-177
Services share of labor, 50f
Services share of labor productivity, 52f
Short-run patterns
  in time-series analysis, 122
Size of economy; see scale effect
Small countries, 4, 67-68, 89-100
  capital inflow influence, 89
  composition of exports, 89, 90
  development pattern, 89-100
  exports, per capita GNP, scatter, 91f
  exports vs. large countries, per capita GNP, scatter, 79f
  government revenue, per capita GNP, 97f
  growth by early industrialization, 101
  import level, 89
  industry share of production, per capita GNP, 99f
  investment, per capita GNP, 95f
  manufactured exports, per capita GNP, 93f, 100
  primary exports, per capita GNP, scatter, 92f
  primary share of production, per capita GNP, 98f
  private consumption per capita GNP, 96f
  resource allocation vs. large countries, 78-88
  saving per capita GNP, 94f
  trade pattern, 71t
Small countries, industry specialization; see industry-oriented countries; industrial specialization countries
Small countries, primary specialization; see primary-oriented countries; primary specialization pattern
Smallholder agriculture, 63n

Social mobility
  and income distribution, 60
Socioeconomic processes, 56
  variables by type of country, 58
Sombart's theory; see declining trade theory
Specification, 141
Statistical accuracy, 164
Statistical data
  definitions, 179-214
Structural change, 3, 4, 10, 56, 132, 135
  and cross-section analysis, 108
  and income range, 19
  large and small countries pattern, 78
  models, 5, 5n
  and transition, 19
Structural characteristics; see structural factors
Structural factors, 9t
  and development policies, 64
  income level effect on, 11
Structural relations, 158
Stylized facts, 19
Supply factor, 5
Sweden, 10
  decline in prime share of production, 129
Switzerland, 10

T

Taiwan, 54
  export pattern, 100
Tax base
  and capital inflow, 128
  income level relationship, 25
Tax ratio
  and income level, 108
Taxation
  and trade, 45
Time
  as a variable, 153
Time series, 11, 117-121
  behavior within and among countries, 120
  comparison of long-run and short-run patterns, 121t
  and cross-country patterns compared, 133
  estimates of, 118-121
  regression equation for 1960s, 131
  sample for, 119

saving and capital inflow
  long-run and short-run estimates,
  127
  short-run experience, 128
  standard equation for, 118, 119
  and trade orientation index, 68
Trade-series data, 167-169
Time trends, 120
  and agriculture developments, 130
  and cross-country pattern, 40, 42
  in developed and less developed
    countries, 116
  and scale effect, 112
  statistical use defined, 18
  in time-series analysis, 120
Timing, 22, 42
  and regression analysis, 66
Total exports; see exports
Trade, 9t
  and capital inflow, 44
  and development policy, 137
  and domestic demand, 40
  Heckscher-Ohlin theory, 33
  and natural resources, 40, 45, 64
  structure per capita GNP, 37f
  tax on, 45
  trade movements, 134
  transformation of, 42
Trade orientation index, 68, 155-156,
  158
  equation for, 69
  measurement of lead or lag, 90
  and resource allocation, 69
Trade pattern, 5
  balanced countries, 72t
  and capital inflow, 66
  classification of, 65-66
  and domestic production, 74
  industry-oriented countries, 73t
  large countries, 70t
  large countries comparison, 76f
  primary-oriented countries, 71t
  scale effect, 74
  small countries, 71t
  small country comparing primary-
    and industry-oriented, 75t
  small countries scatter, 77f
  Sombart declining trade theory, 132,
    132n
Trade processes
  and resource allocation, 113f

Transformation, 8, 19, 89
  lag in, 100
Transition, 8, 10, 19, 122, 136-137
  accumulation role, 31
  factor returns in, 53
  resource allocation role in, 42
  sample division by income level as
    test, 108
Transitional countries
  defined, 102
Tunisia
  exports pattern, 100
Turkey
  exports pattern, 89
  exports share reduction, 131
Two-gap model, 133
  and saving function, 125n

U

USSR, 10
Underemployment
  and population growth, 54
United Kingdom, 10, 54
  decline in primary share of produc-
    tion, 129
United States, 10
Universal factors, 162
Urbanization, 9t, 53-55
  and birth rate, 58
  effect on labor supply, 47
  and income distribution, 60
  and migration, 54
  per capita GNP, scatter, 55f
  trade and production, 54
Uruguay, 54
  primary trade bias, 90
Utilities
  value added per capita GNP, 36f

V

Variable
  errors in, 159
Variable, dependent, 142
  defined, rationale given, 17
Variable, explanatory, 5
Variable, independent, 141

W

Weighted regression, 161-162

AUTHOR INDEX

A

Adelman, I., 56n, 57, 57n, 60, 107n.
    149, 158n, 161n, 162, 213
Ahluwalia, M. S., 138n, 213
Arrow, K., 117n, 213

B

Bacon, R., 149, 149n, 213
Bahl, R., 127, 213
Balassa, B., 106, 131n, 146, 146n, 148,
    148n, 150n, 152, 177, 177n, 213
Beckerman, W., 149, 149n, 213
Behrman, J.R., 119n, 213
Bhagwati, J., 33n, 214
Bogue, D. J., 56n, 214
Bruno, M., 10n, 214

C

C.I.A.P., 158n, 215
Carter, N. G., 19n, 125n, 214
Cheetham, R. J., 5n, 7n, 216
Chenery, H. B., 5n, 7n, 10n, 11n, 16n,
    40n, 47n, 67n, 68, 68n, 69n, 74n,
    78, 88n, 101n, 106n, 107n, 118n,
    119, 125n, 129, 130, 130n, 138n,
    142, 143, 146, 154, 155, 158n, 213,
    214
Clague, C., 152, 215
Clark, C., 32, 177, 215
Cline, W. R., 47n, 215

D

David, P. A., 146n, 150, 150n, 151, 215
Deutsch, K. W., 127n, 132, 215

E

Eckstein, P., 125n, 132, 214, 215
Elkington, H., 11n, 19n, 67n, 68n, 88n,
    154, 214
Enos, J. L., 125n, 215

F

Fei, J. C., 7n, 215
Fisher, A. G. B., 32, 215

Fishlow, A., 63n, 215
Friedlander, S., 56n, 57, 215
Friedman, M., 24n, 215
Fuchs, V., 53n, 215

G

Goldberger, A. S., 159n, 215
Gregory, P., 11n, 215
Griffin, K. B., 125n, 215
Griliches, Z., 160, 215

H

Harris, J. R., 54n, 216
Heer, D. M., 56n, 216
Heston, A., 138n, 148, 150, 150n, 216
Hinrichs, H. H., 25, 45n, 127n, 216
Hirschman, A. O., 132n, 216
Hooley, R. W., 145n, 216
Houthakker, H. S., 6n, 24, 118, 122,
    158-159, 161, 216
Hughes, H., 138n, 214

J

Jain, S., 60n, 61n, 187, 216
Johansen, L., 10n, 216
Johnston, J., 160-161, 163n, 216

K

Kelley, A. C., 5n, 7n, 10n, 216
Kenessey, Z., 138n, 148, 150, 150n,
    216
Kindleberger, C., 132n, 216
Kravis, I. B., 138n, 148, 150, 150n, 216
Kuznets, S., 3, 3n, 4, 4n, 10, 16, 24, 31n,
    32, 34n, 53n, 60, 60n, 63, 89n, 108,
    119, 123, 129, 130, 132n, 135, 141,
    161, 217

L

Landau, L., 123, 123n, 125, 158n, 217
Leontief, W., 10n, 217
Leser, C. E. V., 143n, 217
Lewis, W. A., 6, 7n, 24, 32, 217
Linder, S. B., 33, 217

Lipsey, R. E., 132n, 217
Little, I. M., 106, 217
Liu, Ta-Chung, 144n, 217
Lluch, C., 32n, 34n, 139, 217, 218
Lotz, J. R., 25, 218

M

Maxwell, D. E., 56n, 218
Meerman, J., 61n, 218
Mikesell, R. F., 23n, 122n, 125n, 218
Minhas, B., 117n, 213
Modigliani, F., 158n, 218
Morris, C., 60, 107n, 149, 161, 213
Morss, E. R., 25, 218
Musgrave, R. A., 25, 108, 127, 127n, 218
Myrdal, G., 60, 218

N

Nicholson, J. L., 143n, 218
Nurkse, R., 7n, 32, 218

O

Ofer, G., 11n, 218
Oshima, H. T., 127n, 218

P

Pack, H., 10n, 218
Papanek, G. F., 125n, 218
Peacock, A. T., 127n, 218
Phillips, L., 56n, 218
Please, S., 122, 218
Powell, A., 139, 218

R

Ranis, G., 7n, 215
Rich, W., 57, 57n, 219
Ringstad, V., 160, 215
Rosenstein-Rodan, P. N., 32, 219
Rostow, W. W., 136n, 219

S

Samuelson, P. A., 146n, 177n, 219

Schydlowsky, D., 146n, 219
Scitovsky, T., 32, 106, 217, 219
Scott, M., 106, 217
Shishido, S., 7n, 10n, 214
Shourie, A., 144n, 219
Silver, M., 56n, 57, 215
Sims, C., 11n, 67n, 68n, 88n, 154, 214
Solow, R., 117n, 213
Sombart, W., 132, 132n, 219
Summers, R., 138n, 148, 150, 150n, 216
Syrquin, M., 117n, 146n, 171t, 176, 219

T

Tanzi, V., 152, 215
Taylor, L., 5n, 11n, 16n, 40n, 67n, 68, 69n, 74n, 78, 107n, 117n, 118n, 119, 129, 130n, 138, 143, 155, 214, 219
Temin, P., 130, 130n, 219
Theil, H., 161, 219
Tiemann, A., 60n, 61n, 187, 216
Todaro, M. P., 54n, 216, 219

U

United Nations, 143, 184, 186, 219

V

Vial, Josefina, 150n
Votey, H., 56n, 218

W

Watanabe, T., 7n, 10n, 214
Weisskoff, R., 32n, 60, 219, 220
Weisskopf, T. E., 125n, 220
Williams, R., 34n, 217
Williamson, J. G., 5n, 7n, 10n, 24n, 127n, 216, 220
Willis, R. J., 56n, 220
Wiseman, J., 127n, 218

Z

Zinser, J. E., 23n, 122n, 125n, 218